MARKETS
WITHIN
PLANNING

Socialist Economic
Management in the
Third World

Edited by

E.V.K. FITZGERALD and M. WUYTS

FRANK CASS

First published in Great Britain by
FRANK CASS AND COMPANY LIMITED
Gainsborough House, 11 Gainsborough Road,
London E11 1RS

and in the United States of America by
FRANK CASS AND COMPANY LIMITED
c/o Biblio Distribution Centre
81 Adams Drive, P.O. Box 327, Totowa, NJ 07511

Copyright © 1988 Frank Cass & Co. Ltd.

British Library Cataloguing in Publication Data

Markets within planning : socialist economic
management in the Third World.
1. Socialist developing countries.
Economic development.
I. Fitzgerald, E.V.K.,   II. Wuyts,
M.,   III. Journal of development
studies.
330.9172′4
ISBN 0-7146-3342-9

Library of Congress Cataloging-in-Publication Data

Markets within planning
1. Central planning—Developing countries.
2. Developing countries—Economic policy.
3. Socialism—Developing countries. 4. Capitalism—
Developing countries. I. Fitzgerald, E. V. K.
(Edmund Valpy Knox), 1947–   II. Wuyts, Marc.
HC59.7.M295 1988   338.9′009172′4   88-16192
ISBN 0-7146-3342-9

This group of studies first appeared in a Special Issue on
Markets Within Planning: Socialist Economic Management in the
Third World of *The Journal of Development Studies,* Vol.24,
No.4, published by Frank Cass & Co. Ltd.

Typeset by Essex Photo Set, Rayleigh, Essex

CONTENTS

Introduction

by E.V.K. FitzGerald and M. Wuyts

A greater number of countries than is often realised come under the category of 'Third World socialism' for all the socialist revolutions since 1949 have taken place in the Third World. The list covers all three continents and now includes about 20 nations,[1] the combined population of which is equivalent to nearly a third of the planetary total. They are clearly distinct from the 'dependent capitalist' model upon which so much of the development econmic literature is based, in terms of both the social organisation and the international linkages of their economies. What is more, they are also very different from the model provided by the less industrialised economies of Eastern Europe, such as Bulgaria and Romania. Not only is their productive structure less advanced and their external linkages generally different, but also they have established a national liberation ideology of their own and have learned the lessons of earlier socialist experiences. Usually under severe political and military pressure from former hegemonic powers, these countries have attempted to overcome the immediate problems of poverty, to transform the social relations of production, to establish a new position in the international division of labour, and to initiate a process of rapid accumulation. They have also tried to do this on a basis distinct from the criteria of free markets, private investment and comparative advantage that characterise the rest of the Third World.[2]

These cases are not included in the theoretical corpus of development economics despite the fact that they have not only a distinct strategy with many common features but also their own systemic problems; particularly that of articulating the 'leading' state sector with the small producers on the one hand and with the international division of labour on the other. In recent years there has emerged, none the less, an expanding body of comparative empirical studies of a critical nature, from the standpoint of both development studies[3] and that of Soviet studies.[4]

The initial strategy adopted by most such revolutionary regimes is to concentrate resources behind the rapid expansion of the state sector in order to overcome poverty and transform their economies, which are commonly regarded by their revolutionary leadership (in an initial stage at least) as essentially 'dependent dualist' structures. This has tended to cause severe imbalances in the accumulation process (such as food shortages, inflation and balance of payments difficulties) and has ultimately impeded the process of socialisation itself by causing severe social strain, disarticulating the commercial and administrative relationships within the economy, and effectively reducing real social control, especially by the central government.

The response to this problematic has generally involved in recent years a greater role for markets (particularly those concerned with labour and the exchange of consumer goods from the small-producer sector), more reliance upon financial control over state enterprises rather than administration from the centre, a greater emphasis on the local organisation of social infrastructure and provisioning, and more serious attention to foreign trade criteria in resource allocation.

It is now becoming clear that these changes are neither a tactical response to the world economic crisis, nor a purely political phenomena. They seem to reflect a redefinition of the mode of economic organisation in Third World socialism, although this leads in its turn to further tensions and contradictions. The object of this collection is to analyse this problem of the 'market in planning' in as much depth as possible by means of both theoretical analysis and case studies of a number of such economies in different stages of their transition: particularly China, Vietnam, Mozambique, Zimbabwe and Nicaragua. Our aim as Editors is to contribute to a better understanding of the nature of the macroeconomic management of such economies, and perhaps to the establishment of more effective planning systems.

Socialist macroeconomic management has been undergoing various reforms for some time in Eastern Europe, involving decentralisation of state control over production and distribution (and thus by implication over accumulation as well) in the search for economic efficiency and technological innovation. This has not involved the *replacement* of the plan by the market, but rather the redefinition of planning in terms of the use of value forms instead of material balances to control the economy.[5] However, the task of defining and implementing this 'market socialism' has proved very difficult, particularly because the presence of the state enterprises in product markets tends to be oligopolistic (leading to phenomena such as 'accumulation bias'), while partially decontrolled labour markets are segmented by the emergence of the 'second economy', and foreign trade at capitalist prices requires a redefinition of economy-wide price and profitability criteria.[6]

Apparently similar changes have been taking place in Third World socialist economic management. However, although the immediate motivations may be similar (such as the search for public enterprise efficiency), the strategic aims are for the most part distinct. In 'Second World' socialism, *perestroika* appears to be directed towards achieving international industrial competitiveness on the basis of advanced technology and towards the raising of nonessential consumption standards. In Third World socialism the aims of reform and restructuring seem to be the reduction of external vulnerability and the satisfaction of the basic needs of the population.

Yet it is just as important, if not more so, to avoid a superficial comparison between the adjustments in Third World socialist economic organisation and the 'liberalisation' of Third World capitalist economies under international pressure. The former involves an attempt to rearticulate distinct forms of production, as part of a strategy of industrialisation and social transformation; the latter proposes the reduction of state intervention and elimination of trade barriers in the name of efficiency almost as an end in itself.[7]

In fact, as this collection hopes to demonstrate, the apparent 'dichotomy' between plan and market reflects deeper questions of the nature of economic and social structures, and the best way to transform them. Three of those questions run through this volume: first, the problem of how to articulate very different forms of production and distribution organisation within the economy, especially through market mechanisms; second, the issue of mobilisation of resources for accumulation and their distribution between the state and rest of economy; and third, how labour can be both a factor of production and the dominant historical subject at the same time.

THE ECONOMIC THEORY OF THE TRANSITION PERIOD

Unfortunately there has been little theoretical writing of any depth in the last ten years on the general problem of the transition from capitalism to socialism, so that the works of Bettelheim[8] are still a key point of reference. There has been some debate about the possibility of socialism in more advanced industrial economies[9] in which the transition is discussed (as Marx himself did) in terms of social reorganisation and personal emancipation on the assumption that a high level of development of productive forces has already been attained. All the reasonable consumption needs of the population can be met collectively in a technologically advanced society with a decreasing minimum of socially necessary labour time. If the acquisitive impulse of oligopoly capitalism or the growth urges of state socialist planners can be swept away, men and women can use their 'own' time in increasingly creative and cooperative ways to enrich their lives. At first sight this prospect might not seem to be very relevant for the Third World. Indeed, it might even be interpreted in the negative sense that if 'true' socialism can only be attained under these circumstances, then developing economies have little option but to industrialise as quickly as possible (under dependent capitalism or state socialism) and await a subsequent transition. None the less, there are themes in this debate, such as the fact that socialisation is not coterminous with state ownership or that the collective definition and organisation of basic needs satisfaction is a central element of socialism, that are highly relevant to our problem.

Bettelheim does, however, confront a central issue which does not seem to have been debated sufficiently at a theoretical level, although it is continually discussed in practice. This is the problem of transformation of the social relations of production when the economy is still relatively underdeveloped. Full socialism involves an integrated social division of labour, conscious co-operation in production and social control over the production process. Bettelheim argues that this can only be achieved when there exist a technical division of labour and a centralisation of the production process, sufficient to make such socialisation possible, as well as the material abundance that would eliminate conflicts over resource allocation. Whatever its validity, this conclusion is not very helpful in understanding how a society is supposed to move towards socialisation from a situation of extreme heterogeneity in the forms of production, other than by the expansion of the state sector and its integration with other planned economies.

'Official' writing in developed socialist countries[10] on the economics of transition has an importance beyond its intrinsic merit, because of the inevitable influence such countries have made upon economic policy thinking in Third World socialist countries.[11] This official view[12] admits the existence of a 'mixed economy' during the transition period, but regards the 'socialist' (state) sector as antagonistic to the 'private' sector, which is either capitalist or potentially so, in the case of small producers. Thus the specific task of the state is to replace the private sector as soon as is administratively possible or tactically convenient. Mercantile forms (that is, monetary transactions) are required in order to control the non-state sector effectively; but the socialist (that is, state) sector is centrally planned. This is to be done according to the 'laws of socialist political economy' which establish the correct proportions between Departments I and II and so on. Material balances maintain macroeconomic equilibrium, although economic accounting is used to ensure efficient resource use by enterprises. It is explicitly argued that accumulation should be concentrated in the state and be kept as high as possible so as to accelerate industrialisation, constrained only by the requirement that the per capita consumption of the population should not actually fall. Financial disequilibria are considered to be impossible in a centrally planned system.

Official socialist writing on planning in the mixed economies (albeit 'non-capitalist' or even 'of socialist orientation') of the Third World is somewhat more flexible, because it takes explicit consideration of the small-scale sector, and does not see it as a threat to socialism as such.[13] However, the model employed is that of a dual economy and assumes that all accumulation will be concentrated in the modern (that is, state) sector, which will progressively absorb production and labour from the 'traditional' sector of peasants and artisans. The possibility of planning (identified with socialism) is limited to the state sector itself; so control over the rest of the economy depends upon the trading or financial relationships it may have with state enterprises. There is no concept of the transformation of the small-scale sector itself, let alone of accumulation or socialist organisation occurring there. Recently a critique of this approach appears to have been emerging in Eastern Europe.[14] This does not refer to the experience of socialist LDCs (even members of the CMEA, like Cuba and Vietnam); rather the starting point has been the experience of countries such as Hungary in external trade and the encouragement of small producers domestically. The implications for developing countries are derived from this analysis, which is opposed to the orthodox 'dualist' state industrialisation model, even if it does not take into account the specifics of underdevelopment.

Finally, the theory of 'socialist self-management' is sometimes proposed as a model for the transition economy, as it allows for a large non-state sector.[15] Apart from the evident macroeconomic shortcomings of the Yugoslav economy upon which such theory is ostensibly modelled, the weakness of this approach is that it does not face the central problems of structural transformation. On the contrary, it assumes an almost neo-classical world of independent economic agents (that is, 'worker-owned firms') with no control over the equilibrating market which serves as the expression of social needs.

In another dimension, the recent revival of interest in the NEP is undoubtedly based on its significance as the classic example of mixed economy in transition. The NEP is no longer regarded by historians as merely a tactical policy to revive food production via balanced exchange with peasantry, but rather as a strategic alternative to state expansion and forced proletarianisation.[16] This in turn transforms the notion of 'primitive socialist accumulation' from a question of financing the state into one of the location of accumulation and the conditions of transformation in the long run.[17] However, this concept of a mixed economy cannot simply be translated into the coexistence of large and small enterprise according to respective criteria of efficiency derived from economies of scale and labour incentives as Nove proposes. The issue turns out in practice to be a question of articulating the expanded reproduction of distinct forms of production, which depend upon each other for supplies of labour and producer goods, and for markets, but also have distinct behaviours and internal structures which determine inter-sectoral relationships and thus the macroeconomics of exchange and accumulation.[18]

Some recent attempts to generalise from the experience of the social dimension of the transition stage do take into account multiple forms of production and thus the nature of exchange relations. According to Fagen and Deere [1986] the logic of capitalism is initially subordinated to, and eventually replaced by, a socially determined rationality of production and distribution. The fundamental measures of advance in this transformation are: (i) production and distribution according to the basic needs of the population; (ii) ending of class, gender and ethnic discrimination and access of all to justice, culture, etc; and (iii) reorganisation of state–society relations so as to enable the population to attain a high degree of self-organisation and democratic participation in central decisions. Such a transition is seen as inevitably involving domestic class conflict and international tensions; and is a slow process, lasting generations. For this reason, some would consider such societies as 'proto-socialist', and constituting a distinct path of economic development which is not necessarily unilinear.[19]

Much of the 'radical' literature on underdevelopment sees the transition to socialism as the only way of overcoming dependency on the world capitalist system.[20] Although this approach grossly overestimates the feasibility of delinking from the world economy; the concept of 'convergence' between the needs of producers and what they produce as a characteristic of socialism is useful in the sense that basic services can be locally organised by the population with less recourse to either state or market.

Comparative studies of a more empirical nature on transition economies in the Third World have a natural tendency to concentrate upon 'the agrarian question'[21] and stress the negative consequences for comprehensive rural development of trying to squeeze the peasantry for surplus on which state-led urban industrialisation can be based. A 'twin transition' is posited towards industrialisation and towards socialism; and it is suggested that in practice the former has blocked the possibility of the latter.[22] Although the rural viewpoint of much of this writing leads to an understandable neglect of questions of *national* economy (and particularly the question of macroeconomic management), the critique of forced state industrialisation does provide a useful point of departure. Other studies of a more macroeconomic nature see income distribution as the central political issue in the transition,[23] but do not add much to the analysis of the relationship between plan and market as such.

Finally, the two Editors of this collection have themselves attempted to handle some of these issues elsewhere. FitzGerald[24] adapts the Kaleckian scheme of sectoral balances to the typical structure of a Third World socialist economy, demonstrating the need to maintain consumption levels in the short run (to sustain both peasant exchange with the state and industrial labour productivity) and to base long-run balanced growth on peasant accumulation and adequate attention to exports. Wuyts[25] argues that the attempt on the part of the state to pursue a strategy of state-centred accumulation leads to the development of uncontrolled patterns of private capitalist accumulation within the parallel economy which ultimately erodes the capacity of the state to direct overall economic development. He concludes that planning in this context – while formally all-embracing – *de facto* proves to be illusory.

MARKETS, FINANCE AND PLANNING

The perceived failure of central planning in all the Third World 'socialist' economies discussed in this volume and recent trends towards 'liberalisation' in the more industrialised socialist economies both require careful interpretation. A plausible explanation should include an analysis of the real social relations underlying administrative forms, of the structural implications of attempts to force efficiency (via bankruptcy) on state enterprises, and of the belief that self-help will relieve the state from responsibility for basic needs provision. It has become clear from hard experience that accumulation in the state sector is constrained not only by internal and external exchange relations (which determine the feasible price system), but also by its own administrative limitations. However, it is also necessary to carefully analyse the social organisation of the non-state sector, and identify its own capacity for resource mobilisation, if it is to replace the state.

Perhaps the main conclusion of this book is that it is incorrect to speak of plan *versus* market under such conditions. The central question is not one of whether or not to reinstate the law of value as a means of recovering production efficiency and macroeconomic balance; but rather that of how the law of value is to be managed institutionally so as to articulate the development and transformation of distinct forms of production in such a way as to assure the required mobilisation of surplus and its appropriate strategic investment. Planning can only work if it takes account of real interactions in production and exchange in and between the various heterogeneous forms of production which make up the underdeveloped economy in transition. If administrators attempt to force the plan beyond the constraints imposed by this logic, then independent markets will reappear within the state sector or parallel to it, and they will determine the dynamic of non-state forms of production as well as labour productivity within the state.

Indeed, any market must be structured by state intervention in order to operate. This implies some sort of strategy – even if it amounts to little more than subordination to world markets – and the issue of who benefits from such arrangements. Behind the issue of 'liberalisation' is the question of which social forces are to be 'set free' and within what context. Hence, in the case of transition, the nature of the transformation proposed must be made explicit in terms of the class forces it seeks to mobilise – or contain. Transition strategies define the proposed balance between the expanded reproduction of various forms of production, the consistency of this with production and distribution perspectives, and the consequent allocation of resources.

The opening article by Bettelheim in this collection, on the economic reforms in China since 1979, provides an interesting illustration of this concern with the class character of the attempted transformation. The crux of his argument is that – in the case of China – economic reforms have not resolved the tensions inherent in the Maoist development model and thus do not permit progress towards a more comprehensive form of planning within a broadened conception of socialist development. Rather – he argues – the economic reforms have implied a retreat from planning while opening up largely uncontrolled avenues of private accumulation which fundamentally alter economic and social developments in urban as well as rural areas. The economic reforms propel fundamental changes in the economy which are largely uncontrolled and often unintended as well as being contradictory in terms of the modernisation strategy and generating new tensions at the macro level. Bettelheim concludes that market forces do not operate in a context set by conscious planning, because central planning has been effectively swept aside by the reforms without there being any new system of macroeconomic control to replace it.

In this collection we put forward the argument that financial issues are central to planning in a decentralised economy. An inevitable tension still exists between levels of economic control (planners versus enterprises) and between institutional sectors (state enterprises versus small producers) which must be resolved in administrative and monetary terms. The shift from centralised budget finance to socialist economic accounting requires strict banking controls over surplus and deficit units in the economy, as well as clear profitability criteria for management on a consistent set of prices. Without such conditions there is the danger of a systemic accumulation bias within the state sector, a practice of economic calculation which leads to the unbalanced allocation of resources to other sectors, and the development of inflationary pressures as well as balance of payments difficulties. This in turn makes markets ineffective as part of economic management because enterprise organisation must reflect both the nature of short run efficiency criteria and their relationship to the long run accumulation problem.

The problem of financial imbalances in the context of socialist economic management constitutes the core of the article by FitzGerald. In his article he attempts to provide a theoretical analysis of those aspects of the institutional pattern of Third World socialist experiences which tend to produce a characteristic pattern of macroeconomic and inter-sectoral imbalances generated by state accumulation. Such imbalances can only be understood in the light of an analysis of the systemic forces arising from the specific organisation of economic management characteristic of such economies, their subordinate position in the world markets as primary producers and the existence of a large petty production sector which constitutes an important and integral part of production and exchange.

As his point of departure FitzGerald combines Kalecki's analysis of the 'accumulation bias' in planned economies with Kornai's concept of resource constrained systems and a 'soft budget constraint' in the public enterprise sector. He argues that both forces are also at work within Third World socialist economies, but that in these economies their operation tends to lead to the crowding out of petty producers by the state sector and hence crucially affects the dynamic of production and accumulation. A feasible pattern of planning and accumulation should take account of the fact that the scope for accumulation within the state sector is limited by the conditons of world trade on the one hand and the need to mobilise and transform petty production on the other. In other words, the state is confined between the internal and the external terms of trade. Such a planning system would have to be based more on the management of exchange relations between various sectors of the economy, than on direct production control. This – he argues – would require stricter financial discipline of state enterprises than is usual, and appropriate pricing policies along with more active financial institutions as principal instruments of economic management.

Littlejohn takes up a similar theme when he argues that in developing socialist economies the state sector is often run on the lines of the Soviet central planning model although the organisational conditions may not be appropriate. Typically, exchange relations with the peasantry are supposed to be maintained unaltered while the basis of peasant production is being transformed. With specific reference to the Mozambican experience, the author argues that central planning tends to deny resources to other non-state sectors, so that if the state sector is to develop without crowding out the peasantry, it must enter the intensive, efficient stage from the outset. He stresses the importance of the NEP as a relevant model since it initiated the use of both production capacity directly under state control, and the powers of various state agencies to affect the development of market relations with the peasantry in a socialist direction. However, this requires the development of a smaller but efficient state sector concentrating on particular tasks in transforming the wider economy, rather than the 'statist' concept in which the state sector takes over and controls an increasing proportion of the rest of the economy. Littlejohn suggests that recent Eastern European debates on economic growth are directly relevant to poor economies attempting a socialist transition. Historically, Soviet-type economies witnessed high growth rates for some decades, but subsequently encountered increasing difficulties in maintaining the growth performance of their economies, due to overinvestment and poor control of its efficiency.

Traditional central planning – he argues – involves mobilising resources administratively in 'extensive' development through the expansion of the state sector, which tends to monopolise material and human resources. The tensions which develop within this system require for their resolution a shift towards an 'intensive' phase involving the reorganisation of planning and of its interaction with market mechanisms. This question is not merely one of increasing the scope of the market; it involves rethinking planning itself so as to ensure greater efficiency in resource use rather than merely mobilising more resources.

In his article Spoor looks at the process of transition from a system of 'bureaucratic state finance' towards one based on 'socialist economic accounting' in the context of the post-1975 reforms in Vietnam. His chronologically structured account gives a sense of the 'trial and error' involved in this transition as well as of the practical policy oscillations that occurred. The system of state bureaucratic finance which characterised macroeconomic organisation before the reforms, corresponded to what Bettelheim calls 'imperative central planning'. All state enterprise surpluses were centralised in the state budget while all deficits were financed through budget subsidies: state enterprises therefore operated within a context of Kornai's soft budget constraint. Spoor argues that, while this system may have allowed for the centralised mobilisation of resources, it did little to economise on the use of these resources. Hence the effective availability of such resources to the state was hampered by their inefficient use.

The move towards socialist economic accounting involved hardening the budget constraint to state enterprises as well as granting greater autonomy of such enterprises over part of their financial surpluses. The latter measure is intended to increase labour productivity and the efficiency of state enterprises: the improvement in their financial situation should eventually increase their contributions to the budget. However, Spoor argues that in practice their greater autonomy also involves a higher rate of retention of financial surpluses which deducts from the potential fund available for use by the central state. Furthermore, the case of Vietnam shows how greater autonomy accorded to state enterprises as well as the greater reliance on market mechanisms erodes the capacity of the state to directly allocate resources administratively through the central budget and increases the need for more indirect forms of planning based upon financial intermediation. Spoor argues that this shift raises the question of how to combine the economic requirement for greater financial discipline with the political requirement to guarantee the provision of basic needs to the producing classes.

NON-STATE ACCUMULATION AND THE ORGANISATION OF LABOUR

A third major issue addressed in this volume is the question of the scope for, and the nature of, non-state accumulation in a transitional economy characterised by a predominance of petty producers. Our authors repeatedly stress that in such circumstances planning which, by design or default, attempts to concentrate the accumulation effort virtually exclusively on the state sector tends to become illusory as the capacity of the state to control the use of the economic surplus and to direct overall economic development becomes progressively undermined by uncontrolled pattern of private accumulation within parallel market circuits which in turn erode the cohesiveness of state action itself. A viable strategy therefore needs to combine central direction with sufficient scope for local initiative and accumulation in the context of institutional forms which support an overall socialist policy, and which thus assures the progressive convergence of production with basic human needs. This is the central question raised in Kaimovitz' article on the Nicaraguan experience and in the contribution by

Mackintosh and Wuyts on Mozambique.

Kaimovitz argues that the strategy in Nicaragua followed in the first years after the 1979 revolution was based on a pattern of state-centred accumulation which led to the crowding-out of the peasantry from access to technical resources. He argues that the impact of US aggression and the consequent need to enlist the support of the peasantry led to a change in agrarian policy. The author goes on to argue that these changes were initially perceived as tactical measures necessitated by war rather than by economic design, but gradually amounted to a new strategy based on an alternative approach to the transitional economy. This approach is characterised by three interrelated changes: the move towards the strategic alliance with the peasantry, the notion of organising a 'survival' or 'resistance' economy in the face of aggression, and the shift in emphasis in planning towards 'regionalisation and territorial integration'.

The strategic alliance with the peasantry in Nicaragua entails a significant shift in resources towards the peasantry as well as the greater autonomy of peasant organisations. The centrepiece of the survival economy strategy has been the shift away from a high rate of investment in the state sector towards the maintenance of current capacity and support for the cooperative and private sectors, as well as giving priority to certain sectors and products considered necessary for survival of the revolution itself. Finally, the strategy entails the need for a more flexible response to local conditions in planning by using local markets, and hence a move towards spatial decentralisation in planning. Kaimowitz argues that this set of policy measures provides a more realistic approach to planning transition in Third World economies; especially since few Third World countries have been able to embark on a socialist policy without suffering economic destabilisation and military aggression.

The article by Mackintosh and Wuyts also supports a distinctive approach to economic development and socialist transition in poor economies. The components of this approach are: decentralisation on a basis of the popular planning and control of accumulation; interlinking of investments so that rural production can partly finance social services at the local level; and intervention in markets. The concept of the 'location of accumulation' (in whose hands and within what form of organisation of the social relations of production, accumulation and hence development occur) is of central importance to socialist planning because this will determine over time the relative development of socialised and non-socialised sectors in the economy, and hence whether a socialist transition occurs at all.

Despite the dominant tendency for accumulation to be centred on the state, the Mozambican development strategy contains elements of a more creative approach to planning which aims to promote forms of socialist accumulation both inside and outside the state sector. Mackintosh and Wuyts suggest that production and needs should converge in an interactive process of local collective self-provisioning based on local forms of finance through collective production and taxation, and appropriate forms of state support and redistribution. In this context, they argue that social services potentially form a crucial part of the decentralised economic planning process. The production of social services and the need for local finance to sustain this production can provide an important vehicle for socialised forms of accumulation outside the state sector proper. This process not only involves an administrative reorganisation, but also a distinct concept of planning as a political process and the use of market mechanisms as a tool of socialist planning.

A final theme of this collection is the central position of labour as the social subject in any process of transition. This involves different dimensions of socialist policy: the progressive convergence of production with the needs of the producing classes; the right to work as a fundamental human right and the institutional context through which it is made effective; and the question of workers' control at the point of production and its relation to labour discipline.

White concentrates on the reappearance of an urban labour market in the context of the recent economic reforms in China. Four points emerge from his analysis. First, economic reforms which involve greater financial autonomy of enterprises as well as a greater reliance on market forces will inevitably imply the reappearance of labour markets. Second, for such markets to be manageable and operate effectively, new institutions are needed as a substitute for administrative allocation; that is, markets need an institutional context in order to operate. Third, implicit in White's analysis is the question of whether greater flexibility in labour allocation is achieved at the expense of traditional basic socialist goals such as the right to work or basic needs entitlements. Finally, because reforms in the labour allocation system affect the ideological foundations of socialism, they involve a debate on the legitimacy of the post-Mao regime itself. Struggles over real issues are necessarily involved, but efforts are also made to contain debate and avoid touchy issues.

Moyo approaches this issue of labour in the transition to socialism at a somewhat different level, and in the context of post-independence changes within Zimbabwe. His theoretical starting point is the dichotomy between labour power and labour which involves a number of interrelated and often contradictory processes. The practice of transition requires the transformation of inherited colonial economic structures, while it is also objectively necessary to preserve productive forces so as to avoid economic collapse. However, productive forces do not exist in a vacuum, but rather reflect the prevailing social relations of production: hence labour processes are also shaped by these social relations. This issue is crucial in Zimbabwe because the profitability and productivity of colonial-capitalist enterprises were rooted in extremely oppressive labour regimes based on racial segregation, where firms relied on the state to organise cheap black labour.

Therefore Moyo suggests that transition should address the task of transforming the character of labour processes. This is an immediate problem because independence brought the old labour regimes close to collapse as reflected in the early post-independence strikes and workers' struggles. The need to sustain productivity implies a struggle over the restructuring of labour processes as against reinstating old forms of production organisation. A legitimate concern for the preservation of productive forces can disguise those social forces which oppose the radical reorganisation of the economy. Moyo recognises the need for labour discipline, but he asserts that its specific forms depends on the character of the economic system. The preservation of productive forces does not necessarily oppose discipline or control as against their absence, but rather revolves around the type of control and of labour discipline which emerge within the transition. He argues that in the case of Zimbabwe the dominant tendency has been to fall back on the logic of old labour regimes rather than come to terms with their transformation.

The articles which make up this Special Issue of the Journal are not entirely consistent in approach, but their coverage and common concern do challenge the simplistic notion which would oppose 'plan' against 'market', or regard any recourse to market mechanisms in socialist economies as evidence of the inherent superiority of capitalism. Socialism inevitably involves a strongly managed economy and attempts to plan (that is, socially control) production according to the interests of the producing classes. Various contributors to this volume argue that this requires not only planning adapted to the market where it exists, but also intervention so as to restructure markets in accordance with socialist objectives.

Unfortunately some key issues which relate to the problem of markets within planning in socialist transition have been dealt with marginally or not at all in this collection. Probably the most important is the relationship between the national economy and world markets. The issue of foreign trade policy is touched upon by FitzGerald and Littlejohn, but problems such as donor pressure and foreign exchange constraints remain an important area for further research.[26]

NOTES

1. Szajowski [1981] gives a catholic listing in the introductory survey to his edited series of books on 'Marxist regimes'. It includes Afghanistan, Albania, Algeria, Augusta, Benin, Capo Verde, China, Cuba, Ethiopia, Ghana, Guinea-Bissau, Grenada (1979–83), Guyana, Kampuchea, Korea (PDR), Laos, Madagascar, Mozambique, Nicaragua, Surinam, Vietnam, Yemen (PDR), Yugoslavia and Zimbabwe. Clearly there could be arguments as to his inclusions (for example, Surinam) and exclusions (for example, Chile, 1970–73) but the numerical importance of the category is clear. We shall accept such a grouping as an empirical fact, and not attempt a taxonomic definition of what constitutes a 'socialist LDC' in the abstract; nor what 'true socialism' might be.

2. For a general discussion of this problematic, and its socio-political dimensions, see Fagen and Deere [1986]. A large number of cases are surveyed in Jameson and Wilber [1984].

3. White et al. [1983] and Saith [1986] contain surveys which, broadly, accept the premise that the construction of socialism is a valid objective of national economic strategy.

4. Morawetz [1980], Wiles [1982] and Desfosses and Levesque [1975] all attempt to apply conventional criteria of 'economic efficiency' without defining this in terms of the wider concept of structural transformation implicit in a revolution, the desirability of its eventual outcome or indeed its capacity for survival.

5. Ellman [1979] and Wilczynski [1982] give perceptive surveys of these reforms.

6. This is already implicit in the theory of the 'shortage economy' in Kornai [1980], but it is made explicit in Kornai [1986] in relation to the Hungarian reform experience.

7. Fitzgerald and Vos [1988] explain in detail the distinction between a 'structuralist' and 'neo-orthodox' approach macroeconomic management. IBRD [1985] is a typical example of an attempt to apply neo-classical economics to an evident case of structural transformation.

8. Particularly his general theorisation of the economics of state-led transition from capitalism to socialism [Bettelheim, 1975] and his analysis of the implications of using value forms to assess economic efficiency [Bettelheim, 1976]. Some of these theories are reflected in

Bettelheim's contribution to this collection, and are also taken up in the chapter by FitzGerald.

9. Mandel [*1986*] gives this case eloquently. Brus [*1972*] gives a similar argument from the viewpoint of Eastern Europe.

10. Particularly that of such bodies as the Soviet Academy of Sciences, and distributed by Progress Publishers on a subsidised basis throughout the Third World. Apparently all such 'manuals' are currently under revision due to *glasnost*, but they remain relevant for the period to which the country studies in this volume refer

11. This is experienced in a number of ways: influence on local official ideology (particularly from *before* the revolution); training of planners and party cadres; and through econmic advisory work.

12. Rumantsiev [*1979*] is the leading orthodox 'manual' in the field.

13. Smirnov [*1980*] is the standard Soviet textbook for Third World economics students.

14. Bablewski [*1987*] surveys and contributes to this debate from a Polish viewpoint. Much of the argument had in fact been anticipated by Kalecki in the 1950s.

15. Horvat [*1982*] has attempted to generalise this (ostensible) Yugoslav system of economic management to a general 'political economy of socialism', which has clearly influenced the concept of 'feasible socialism' put forward by Nove [*1983*].

16. Harrison [*1986*] has an excellent discussion of this reappraisal, which is also the subject of Littlejohn's article in this collection.

17. Ellman [*1979*], Saith [*1986*] both make this point.

18. This question is central to the work of Kalecki [*1986*] on the planned economy and provides the point of departure for the chapter by FitzGerald in this volume.

19. This concept is defined in White [*1983*]; it implies the possiblity of reversability.

20. Thomas [*1974*] is a lucid exposition of this approach, arguing also that adequate industrial scale economies can be obtained from domestic markets for 'essentials' once income has been redistributed.

21. This is, indeed, the central theme of Saith [*1986*], White and Croll [*1985*] and White et al. [*1983*].

22. Bideleaux [*1985*] elevates this to a general proposition on 'communist development strategies'; but see Kitching [*1981*] for a mordant critique of this sort of approach as 'populist'.

23. Griffin and James [*1981*] make this the central element in their approach, while Griffith-Jones [*1981*] stresses the political consequences of inflation.

24. Fitzgerald [*1988a, 1988b*].

25. Wuyts [*1985, 1988*].

26. Comparative data is presented in Stallings [*1986*], while Cassen [*1985*] contains useful material on Soviet economic relations with Third World socialist countries. There are also some analytical remarks in FitzGerald [*1986*].

REFERENCES

Bablewski, Z., 1987, 'The Evolution of Development Theory of Socialist Economics' (paper delivered at the EADI conference, Amsterdam).

Bahro, R., 1978, *The Alternative in Eastern Europe,* London: New Left Books.

Bettelheim, C., 1975, *The Transition to Socialist Economy,* Brighton, Sussex: Harvester.

Bettelheim, C., 1976, *Economic Calculation and Forms of Poperty,* London: Routledge & Kegan Paul.

Bideleaux R., 1985, *Communism and Development,* London: Methuen.

Brus W., 1972, *The Market in Socialist Society,* London: Routledge & Kegan Paul.

Cassen R.H. (ed.), 1985, *Soviet Interest in the Third World,* London: Sage.

Desfosses, H. and J. Levesque (eds.), 1975, *Socialism in the Third World,* New York: Praeger.

Ellman, M., 1979, *Socialist Planning* Cambridge: Cambridge University Press.

Fagen, R.R. and C.D. Deere (eds.), 1986, *Transition and Development: Problems of Third World Socialism,* New York: Monthly Review Press.

FitzGerald, E.V.K., 1985, 'The Problem of Balance in the Peripheral Socialist Economy: A Conceptual Note', in White and Croll [*1985*].

FitzGerald, E.V.K., 1986, 'Notes on the Analysis of the Small Underdeveloped Economy in Transition' in Fagen and Deere [*1986*].

FitzGerald, E.V.K., 1987, 'Kalecki on Planned Growth in the Mixed Economy', *Development and Change*, Vol. 19, No.1.

FitzGerald, E.V.K., 1988a, 'Kalecki on the Financing of Development: Elements for The Macroeconomics of the Semi-industrialised Economy', *Cambridge Journal of Economics* (forthcoming).

FitzGerald, E.V.K., 1988b, and R. Vos, 1988, *Financing Economic Development: a Structural Approach to Monetary Policy*, London: Gower.

Griffin, K. and J. James, 1981, *The Transition to Egalitarian Development: Economic Policies for Structural Change in the Third World*, London: Macmillan.

Griffith-Jones, S., 1981, *The Role of Finance in the Transition to Socialism* London: Pinter.

Harrison, M., 1985, 'Primary Accumulation in the Soviet Transition', in Saith [*1985*].

Horvat, B., 1982, *The Political Economy of Socialism*, Oxford: Martin Robertson.

Jameson, K.P. and C.K. Wilber (eds.), 1984, 'Socialism and Development', special issue of *World Development*, Vol.9, No.9/10.

IBRD, 1985, *China: Long Term Development Issues and Options*, Baltimore, MD: Johns Hopkins University Press.

Kalecki, M., 1986, *Selected Essays on Economic Planning*, Cambridge: Cambridge University Press.

Kitching, G., 1981, *Development and Underdevelopment in Historical Perspective*, London: Methuen.

Kornai, J., 1980, *The Economics of Shortage*, Amsterdam: North Holland.

Kornai, J., 1986, 'The Hungarian Reform Process', *Journal of Economic Literature*, Vol.24, No.4.

Mandel, E., 1986, 'In Defence of Socialist Planning', *New Left Review*, No.159.

Morawetz, D., 1980, 'Economic Lessons from Small Socialist Developing Countries', *World Development*, Vol.8, No.5/6.

Nove, A., 1983, *The Economics of Feasible Socialism*, London: Allen & Unwin.

Rumantsiev, A., 1979, *The Political Economy of Socialism*, Moscow: Progress Publishers.

Saith, A., (ed.), 1985, *The Agrarian Question in Socialist Transitions*, London: Cass.

Smirnov, G., 1980 *Planning in Developing Countries: Theory and Methodology*, Moscow: Progress Publishers.

Stallings, B., 1986, 'External Finance and the Transition to Socialism in Small Peripheral Economies', in Fagen [*1986*].

Szajowski, B., (ed.), 1981, *Marxist Governments: A World Survey*, New York: St. Martin's Press.

Thomas, C.Y., 1974, *Dependence and Transformation: The Economics of the Transition to Socialism*, New York: Monthly Review Press.

White, G., R. Murray and C. White, 1983, *Revolutionary Socialist Development in the Third World*, Brighton, Sussex: Harvester.

White, G., 1983 'Revolutionary Socialist Development in the Third World: An Overview', in White *et al.* [*1983*].

White, G., and E. Croll, (eds.), 1985, 'Special Issue on Agriculture in Socialist Development', *World Development*, Brighton: Harvester.

Wilczynski, J., 1982, *The Economics of Socialism*, London: Allen & Unwin.

Wiles, P. (ed.) 1982, *The New Communist Third World*, New York: St. Martins Press.

Wuyts, M., 1985, 'Money, Planning and Rural Transformation in Mozambique', in Saith [*1985*].

Wuyts, M., 1988, *Money and Planning for Socialist Transition: The Mozambican Experience*, London: Gower.

Economic Reform in China*

Charles Bettelheim**

Since 1978, China has undergone a series of radical economic reforms which officially constitute a logical step in the 'initial stage of socialism', and imply a transition from central planning to a mixed economy. The author argues that in fact the transition taking place is from a soviet type of state capitalism towards private capitalism. The rural reforms involve the restoration of pre-revolutionary production relations, while the urban reforms introduce new capitalists drawn from the ranks of the state administration, to the detriment of the poor and unskilled. There has been a retreat from Marxism as the official ideology, and the legitimacy of the regime is now based on modernisation as a national goal.

In December 1978, the Eleventh Central Committee of the Communist Party of China[1] put the reform of the economy at the head of the agenda for its third plenum and the first official documents on the reforms were issued by the Council of State in December 1979. In the event, the agrarian reform was the first to get under way; in some cases in advance of the official documents. Nine years later, the Chinese economy is fundamentally different from what it was when Mao, the founder of the CPC, died.

The changes (*bouleversements*) that the economy and society of China have experienced go far beyond simple 'adjustments'. Indeed they can be said to constitute a 'new revolution' (*nouvelle révolution*). Thus we must review the evolution of the situation before 1978 in order to ascertain why the 'Maoist model' of development was apparently abandoned so suddenly.

ECONOMIC DEVELOPMENT IN 'MAOIST' CHINA

For those who have always held a critical view of Maoist China, the reason for abandoning the previous 'model' is simple: it was 'inefficient'. The official figures showed that China could not continue to follow the same road: so at all costs it had to take a 'new direction'.

Reality is not so simple. The 'model of development' which took shape under Mao's leadership was certainly not 'perfect' (any real social system has contradictions and imperfections) but the economic and social results obtained were far from negligible. However, certain aspects were less and less

---

* *Translator's note*: Technical accuracy has been given precedence over literary style in this translation, and where the terms are coined by Bettelheim himself the French version is also given. Proper names and bibliographical references have been left as in the original manuscript – E.V.K.F.
**École des Hautes Études en Sciences Sociales, Paris.

compatible with the desire for rapid 'modernisation' which inspired the Chinese leadership of the post-Maoist era, nor were they compatible with the aspirations of significant strata of the Chinese people.

I think it is appropriate to consider the years 1956–78 as covering the essence of the Maoist period. In effect, 1949–55 corresponds to the establishment of state power by the CPC and the construction of the 'new democracy' (*démocratie nouvelle*), but this did not affect individual peasant farms and the process of industrial transformation had not yet begun. From 1955–56 onwards things were quite different. As far as 1978 is concerned, two years after the death of Mao, the structural and political changes were still of a relatively secondary character.

The overall results obtained from 25 years of 'Maoism' are considerable, above all, if we allow for the 'black years' (*années noires*) after the 'great leap forward' followed by the onset of the 'cultural revolution'.[2]

The statistics on the broad aggregates over long periods are still in dispute, and should not be considered as anything more than orders of magnitude. In the discussion that follows I will use the recent official economic indicators, which are generally accepted by foreign analysts, albeit with some reservations. These figures suggest an overall rate of growth of national income between 1952 and 1978 (based on sectoral output) of 4.4 per cent at 1980 prices. This is not a very high rate of growth, but it is respectable (*honourable*) if the events of the period are taken into account, and income per head did rise by 2.5 per cent per annum.[3] However, these positive results should be qualified by the fact that agricultural output was growing at only 2.0 per cent per head.[4]

This growth pattern did not contain an expansion of industrial employment sufficient to permit a reduction of rural over-population. Thus, between 1957 and 1978, although the proportion of the workforce in agriculture diminished from 81.2 per cent to 73.8 per cent and that in industry rose from 7.6 per cent to 15.5 per cent; the ratio of average labour productivity in agriculture compared to that for production as a whole fell from 0.7 to 0.5[5] because annual productivity growth in agriculture was only 0.2 per cent while that for industry and construction was 2.8 per cent.[6]

As a whole, this 'Maoist period' saw an expansion of 25 points in the share of industry in national product over the two decades, which rose from 16.8 per cent to 41.7 per cent.[7] As K.C. Yeh points out, it took Great Britain 40 years (from 1801 to 1841) to increase its industrial share in national product by 11 points, and 45 years for Japan (1878–82 to 1923–27) to raise this indicator by 22 points. However, the negative aspects were:

> (a) the poor progress of agricultural productivity due to a serious rural overpopulation and a poor utilisation of this workforce which slowed down industrial development potential.
> (b) a reduction of the share of services in the national product, which fell from 24.5 per cent to 20.4 per cent during the period under consideration, contrary to the experience of other developing countries.
> (c) the growth not only of rural overpopulation but also of urban unemployment, which has not been properly estimated; by 1978 it reached approximately ten millions, out of a total urban population of 172 million.

(d) the reduction in the marginal efficiency of investment, which fell from 0.75 in 1962–65 to 0.25 in 1970–75, indicating a growing underutilisation of capital due to the duplication of production capacity arising from the state of transport infrastructure; this underutilisation is also linked to insufficient production of energy and raw materials, as well as the frequent breakdowns of overworked and poorly maintained plant.

These factors, among others, contributed to the 'Maoist model' of development being abandoned in favour of far-reaching economic reforms.

THE DETERMINANT FACTORS IN THE 'NEW COURSE' OF ECONOMIC POLICY

The factors which directly determined the abandonment of the 'Maoist model', inspired by Soviet model established in the 1930s,[8] are many. It would be a gross oversimplification to search for a single cause, or even to suggest that one factor was more decisive than others. It is not even possible to establish a heirarchy of the factors which have influenced the adoption of the 'new economic course'; in effect, this 'adoption' was a *continuous process* during which the reforms and economic measures interacted, so that each measure or reform was subject to the influence of factors different from those which influenced the measures adopted earlier on. Among these factors there are certain consequences of the 'New Course' itself, which frequently required further reform measures.

We may list briefly the principal factors which contributed directly to the abandonment of the 'Maoist model':

(a) factors connected to agricultural structures and policies, among which figure the discontent of an important part of the peasantry as to the system of popular communes and the imperative planning (*planification impérative*) system which obliged them to produce crops they considered to be unprofitable and which was not conducive to rapid agricultural development, reducing investment where it could have done most good (especially if it had received higher state purchasing prices) and discouraging local initiatives.

(b) the neglect of light industry, transport, energy and services as against heavy industry,[9] which contributed to the tendency for the standard of living of workers and peasants to stagnate, above all, from 1966 onwards.

(c) the excess of effective demand over aggregate supply, due to an extremely centralised and ineffecient planning system, to a very high rate of investment, and to a system of administered prices which did not reflect either the costs of production or the relation between supply and demand. These problems led to widespread scarcity and the imposition of rationing, as well as the growth of a heavy bureaucratic apparatus and a deterioration in the efficiency of resource use.

(d) the administration of 'detailed imperative planning' which grew more unrealistic to the extent that production became more complex and diversified, and involved an increasing waste of resources and the

appearance of bottlenecks preventing the development of the economic
sectors necessary for more rapid growth of production as a whole and a
greater satisfaction of the basic needs of the population.[10]
(e) a system of state enterprise administration which, faced by the
demands of complex technologies and the need for diversification, did
not leave initiatives to the managers nor itself promote the absorption of
new techniques and the modernisation of equipment, production
systems and products.

These defects in the system, established from 1956 onwards, were
aggravated between 1966 and 1975 by heightened political struggle and
personal rivalries within enterprises and government departments during the
Cultural Revolution. The statistical system broke down[11] and the training of
engineers and specialists was retarded, as was the level of technical
knowledge.[12]

These appear to be the principal factors which, under the particular
circumstances, caused China to abandon the model of organisation and
development, and the forms of management dating from 1956 and essentially
maintained until 1975.

None the less, beyond the specific conditions which contributed to the 1978
reforms in China, we must ask if at some point the weaknesses of imperative
central planning (accentuated by the increasing technical complexity of the
economy) make drastic reform necessary in 'Soviet-type planning' in general.
On this question, it seems to me that the answer must be in the affirmative.[13a]

I believe that Soviet-type central planning (in reality we should call it
'Stalinist') permits during one or two decades an exceptionally high rate of
growth but creates at the same time tensions which require the application of
anti-democratic and repressive measures. This type of planning generates
both fundamental disequilibria and an illusion of control over the economy.
These problems can lead to a social and economic crisis of the sort
experienced by the Soviet economy in the 1970s. In order to overcome this
crisis, and the consequent breakdown of the economic system and social
relations, the abandonment of detailed central planning becomes necessary.
As to the nature of the consequent reforms, in order to be effective they should
in my opinion combine long-term planning, implemented mainly through
'economic levers' (*leviers économiques*), with the use of market mechanisms.

In the event, the tentative reforms of the 1950s in the USSR and Eastern
Europe responded to the decline of growth rates and to the violent explosions
of popular discontent: in 1953 in the Soviet sector of Berlin, and in 1956 in
Poland and Hungary. Except in Hungary, these reforms were halted for
various reasons but the 'reform movement' has continued, developing
underground at the theoretical level and contributing to partial reforms in
various countries. The Polish economist, W. Brus, has thus been able to
distinguish three 'waves' of reform in Eastern Europe[13b] which the
conservative opposition and, above all, the Soviet Union, has been able to halt
– by military pressure if necessary. Since the arrival of M.S. Gorbatchev we
have seen a 'fourth wave' beginning in the USSR itself, even more radical than
its predecessors and with the additional merit of stressing democratisation

and 'transparence' (*glasnost*). Only the future will tell where this wave will go or what its effects will be.

These remarks should indicate why in China, before initiating the reform process officially in 1978, proposals to reform the existing system had already been discussed, although with considerable prudence, because the CPC is even less tolerant in ideological matters than the CPSU. Some of these propositions emerged as practical decisions. For example, a series of measures adopted by the Council of State in 1957 increased the powers of state enterprise managers, transferring the great majority of light industrial enterprises to provincial governments and limiting, in principle, to 12 or 14 the number of obligatory targets assigned to these enterprises. The articles published in 1977 by Xue Muqiao contain a description of certain partial reforms already adopted and of some aspects of the debate that had taken place in China on this question.[14]

In order to understand the implications of the reform process initiated officially in 1978, we should recall the social and economic conditions which engendered it, and the socio-economic system upon which it was to act.

THE SOCIAL AND POLITICAL CONDITIONS OF THE REFORM PROCESS

Since 1977 in certain provinces, especially in the interior such as Cangsu and Sichuan,[15] a strong peasant movement was pressing for decollectivisation. This base movement was to be one of the first detonators of the transformation of the relations of production in the countryside.

On the purely political level and at the top of the CPC, the turn towards reform was taken at the Third Plenum of the Eleventh Central Committee, which signalled the victory of the Deng Xiaoping line over that of Hua Kuofeng, then prime minister and successor to Mao in the leadership of the CPC. The victory of Deng, who had been identified for a long time with radical reforms,[16] had been foreshadowed by his readmission to the Central Committee, the recovery of his functions as deputy prime minister and vice-president of the Party, and by the return in force of his supporters to senior CPC positions in July 1977. It is linked to sympathy with, and loyalty to, Deng, as much as support for his economic ideas, on the part of numerous provincial authorities, and a large part of the military authorities, as well as the population as a whole. Deng thus had the political means which permitted him, with a programme essentially made up of slogans although based on economic and political analysis, to steadily displace Hua, who was considered as the spokesman for a 'conservative' and 'neo-Maoist' tendency favourable to the maintenance of a highly centralised system.

The fall of Hua became inevitable in February 1980 after the eviction of his allies from the Politburo, In September, he resigned as prime minister and was replaced by Zhao Ziyang. His defeat was complete by June 1981, when he lost his post as president of the Party and was replaced by Hu Yaobang. In the autumn of 1982 he was dropped from the Politburo itself, and the victory of Deng was assured. None the less, since December 1978 Hua had ceased to be the supreme leader of the Party, so that 1979 can be said to mark the beginning of the 'age of Deng' (*ère denguiste*).

Before turning to the main aspects of the Deng political line and its implementation, a question must be addressed: was this line directed towards the reform of the existing socio-economic system, or was it to substitute another? The answer to this question is necessarily open and partly hypothetical. My own answer is derived from my judgement today as to what the 'Maoist system' was, as to what Deng seems to want to do and what has been done under his leadership. These latter two have not always been identical, because the requirements of a contradictory socio-economic situation have obliged Deng to take measures against his wishes. The resultant is the *effective* political line followed since 1978.[17]

WHAT ECONOMIC SYSTEM WAS TO BE REFORMED (THAT IS, MODERNISED) AND HOW IS THAT SYSTEM CHANGING?

Having studied the Soviet system,[18] which is very similar to the Chinese, I believe I can answer the first question in the sense that the system established in the USSR during the 1930s, and fundamentally unchanged since, constitutes a particular form of capitalism. State capitalism (*capitalism d'état*) directed by a single party participates directly in all essential economic decisions. It might even be defined as 'party capitalism' (*capitalisme de parti*) where the ruling class forms a 'party bourgeoisie' (*bourgeoisie de parti*).[19] In the expression 'party capitalism' the essential term from the economic point of view is that of capitalism. I employ it because the system is characterised, like all capitalist forms of production, by a double separation: the separation between production units which means that output takes the form of commodities with a price; and the separation of the producers from their means of production which means they are obliged to sell their labour power for a wage determined by those who control the means of production. We can find this double characteristic in the Chinese economic system. We can also find, at least until the reforms initiated by Deng Xiaoping, the sole party at the head of the state.

I believed for a long time that China was ahead of the Soviet Union, having advanced further along the socialist road (*voie socialiste*). The Cultural Revolution and its aftermath, followed by the policy of the CPC since 1978, have forced me to abandon this position as no longer realistic and to insist upon the effective social relations (*rapports sociaux effectifs*) disguised by ideological discourse.

Recent events and publications on contemporary China and on the 1949–78 period,[20] as well as my own direct knowledge of the country and that of colleagues, allow me to state that:

(a) after 1955–57, China entered a state capitalist road (in the form of party capitalism) after the 'collectivisation' of agriculture and the elimination of private capital and individual enterprises.
(b) after the 1978 plenum, as a result of the peasant movement and subsequent struggles, China entered an unprecedented 'new road' following decollectivisation and a drastic reduction in the economic role of party and state. These are the main changes we must study.

In brief, it appears to me that these changes could develop in either of two directions. One is that of a 'mixed capitalist system' (*système capitaliste mixte*), also without precedent, in which the state, the party, private capitalists and various kinds of enterprises all play a certain role although their relative importance cannot be forseen, as it depends upon the evolution of a trial of strength in the economic, social and political fields. The other is that of a 'predominantly private capitalist system' (*systeme capitaliste à dominante privée*) but with a substantial role for the state apparatus, and a less certain role for the party, which may even be displaced by a multiparty system under the pressure of social tensions.[21]

The Deng political line appears to be engaged in the former of the two possibilities outlined above, which permits the single party to play a considerable role, albeit more limited than before. This role will lead sooner or later to open conflicts between the social classes that do not attain expression through the party, and who will struggle for the development of democratic forms. Of course only history – with all its uncertainties – will allow us to know where China is going at present. For the moment we shall examine the major changes since the beginning of the 'Deng period' and their consequences.

'DECOLLECTIVISATION' AND THE TRANSFORMATION OF THE RELATIONS OF PRODUCTION AND DISTRIBUTION IN THE COUNTRYSIDE

What might be called for convenience 'de-Maoisation' (*demaoisation*) did not start immediately after the death of Mao in September 1976, but rather during 1977 in the form of a 'decollectivisation' arising from the spontaneous movement by part of the peasantry. The official 'de-Maoisation' (which was never called this, of course), started in December 1978 after the Third Plenum of the Eleventh Central Committee. In the opinion of M.C. Bergère, this plenum 'marks as fundamental a turning point in the history of the People's Republic of China as the 20th Congress in that of the Soviet Union'.[22] This view appears correct to me.

Personally, I believe that at the economic and social levels, the Chinese reforms are much more radical than those which the USSR attempted in 1956 because they affect the relations of production and distribution themselves. However, the 'perestroika' of Gorbachev, if it is completed, could open a much wider perspective than that presaged by the Chinese reforms because the proposed democratisation and 'glasnost' are potentially capable of over-throwing the structure of political relations which the USSR has known for seventy years – and which to a great extent reproduce the absolutist structures of Old Russia.

In any case, the decisions taken by the plenum in 1978 'officialised' what the peasant movement had initiated; they opened the door and became part of a much larger 'strategic turn',[23] made up of the 'four modernisations' in agriculture, industry, defence and science. The watchword of modernisation had already been proclaimed in 1964 and again in 1975 by Zhou Enlai. It had no practical consequences, first, because of the Cultural Revolution, and second, because the death of Zhou himself had rapidly placed economic decision-making in the hands of Hua. Only in 1978, when he in his turn went, did a new period begin.

As far as agriculture is concerned, the turn rapidly led to the dissolution of the 'popular communes'. In almost all cases, they were replaced by private agricultural units (*explotations agricoles privées*). The land is still formally 'social property' but it is rented for a (renewable) period to peasant households. This is what might be called a 'silent revolution',[24] which arose from the insatisfaction of a large part of the peasantry with collective forms of farming because of the consequent bureaucratisation and distribution of income that did not correspond to individual effort.

During a visit to China in 1983, H. Marchisio noted the number of peasants who criticised the collective production system because the efforts of the more active workers were cancelled by the laziness of others, which reduced the growth of output and incomes: 'whether one works a lot or a little makes no difference, and whether one works well or badly, its the same thing'.[25]

By the end of 1984, it was clear that a new rural China had been born. The decollectivisation movement extended to the whole country, although organisation of production in brigades did survive in some places. Peasant families arranged for their land to be assigned to them through contracts signed with the sub-units of the communes, normally the production brigade itself. Usually these contracts were for three to five years, but since 1984 they have been extended to 15 years and sometimes even to 30. Almost everywhere, the instruments of production are sold or leased to peasant families.

At the end of 1985, there was another important decision: those peasant families who were obliged to deliver a minimum quantity of cereals, meat, fish, fruit or vegetables at prices below those of the market, saw such contracts eliminated. Henceforth, the peasants were only subject to various local taxes and the payment for supplies purchased from the state. That part of production that they do not consume themselves is freely sold either at variable prices according to the market situation or to the state at fixed prices.[26a] Private agricultural enterprise is thus highly profitable, although not landownership as such. Under certain conditions, a peasant who abandons farming can nowadays 'transfer' to someone else his rights to the land.

Private cultivation (*exploitation privée*) based upon the 'household responsibility system' (HRS) became widespread by 1982. In its advanced and most widespread form (baogan daohu), the agricultural cultivator is in the position of being a contractor (*fermier*) where the proprietor is the state itself or a sub-unit of the former communes, which are no longer centres of political power. In 1982 the former local centres of government (xiang) were reinstated, and were almost all operating by 1984.

These fundamental transformations in the Chinese countryside since 1978 have had considerable consequences both agriculture itself and for rural off-farm activities.

Since 1978, the gross value of agricultural production (in the strict sense of the word) has grown by around six per cent a year, and that for stock raising by nine per cent. This growth is due both to greater volumes of production and to the more rapid growth of those crops with the most advantageous prices. Also the output of cereals has risen at about four per cent per annum, edible oils by 14 per cent, and meat by nine per cent.[26b] These results have been obtained by a better use of resources than under the previous objectives set for the communes; more motivation on the part of peasants on privatisation and higher prices for their marketed output. However, these new prices still do not make agricultural labour as remunerative as other activities; so an agricultural household must obtain authorisation in order to move to other activities, and various administrative measures exist to limit the rural exodus. Nevertheless, the higher prices paid by the state have not been entirely passed on to consumer prices in government stores, which required subsidies of some 37 billion yuan in 1984 (about a quarter of central government expenditure) although, since then, higher consumer prices have reduced this burden.

A significant improvement in the economic situation of the peasantry in terms of adequate income from cultivation, without state subsidies or prejudice to urban consumption, would have to be based both on larger and better-equipped peasant farms, and on more non-agricultural employment because there is practically no new land to be cultivated, at least without enormous investment. Present policies favour off-farm employment in the countryside itself, in the market-towns and villages, because the larger cities still have large numbers of unemployed.

At the same time as agriculture has gone through these transformations, new workshops and small factories have sprung up in the countryside. These initiatives are usually due to production brigades or collectives of workers, but they can equally be set up by rural families specialising (with or without authorisation) in non-agricultural activities. Sometimes the workshops placed under the direction of a brigade are in fact managed by a rural family. These changes are the source of additional income which can be reinvested, contributing to an 'industrial network web' (*tissu industriel*) and essentially creating private rural capitalism: in effect, certain families have rapidly returned to the use of wage labour.

The new constitution has made these social and economic transformations official. A resolution of the Central Committee in October 1984 defined the urban and rural 'individual enterprises' as an 'indispensable complement to the socialist economy'. Theoretically they could have, at most, eight salaried employees; but, in fact, this limit was generally exceeded, and was subsequently abolished.[28] Since 1978 these 'new' social relations (which are really those which obtained before the transformations of the 1950s and 1960s) have extended themselves throughout the Chinese countryside, relations which are essentially mercantile or capitalist, and which permit the growth of private savings and investment.

By the end of 1984, 25 million rural families (that is, 14 per cent of the total), were engaged exclusively in non-agricultural activities. To these should be added those which carry on farming jointly with other activities. The richer families among them form a rural capitalist class. A large part of their agricultural and artisan production is sold in local urban markets.[29]

The productivity gains in agriculture and higher prices have raised average peasant incomes enormously, and have reversed the notable tendency to stagnation, especially in marketed output. They have also removed the major obstacle to modernisation and industrialisation represented by the reduced agricultural marketed surplus available in the early 1980s.[30]

Recent data do not permit a detailed analysis of industrial and agricultural production, although some broad indicators are significant.

OVERVIEW OF THE RURAL AND AGRICULTURAL SITUATION IN THE SECOND HALF OF THE 1980S

The aggregate figures for industrial output by forms of property in 1985[31a] are as follows: state enterprises 40.6 per cent; collectives 36.7 per cent; other forms 22.7 per cent. The value of industrial production was thus less than half the total by 1985, while the collective enterprises run by local authorities accounted for a third, and other forms (both individual and capitalist) of property almost a quarter. It should be noted, however, that the real state share is underestimated because of the pricing system which depresses state prices, while the 'collective' sector is, in fact, mostly co-operatives, the rapid growth of which are a sign of vitality as they are established on a voluntary basis. Although the official figures[31b] indicate a much lower weight for the private sector (some two per cent of industry and 16 per cent of retail commerce in 1986) the central government does seem to be worried by this phenomenon, perhaps because of the possibility of there emerging an economic (and even political) power independent of itself. Non-state forms of industrial production are developing more rapidly in rural areas than in the towns, although even here their role is far from negligible,[32] causing a rapid rise in off-farm incomes.

In his report to the Twelfth Party Congress in October 1987, the interim secretary-general Zhao Ziyang stated that the average incomes of the rural population had almost doubled in nine years.[33] This growth is due to both higher peasant earnings and the impulse of off-farm incomes, as agriculture is producing more with less labour. This impulse will continue in the years to come, and stands out in the report by Zhao Ziyang, who insists upon the importance of the development of a market economy (which he evidently refuses to identify with capitalist development) and of non-state forms of property.[34]

The contribution of artisan activities, services and rural industries in market towns and villages should be such that by the year 2000, out of a total workforce of 850 million, some 450 millions would still be rural, but only a third of these would be farmers. Some 20 per cent would be employed in subsidiary activities (storage, forestry, fisheries, etc.) and 40 per cent in industry, construction, commerce and public services (only ten per cent in the towns themselves). If these forecasts are realised, the market towns will number some 60,000 with a population of 300 millions, compared to some 2,700 with a population of 60 million in 1982.[35] This represents an enormous transformation, and, although recent developments indicate that it is not impossible, it certainly faces enormous obstacles. Not the least of these is the requirement for a ten per cent annual growth rate in off-farm activities.[36]

THE ECONOMIC CONTRADICTIONS IN THE CURRENT TRANSITION
REPRESENTED BY THE 'DECOLLECTIVISATION' AND 'PRIVATISATION' OF
MANY ACTIVITIES

The process initiated in 1978 also contains both positive and negative elements, among which we can mention the following ones.

The growth of average incomes is positive, as is the increase in labour productivity, the marked improvement in resource use, the spectacular expansion in marketed output and the rise in savings. The rise in savings is particularly significant in the rural sector, although it is not entirely a positive phenomenon because it is partly in the form of 'forced' saving through the uncontrolled expansion of bank credit and the effect on the poor of price liberalisation.

In order to mobilise this rural saving and direct it towards investments conducive to rapid and balanced economic growth, the role of the Agricultural Bank of China and the Rural Credit Cooperatives has been restored and they have been given greater freedom to fix rates of interest on deposits and loans, taking into consideration local conditions. At the same time, the authorities have allowed private credit groups to emerge, and even private moneylenders.[37]

These measures have not prevented part of the rural savings from draining off to the towns in order to finance hotels in Peking, for example,[38] even though the profits from rural investment are considerable. This is particularly true of small enterprises whose profits are insufficient and must depend upon external financial resources to expand.[39]

If this is the case for small on-agricultural enterprises, it applies even more for the financing of investments urgently needed for the modernisation of farms, improved storage facilities and rural infrastructure which are short of funds, despite increased rural saving. This problem is all the more serious because the funds available from the central government, either directly from the budget or indirectly through the banks, have declined in recent years as a result of both decentralisation itself and the government's own concentration on industry, energy and transport.

In his report to the Thirteenth Congress, Zha Ziyang evoked this problem when stating:

> In parallel with the deepening of the rural reforms, the State, the collectives and individuals should invest more in agriculture; local authorities should devote a greater proportion of their financial resources to multiply rural infrastructure (especially hydraulic projects), combat floods, droughts and other natural disasters, and improve the basic conditions of agricultural production. Land management will be strengthened and the reduction in the cultivated area will be halted . . . .
> We must increase the production and distribution of chemical fertilizers, plastic sacks, insecticides, herbicides, diesel, agricultural machinery, etc. in order to reinforce the material underpinning of agricultural production.[40]

The recent growth in agricultural production (which allowed an aggregate output growth of 12 per cent in 1985, and high rates in the subsequent two years) and the targets fixed for the coming years to meet nutrition and employment targets in relation to demographic growth, require an extremely high rate of accumulation. This had already reached 30 per cent of national income in the early 1980s. It also requires a more rational allocation of investments and an effort to improve the quality of goods exchanged with the peasantry.[41] These conditions have not been met, which has led to an imbalance between supply and demand, and an 'overheating' of the economy.

This overheating is translated into a serious inflationary pressure (which is not properly reflected in the official figures) and intersectoral disequilibria which required a reduction in the growth rate. From 12.3 per cent in 1985, according to government forecasts it should have been reduced sharply in 1986 and 1987, but this was not the case. In the first five months of 1987, industrial production rose by 14.6 per cent even though its annual target was 7.5 per cent, leading to even more bottlenecks. The failure to reduce this overheating demonstrates the weakness of the instruments that the State controls in order to ensure the macroeconomic regulation it desires.

SOCIAL CONTRADICTIONS IN THE COUNTRYSIDE

Even though decollectivisation (or rather, the abandoning of centralised agricultural planning) and farm price liberalisation have had a positive effect on aggregate agricultural output and marketing, supporting a high national growth rate, this has not been of benefit to the entire population, due to the emergence of social inequalities. Differentiation has increased between families in the same village. The richer families generally have the best land and more and better means of production than poor families.[42] These inequalities have also grown between villages (especially favouring those near the towns) and between regions. These effects are generally cumulative, so that those families who were initially better off grow richer – they manage their farms better and are not so subject to natural disaster – and the others get poorer, or at best experience slower income growth.

We do not have very much information on rural social differentiation, only the results of some local surveys. In the prefecture of Chuxian (Anhui province) which was one of the first to adopt the 'household responsibility system' we know that the general increase in income was accompanied by greater inequality. As early as 1981, 1.2 per cent of families had attained an income per head of 500 yuan, while another five per cent earned less than 60 yuan, a considerably greater spread than before decollectivisation. Chuxian is considered to be representative of the underdeveloped third of the Chinese countryside.[43]

The development of property (from tractors to shares in enterprises) has favoured the accumulation of private wealth. In March 1983, W. Hinton met a peasant in the district of Fenyang (Anhui) who owned two tractors which earned him 1,000 yuan a month each, which allowed him to pay off their cost in six months. Another peasant had become a merchant, earning 20,000 yuan a year, and although he paid three-quarters of his income in tax, the remainder was 14 times that of the average income in the district. Hinton adds this comment: 'He could reinvest this money in his own business, buy shares in

new industrial enterprises under construction . . . and reinvest his new income
. . . . Commercial freedom threatens to create merchant princes once more'.[44]

This type of wealth creation is encouraged by the new political line, the promotors of which affirm that this will lead to a general improvement and that classes based on private property cannot emerge. This is incorrect, of course, because to be the owner of tractors, to hold shares in enterprises based on wage labour, or to manage a commercial business with waged employees, is obviously to be a private capitalist. This is what K. Lieberthal, among others, argues when he considers that the newly rich classes in many rural (and urban) activities 'will inevitably generate pressures to increase their social and political power'.[45] The silence of the CPC on this point indicates an official refusal to recognise the reality of this tendency, which in fact has the effect of reinforcing it. Lieberthal indicates that the potential activities of these rich peasants extend from local charity to the financing of higher studies for their children. According to certain leaders of the CPC, these activities recall the role of the enlightened gentry (*gentry éclairée*) before 1949. This comparison, which seems to idealise the true situation, is consistent with certain remarks made by the vice-premier Wan Li who evokes, in relation to the better-off rural classes, the 'sound traditions . . . of the representatives of the advanced forces of production in the countryside'.

It is essential to recall that these new rich are not necessarily the most capable or hardworking peasants, but rather are often former cadres of the brigades and production teams, young educated men, demobilised soldiers or skilled workers from industry and commerce. A 1984 survey in one county of Shanxi revealed that only five per cent of the new rural capitalist class (the survey talks of 'prosperous households') are 'peasants with experience in management', and all the indications are that this is a fundamental trend.

The place of the lower and middle cadres in the formation of a well-to-do stratum and a new capitalist class is a phenomenon also to be found (although less markedly) in the towns. It merits attention because it strengthens the close links between the administration, the party apparatus and the new private bourgeoisie; links which in turn create corruption. Indeed, it would appear that the new private bourgeoisie has entered business without habits of enterprise and profitability (*calcul économique*) but rather with routine administrative ones. Thus a general characteristic of this new social system is that it has been built up in a context of existing 'clientalism' modified to the new environment.[48] What we are seeing is a process which J. Oi has called 'commercialisation of the rural cadres'.[49]

According to M.C. Bergere, there existed in 1985 some 25 million rich rural households, representing 13 per cent of all rural households, and receiving some 3,000–5,000 yuan a year, compared to an average of 1,000–1,500. At the same time:

> the gap is deepening between the income of those peasants remaining on the land and those employed in the new artisanal or industrial enterprises. In the region of Wuxi (Jiangxi) . . . the difference between the income of the former and the earnings of the latter is so great that the local authorities decided, in September 1985, to subsidise cereal farmers

to prevent them from leaving the countryside.[50]

In 1987, the Chinese authorities recognised that 100 million people (mostly rural) were suffering from extreme poverty.[51] The help extended to poor peasants is feeble, so they tend to abandon agriculture altogether. In order to avoid a massive rural exodus, the government has promoted village industry and rural artisan activities, but this has not prevented a large number of peasants from leaving their villages: they crowd the main streets of large and medium towns.[52] The lands they abandon are 'sold' (that is to say, the right to use them is exchanged for money) to the peasants remaining in the village or are reallocated administratively.

This social polarisation in the countryside is quite contrary to the egalitarian ideology of a peasant-based party. It is a source of tension and poor peasants have attacked their richer neighbours 'robbing their goods and destroying their equipment'[53] but little is known of these social conflicts.

Women are the main victims of 'decollectivisation'. In effect, wives and daughters of peasant families are once again working under the household head for no pay, whereas in the commune system they earned 'workpoints' which gave them a certain independence.

Another negative consequence of 'decollectivisation' is the partial disappearance of medical and social services, as well as rural education, because these were financed by the communes and the work brigades. The report by Zhao Ziyang to the Twelfth Congress foresees that the unfavourable situation of the rural regions will be partly overcome by the end of the century when, he states: 'primary education will be generalised in the urban centres and in almost all the rural regions' when 'the GDP will have doubled and will allow people to achieve reasonable comfort'.[54]

These forecasts seem somewhat optimistic if we consider the extent of the urban and industrial problems that remain to be resolved, and the negative effects of the widening economic and social inequalities, factors which the Twelfth Congress did not attribute sufficient importance.

GENERAL REMARKS ON THE URBAN AND INDUSTRIAL REFORMS

Before discussing non-rural problems, three general remarks are in order:

> (i) these problems are much more complex than the rural ones, because the policy of technical and industrial modernisation which the CPC has decided to apply to China requires entirely new structures. These structures must be adapted to the needs of socio-economic development not only of China but also of twentieth-century international economic relations. To a great extent they must be invented, in contrast to the rural sector, where to a great extent it is the former social relations which are being restored in specific forms. This means, of course, that these social relations will have to be fundamentally transformed, but this is not yet a major issue.
> (ii) the divergence in views is still considerable at all levels upon what the urban and industrial reforms are needed in order to reach the objectives set by the CPC, not least because of their novelty. In fact, these reforms

have hardly started, despite appearances to the contrary. It is only possible to give a brief description of them and some provisional conclusions as to their implications.

(iii) these reforms are essentially concerned with the enterprises, the wage system, prices, management and planning. They require analyses of four points in particular: the development of the urban private sector; the drastic reduction of the role of 'imperative' planning; changes in the management and price systems; and the credit system and demand management.

Since 1979, there have been many attempts to increase the efficiency of the management and planning of enterprises. A number of measures have been applied, which are sometimes contradictory. Moreover, the problems linked to urban reforms have generated considerable agitation without leading to a clear direction. Only in October 1984 did the Central Committee decision on 'reforms of the economic structure' recognise the ineffectiveness of the partial decisions taken previously and affirm its desire to carry out an urban economic 'revolution'. The principal aspects of this 'revolution' should minimise the role of government in the administration of enterprises, which would then gain their autonomy and be forced to compete with private firms. Simultaneously, the scope of 'imperative' planning is gradually being reduced as market forces grow in importance due to the price reforms.

(a) The Development of the Urban Private Sector

It should not be forgotten that the urban reforms were initiated in 1978–79 when the urban private sector was already expanding rapidly. They have been aided by the pressure from millions of young people looking for work and by a revision in the definition of socialism. As to the first point, the following figures may be useful:

PERSONS ENTERING THE URBAN WORKFORCE
(millions)

1978	1979	1980	1981	1982	1983	1984
5.44	9.03	9.00	8.20	6.65	6.28	7.22

Source: Statistical Yearbook of China 1985, p.735.

The years of greatest tension – which provoked serious discontent, demonstrations by young people and violence – were those between 1979 and 1981. During these years the authorities naturally gave priority to the rapid increase of employment. These tensions arose from the stagnation in urban employment since 1966 and the return to the towns of millions of young educated people (jeunes instruits) sent to the countryside during the Cultural Revolution.

On the ideological plane, the idea began to appear that China was still in what was henceforce known as the 'primary stage of socialism'. According to this concept (developed at length by Zhao Ziyang in his October 1987 report, but of earlier origin) many different forms of enterprise can coexist with state enterprise[55] and expand, which is a characteristic of *socialisme à la chinoise* in its primary stage.

In fact, along with the establishment of millions of small private firms, small and medium state enterprises were converted into private firms of diverse juridical nature. Usually they were leased, but in practice (and this is more or less acknowledged officially) they usually seem to have become private property in the form of cooperatives where the shares are distributed to the workers and yield a dividend in the normal way. Moreover, the authorities have decided to privatise all those unprofitable and medium state enterprises.

Towards the end of 1984, there were some 4.2 million stores and workshops owned by urban families, which employed some 5.4 million workers.[56] Many of these small individual enterprises were set up by young people unable to find employment, who entered business in order to obtain a modest income. However, although these private enterprises do provide employment, they also provide large incomes for their managers. They have come to constitute one of the main forms taken by private urban capitalism and exist in industry, commerce and transport.

One of the most typical cases is that mentioned by W. Zafanolli, of the Minsheng private navigation company, with five vessels and 160 crew which has been able to compete on the Chongqing–Shanghai route against the subsidised national company with 5,000 employees.[57]

(b) The Drastic Reduction in the Role of Detailed and Centralised Imperative Planning

One of the most striking changes is the drastic reduction in the scope of 'imperative planning',[58] which symbolises the profound transformation in economic relations which has occurred in China during recent years. Since 1979, the planning system has been reformed by reducing the number of state enterprises subject to the plan and the number of fixed targets. In subsequent years, the plan was further reduced. In October 1984, the plenum of the Central Committee decided to reduce to 50 the number of products covered by compulsory planning; the level of output of other products is (in principle) directly determined by market mechanisms, by competition between enterprises and, indirectly, by an indicative plan which should use 'economic levers' (*leviers économiques*) such as credit and fiscal instruments.[59]

We do not have precise and detailed statistics that would reveal how the reduction of imperative planning is progressing in industry; in agriculture it had been practically abolished by 1985. However, we can estimate that as a whole the central plan for 1977–78 covered about 50–55 per cent of gross industrial production, the proportion varying from 100 per cent for the centrally administered firms to 20 per cent for collective rural enterprises.[60] By 1984, the central plan did not include more than 30 or 40 per cent of gross industrial output,[61] and this proportion has since continued to decline. This change has been accompanied by radical modifications in the price system, as well as in the management and finance of enterprises.

(c) Transformations in Enterprise Management and the Price System

The reform of state enterprise management and of the price system in China has been carried out in a number of steps. It is designed to ensure a better use of available resources and to make official regulations on management consistent with the real activities of enterprises because, before the reforms, a facade of centrally planned management disguised an incalculable number of undeclared operations. This situation appears to exist in all centrally-planned economies to some extent, but in China it had reached 'a degree quite out of proportion with previous experience', according to F. Lemoine.[62]

In the first stage (from 1979 until the autumn of 1984) the measures adopted tended to simplify planning, by limiting the number of plan indicators, substituting bank credit for budgetary investments, and by authorising enterprises to sell freely any output above the plan target. Enterprises were allowed to retain a greater part of their profits, weakening the centralised system of resource allocation, and large numbers of enterprises in the same branch were concentrated in large corporations which plan their production and distribution internally.

These partial reforms were shown to be largely ineffective: they could not force the enterprises to reduce their costs, or get them to stop selling illegally (indeed such sales were encouraged by the official authorisation of a poorly controlled 'free market'), avoiding taxes, and distributing bonuses to all employees – even though these were supposed to reward the most productive among them. Moreover, all the financial calculations (*calculs économiques*) were without meaning because they were based on prices fixed since the 1950s and which did not correspond to costs or to scarcity, although the firms themselves expanded as much as possible the output of those products with high prices, and reduced that of those with low prices, in order to maximise profits. When 'free' and 'fixed' prices exist simultaneously, financial calculations become very problematic.

The plenum of October 1984 gave a new direction to the reforms and reduced the role of the imperative plan still further. All those products not included in the plan became subject to the mechanisms of a free market which was supposed to be regulated by a system of indicative planning using controls over credit, taxation and some key prices . . . . At the same time, the powers of enterprise managers were increased, while in theory they were supposed to be controlled in their turn by the trades unions at the firm level. However, these unions do not usually fulfil this role of countervailing power because their leaders are more concerned with the growth of production (the priority for the CPC of which they are members) than with the claims or wishes of the workers. Thus their prestige is virtually non-existent.

The existing production capacity, the rise in marketed agricultural production and the initiative of an enormous number of economic agents, all generated a rapid growth in industrial production, urban employment and monetary expenditure. However, it cannot be said that this indicative planning had any more influence over the functioning of the economy or the production structure than imperative planning. The Chinese economy still suffers from many disequilibria, bottlenecks, and price rises which generate a strong inflationary pressure.

A remarkable aspect of this situation is that it corresponds to an attempted transition away from an economy dominated by sellers (with its shortages, deteriorating quality, etc.) towards an economy dominated by buyers. All the historical experiences indicate that this transition is among the most difficult. In spite of the disequilibria we have discussed, it seems to me that China enjoys relatively favourable conditions for this transition due to judicious use of a price system with two or more levels.

Sufficient studies are not available on the way in which this price system operates in China. However, we do have some partial analyses which throw light on certain effects of this price system and permit some conclusions. A good example is the CESRRI study.[63]

Before examining certain results of this inquiry, it is worth underlining that once the new price and management system has progressively freed prices for part of production, shifting it partly from planned distribution to market mechanisms, and increasing the portion of profits retained by enterprises, these retained profits are allocated to productive investments within the firm and to the development of certain social activities (bonuses, housing, etc.) for the workforce; but they are also invested in activities outside the enterprise. To this end, enterprises can enter into agreements among themselves, create new firms (even under certain conditions, with mixed capital held by the state and the private sector) and make loans. Under the new system, enterprises may also borrow from state banks, from other firms or from the public, especially by issuing bonds. State industrial enterprises can also engage in sub-contracting and set up affiliates in very diverse activities, such as transport, commerce, and hotels.

The managers of state enterprises have wide powers in personnel administration, which is their sole responsibility: the manager decides on hiring and dismissals (although this latter is unusual), and on promotions bonuses and punishments.[64] The main objective of enterprise activities is to guarantee the expansion of their output so as to increase their profits and eventually their internal investment.

After these changes in the functioning of the state enterprises, they have been supposed to operate more and more like private capitalist firms, subject to a limited number of administrative controls. However, these state managers do not yet behave like capitalist managers because a kind of behaviour has emerged, based on the 'paternalism' of the old system and a sort of 'collaboration' with their workers. The form taken by this collaboration in a market dominated by sellers has had far from favourable effects on the reorganisation of the labour process, enterprise modernisation and increased efficiency.

Commenting on the reform of the price and management system, the Chinese economist Xue Muqiao states that the objective of the reforms is to give real autonomy to the enterprises, to make them responsible for their own profits and losses, and to replace political directors with managerial ones. Xue stresses that this reform requires a transformation of the systems of planning, finance, banking, commerce and wages. If the urban reforms are only partially implemented, they will encounter serious difficulties.[65]

The difficulties to which Xue Muqiao refers consist among others in the resistance to change on the part of local and provincial cadres. These cadres frequently demand that managers obtain 'authorisations' for all sorts of purposes from them, even though these authorisations are legally useless. The significance of these requirements is that the cadres obtain their bribes (*pots de vin*) in this way. To combat this phenomenon, the application of the rule of law to everyone is stressed – albeit with only partial success.

The powers granted to directors and local authorities by various central government decisions in order to promote decentralisation are often used by the leading cadres of these institutions for their personal gain. Such 'economic crimes' are severely punished when they are discovered: for example in the first half of 1986 nearly 19,000 people were arrested for such crimes, twice as many as in the same period of 1985. In January 1986 Hu Qili, a member of the politburo announced a further strengthening of the campaign against corruption among the cadres.

This fight against corruption should also play an educational role: according to Hu Qili 'it is necessary to execute one in order to warn a hundred'.[66] This phrase expresses well the brutal determination with which the campaign against corruption (*répression économique*) can be implemented; but although such crime can be limited, it cannot be eliminated because the country is so large and the central authorities have little information about what goes on in the various localities, where in any case the cadres work together in a clientelistic network.

In spite of the negative consequences (officially considered to be transitory) on the behaviour of certain directors, economic cadres and administrators, the reforms forsee a growing autonomy for the enterprises and the transformation of the price system is continuing. More and more the management of enterprises is being distinguished from the concept of state property: the main manifestation of this concept now being the nomination of enterprise directors by the political or administrative authorities, on 'the recommendation of the Party'. These nominations are supposed to give weight to the technical and managerial capacities of the directors, who are also assessed by examinations and competitions, as well as by their own balance sheets.

Taking these points into account, we can examine some of the results of the CESRRI survey. The survey shows that the new system has strongly motivated the state enterprise managers to increase their profits, and has effectively increased the autonomy of firms. The proportion of raw materials bought on the market by firms in the sample (as opposed to planned allocations at fixed prices) rose to 44 per cent in the first half of 1985, as opposed to 27 per cent in 1984. Since the end of 1984, 77 per cent of the enterprises surveyed had felt it necessary to adapt production to demand, while 90 per cent had decided to sell at least part of their production on the open market, although the rest still went to state organisations at administratively determined prices.[67]

Thus the 'two-tier' pricing system was extended rapidly, as an intermediate step between administered prices and distribution and prices determined on the open market, at higher levels. Beyond a certain threshold, those operations made on the open market have a considerable marginal impact and lead to a notable saving in raw materials. As early as 1984, 300 enterprises which had decided to supply themselves through the market had reduced their use of steel per unit of output by 18 per cent.[68] Enterprises obtaining supplies on the open market at higher prices also run much lower stock levels. Various methods of calculation indicate that the extension of operations through the market substantially modifies the way in which enterprises behave.

The enterprise reform of 1984 has since been extended to new firms and new products. However, there are still many weak points, particularly those related to the system of prices, wages and investment finance. This last depends upon banking practices which have not been adapted to the new conditions, and the losses absorbed on their loans are increasing.[69] In order to strengthen enterprise responsibility they can be bankrupted, but this sanction, due to its effect on employment, is rarely used.[70a] It appears that the reform will still have to establish the logic for a new system, with the objective of gradually moving to what might be called an economy 'which achieves an organic combination of plan and market'.[70b]

One of the consequences of the loose management of the banking system which has prevailed since 1984 has been the swelling of the monetary stock and a constant surplus of demand over supply, as the money in the hands of the population has grown more rapidly than the national income.[71]

(d) The Expansion of Credit, Decentralisation and Excess Demand Growth

After 1983, by placing the Popular Bank of China at the head of the banking system, the economy had in theory an institution which could play the role of a true central bank and control the other banks (and the rural and urban credit co-operatives), the insurance companies and an investment company linked to an international investment trust.[72]

The banking system is in practice decentralised, and its local and provincial branches are subject to pressures from the relevant political authorities. In fact, their activities are poorly controlled from the centre, which does not manipulate the interest rate (set too low to dissuade borrowers) but, rather, regulates the kind of loans that may be made and fixes quantitative targets. These regulations are badly applied not only because the provincial and local bank branches are subject to local political authorities, but also because the staff form part of a network of clientelism and interpersonal relationships (quanxi) which determines the greater part of their decisions. Similarly, the share of profits which each enterprise may retain, and the tax exemptions it may benefit from, depend on a series of negotiations the result of which is often an excessive expansion of credit and investment.[73] As the reforms advance, these investments depend less and less on the allocation of budgetary funds, and more on other sources, particularly from the banks.[74] However, the extent of these resources and their distribution depends to a great degree upon the strength of sectoral an regional interests and their success in overriding national priorities.[75]

In effect, the Popular Bank of China intervenes too little and too late, which tends to create a macroeconomic cycle rlated to a succession of 'soft' and 'hard' credit restraints,[76] although never sufficient to correct the excess of demand over supply and thus reduce inflation. The inflationary pressures ceate price rises which have officially ranged from 5.5 per cent to 9.0 per cent in recent years, although observers estimate that prices rose by betwen 15 per cent and 20 per cent in 1985.[77] The rate of inflation fell in 1986, but rose again in 1987, leading to a marked depreciation in the Chinese yuan.[78]

Price inflation is maintained by rising labour costs. This has generated – in situation where investment is also uncontrolled – to a rapid expansion of light industry and a slowdown of heavy industry, which creates the danger of structural disequilibrium because the production of means of production is not keeping up with investment. Recourse to foreign capital – which has been officially encouraged since 1979 – is still minimal and does not cover these shortages. Further foreign borrowing would also result in a degree of external indebtedness that would discourage future investors, so it is not encouraged.[79]

As far as investment efficiency is concerned, the particularly rapid growth of investment in 'unproductive' sectors such as housing should be noted. In the Sixth Plan this sector absorbed more than 40 per cent of the investment allocated to capital construction. This is mainly due to the current practice of redirecting the funds allocated to the reforms themselves and to technological restructuring, towards housing, which incidentally reduces considerably the significance of the watchword of 'modernisation' which is central to the Deng policy. During the Sixth Plan, productive capital construction was only 6.4 per cent higher than in the Fifth Plan, while unproductive construction was 128.8 per cent higher.

This problem was compounded by the new investments in thousands of small light industrial units, too small to use modern technology.[80] The spatial dispersion of small production units reflects, as in the case of Yugoslavia, the breadth of the pressures excercised by the regional and local authorities and threatens also to lead to duplication and high production costs.[81]

In his article on investment disequilibria, T. Pairault throws light on the danger these problems represent for the future development of the Chinese economy. The investment pattern has evolved to the detriment of basic industries and has worsened bottlenecks, while its economic logic is still weak. Although fixed capital formation totalled some 300 billion yuan in 1986, national product only increased by 80 billion yuan; the share of state revenues in national income fell to 25.0 per cent (compared to 31.9 per cent in 1979); and the official instructions to increase investment in energy, transport and technological modernisation were largely ignored.[82]

These disequilibria have not yet revealed their full effects for two reasons:

(a) higher raw materials prices force profit-maximising enterprises to economise on inputs, including energy. These efforts have met with considerable success but seem to have reached a natural limit which can only be overcome by large new investments and extensive retraining of the workforce.[83]

(b) part of the new income does not increase consumption demand but is saved in various forms, such as debentures and shares issued by state firms and joint ventures with the private sector. According to B. Naughton the negative consequences of significant budget deficits and lax bank finance of investment are 'almost balanced' by these forms of saving, to which not only private individuals contribute, but also enterprises unwilling or unable to invest in their own expansion or in the creation of subsidiaries.

The issue of securities has been very successful, due to their high rate of return (nine to 11 per cent per annum) but they do not seem to have reduced inflation very much.

THE TRANSFORMATION OF THE WAGE SYSTEM

After the plenum of December 1978, the Party and the government were forced to reform the wage system that had gradually been constructed since the foundation of the People's Republic, because it was considered to work against labour productivity growth and to be generating continual increases in labour costs. In 1983 96.8 per cent of workers in state enterprises enjoyed the status of 'permanent employees' having been attached to the same firm where they were first employed, although originally this status was supposed to be applied only to college or university graduates. This status turned each state enterprise into a 'little club' (*petite societe*) within which employment tended to become hereditary. Each firm supplied its own medical services, insurance, housing schemes, child care and retirement pensions. Wages were increased principally according to length of service. The system of permanent employment favoured laziness and severely limited the mobility of labour between enterprises, sectors and regions.[85]

The supporters of the economic reforms have attacked this system, and have pejoratavely called it the 'iron rice bowl'. A lengthy conflict ensued between the reformers and the supporters of the existing system, who claimed that it was a 'socialist form', citing Marx to the effect that life should not be reduced to the division of labour. The workers themselves are generally in favour of maintaining the system as they do not wish to lose their job security. Many enterprise managers are unenthusiastic about changing a system to which they are accustomed and which has allowed the establishment of a paternalistic environment and has made it possible to interest the workers in greater profits through bonus schemes unconnected with labour productivity.

The opponents of the system are mainly from among the economic reformers themselves, young 'scientific' managers, and those employees who expect to improve their earnings with productivity-related bonuses. Even though the supporters of reform have been able to demonstrate that permanent jobs retard technological progress and prevent young people from entering employment, resistance to the elimination of this system has been so great that only in April 1983 was the principle accepted of experimenting with limited and renewable contracts.

Outside the state sector there exist a large number of wage earners who do not benefit from this status. R. Low[86] identifies three kinds of temporary labourers in this category:

(a) those who work in the small rural factories, who totalled some 20 million in 1980 and earned about 374 yuan a year. They also work in the fields, and by all indications have increased greatly in numbers since 1980.

(b) the peasants hired by an enterprise from a peasant work team. Their number must have diminished since 1978 in favour of the first category, because the team receives part of the wages.

(c) seasonal workers in cane-cutting, terracing, building and so on. There is no reliable information on their number or earnings, but given the expansion of construction activity since 1980 this category must be growing rapidly.[87]

Compared to these categories of workers, those who have job stability are privileged. They also constitute one of the key social bases of support for the regime, which is why part of the CPC leadership hesitates to alter their status.[88]

Apparently the reformers were – and are – even more enthusiastic about a 'labour contract system' than about industrial modernisation because it means labour mobility and the establishment of a close link between individual productivity and earnings. They argue that between 1978 and 1982 labour productivity hardly increased at all while average real wages rose substantially.[89] In any case, since 1978 labour productivity has risen less rapidly than nominal wages, generating increased labour costs and greater aggregate demand.

Despite the official decision to push forward with the labour contract system, by 1986 it still only affected about three million employees in the state sector, which is a minuscule proportion of the 86 million employed in this sector alone.[90]

Since 1984, the theme of the labour contract has occurred frequently in official speeches. Zhao Ziyang made reference to it in his political report of October 1987, denouncing the practice of what is known as 'eating out of the same pot' as egalitarianism:

> We must continue to overcome this tendency with ideological work and practical measures. Where the conditions are appropriate . . . payment according to standardized piece work should be generalised . . . . It is necessary . . . to make sure that the average rate of increase of wages and bonuses does not exceed that of productivity . . . and that the growth of the consumption fund does not exceed that of the gross national income disposable.[91a]

These declarations demonstrate that the direction of wages policy has been the same over a number of years, but that it clashes with a contrary trend based on the passive resistence of workers and the attitude of many managers and cadres at the grass roots. The influence of these groups is capable of creating a policy which is in effect quite different from the official one.

So that the reforms can continue in depth, it is necessary to re-establish the aggregate and structural equilibria of the economy and to change the mentality of the workforce. This requires more than speeches and the formulation of general policies. It requires the creation of the social conditions and institutions which can inspire the trust of the workers and ensure them advantages equivalent to those which they had enjoyed in the 'little clubs' which the state enterprises always represented. Thus among the problems raised by the application of the reforms are to be found a system of guaranteeing social security, general medical services, and free education; all of which poses serious financial problems in a period when the state share of national income is falling.

OVERVIEW, PERSPECTIVES AND QUESTIONS

Leaving aside for a moment inequalities and economic contradictions, it would appear that the changes that China has experienced since 1978 have agiven a new impetus to an economy which had (according to the Party itself) lost its dynamism and an agriculture which had not expanded fast enough to support industrialisation or higher standards of living. During the period which began at the end of 1978, agricultural and industrial output have grown remarkably, essentially as the result of the increase in marketed farm production and, to an extent, difficult to measure but none the less undeniable, the economic reforms. The initiative of a myriad of small private enterprises, operating more flexibly than the state apparatus, has well adapted production to current demand for consumer goods, although not to the future need for the producer goods required to support steady economic growth.

Between 1980 and 1986 the gross value of agricultural production grew at 10.4 per cent per annum, due to the expansion of the most profitable crops. The index of industrial production rose by 10.1 per cent per annum, and that for light industry by 12.5 per cent.[91b] Industrial expansion was accelerated despite a macroeconomic 'overheating' marked by shortages of energy and raw materials, and a serious increase in imports which it was necessary to restrain in 1987 due to heavy external indebtedness. The economic restraint was not as strong as had been foreseen, and in fact during the first three-quarters of 1987 industrial production rose at an annual rate of 15.3 per cent, about double the planned rate.[91c] These figures confirm that the political power centre does not possess any real means of controlling the economy. This lack of control already existed in the times of 'imperative planning', but it was exacerbated by the relaxing of planning itself and by the measures of decentralisation which accompanied it.

The monetary incomes of the peasantry have risen faster than production because agriculture has been progressively less subject to forced deliveries at low fixed prices, and farmers have benefited from higher market prices except in cases of gluts. Between 1980 and 1985, the annual income of a peasant has gone from 191 to 400 yuan; in 1987 it should have reached 500 yuan. Meanwhile, the average urban wage went up from 762 to 1176 yuan[92] at current prices, although the increase in real terms is less due to price inflation, especially for food.[93]

These favourable results in the aggregate should not disguise what Tuan Jiyuan said in January 1986: there are real difficulties caused by the rapid rise of wages in certain industrial sectors (although the real income of some families has fallen), the excessive rate of investment in relation to the macroeconomic balances, and the over-emission of money and the fall in exchange reserves.[94] He was of the opinion that the 'necessary measures' had been taken to redress the situation. However, experience has shown that it has not been possible to eliminate more than a part of what he called 'the factors of instability[94b] and that the regional and social inequalities continue to grow while the structural disequilibria get worse. Indeed, certain inequalities are even accepted by the regime with the argument that 'someone has to get rich first', presumably on the grounds that they will blaze a trail for the rest, although there is nothing to prevent the former from getting even richer while the latter follow them more slowly or not at all.

In any case, the Thirteenth Congress has confirmed that the reforms are going ahead. Deng Xiaoping is still the top leader and has retained the key role of controlling the armed forces, even though he has given up his other functions. The other octogenarians have retired and a 'new generation' aged 65 or less, more favourable to the reforms, has joined the Politburo.[95]

The Thirteenth Congress possibly marks another step forward in what has become known in China as the 'combination of Marxism and practice', the first two historic steps having been the adoption by the CPC of the idea of the 'new democratic revolution' proposed by Mao in the 1930s, and the December 1978 meeting of the Central Committee following the Eleventh Congress. This meeting gave priority to objective of the 'four modernisations' in place of the Maoist concept of the 'permanent class struggle in socialist society'. This new objective is now closely linked to the idea that 'China is at present in the first stage of socialism' which should last a century according to Zhao in his report to the Thirteenth Congress.[96]

The economic section of this report insists once again – as in previous years – that the need to develop the productive forces as rapidly as possible requires varied forms of property, a struggle against 'egalitarianism', a policy of 'openness' and 'economic and technical cooperation with foreign countries'. He also insists that it is essential to distinguish between ownership and management, judging that the relations between the state and enterprises should always be detailed in contracts. Speaking of enterprises (and including the state by implication) he praises 'healthy stimulation' which permits notable adminstrators to be rewarded or punished, thanks to market competition and the personal responsibility system. This should 'make people respect work discipline' and allow 'the creativity of employees and workers' to be expressed.[97]

That part of the report dealing with the 'reform of the political system' contains few novelties, but it is important because it reaffirms that excessive democracy cannot be permitted to the detriment of state laws or social stability.[98] While talking of the 'progressive improvement' of democracy, of socialist legality at the service of economic reform, of internal and external openness, and of the struggle against bureaucratisation, Zhao repeats that the country should be content to remain 'under the leadership of the Communist Party', functioning on the principle of 'democratic centralism' – which concentrates power at the top of the Party. It is true that Zhao mentions co-operation and consultation among a number of political parties, but to date this has been no more than a parody and there is no indication of change in this regard.[99] On the contrary, Zhao declared that 'the separation of powers or alternation of parties in government as in the West' should never be introduced.[100]

It should also be borne in mind that the press tends to highlight the darker side of what is going on and the abuse of power by various institutions. Thus, since 1986, the press has denounced a number of cases of torture in prisons and police stations which violate the constitution.[101]

These points raise a number of questions which I cannot pretend to be able to answer properly. The first, to which I have already given a preliminary reply, is that of the nature of the socio-economic system which is now dominant. In my opinion China is not 'socialist' in the sense used by Marx and in which the leadership makes its claims. China was a state capitalist (or 'party capitalist') society before and, today, it is one where state capitalism is combined with a number of other varieties of the capitalist mode of production, and with a large petty mercantile production sector which does not rely on wage workers.

In this mixed system, market forces work openly and their existence is recognised and ideologically justified by reference to a notion of the 'initial stage' (*étape primaire*) of socialism. More and more these market forces are outweighing planning, to the extent that the latter has become incapable of exercising real control over the economy. The current 'mixed system' is supported by the great majority of the peasantry, part of the intelligentsia (especially the technocrats) and the top leadership of the Party. The signs of a temporary crisis are obvious, but there is nothing to indicate that they are serious enough to force China into an 'anti-reform' course.

The writings of the theoreticians and ideologues who advise the political leadership and influence 'public opinion', or its equivalent, all support the extension of market mechanisms, albeit under certain control. They even suggest the enlargement of the 'capital market' in order to mobilise savings, although for some time these could accumulate within enterprises because of the bottleneck created by the lack of producer goods output. These steps to mobilise savings were taken in 1986 and, above all, in early 1987. The strategy design assumes that 'socialism' in the traditional sense of the word will take a long time to come in China.[103]

Another problem of considerable importance is the capacity of the state to 'dominate' or 'control' the movements of the economy and of civil society, a problem which faces China just as it does the other so-called 'socialist' countries, the industrialised capitalist nations, and the Third World.

After attempting to control the economy by 'imperative planning' and 'political and ideological struggle' which increasingly impeded the development of productive forces while generating excessive tension and intolerance, China has adopted since 1978 a more 'open' political line (although deviation from that party line is not allowed) and an economic system which combines market mechanisms with state intervention. Although the economic strategy has been successful in terms of growth rates, it has proved deceptive in terms of macroeconomic control and social criteria, which have never responded to the 'directives' or 'orientations' of the party and the government, allowing a number of imbalances and contradictions to get worse.

The regime aspires to administer everything, to the point that it has been called 'totalitarian', but this does not really obtain in practice, although the desire for total domination (*l'aspiration à une domination totale*) has been and is present in party ideology. The economy and society, however, have shown themselves to be both opaque and resistant. 'Opaque' in the sense that nobody really knows precisely what is going on in the economy; all that is known are certain trends and current phenomena and their approximate magnitude. 'Resistant' because institutions such as the civil service, the police, or the provinces disobey or hinder orders given 'from on high' when they consider them inconvenient. This does not mean of course that a determinate policy cannot be at least partially implemented, as the birth control policy indicates. It seems that the population growth rate has fallen to 1.1 per cent[104] which will – if maintained – limit the Chinese population to some 1.2 billion by the year 2000. In quite another area, in 1987 the Chinese government appears to have been able to control, provisionally at least, the serious foreign trade deficit.[105]

This opacity and resistance to state power by economy and society pose serious problems for China because basic industry has not developed at a rate sufficient to equip the factories and workshops to handle the enormous influx of manpower in the coming years.[106] Much more investment has been concentrated in light industry than the government wished; while the small size of most of the new firms, their backward technology despite the watchword of modernisation, and the poor quality of their products, means that their output is difficult to export in exchange for machinery. This poses a serious employment problem for the future.

It appears that the development strategy and system of economic control that China has relied upon since 1978 will have to be replaced by a new combination of more active indicative planning and a new role for market mechanisms, particularly a better use of bank loans and differential interest rates.[107]

In order to resolve the immensely complex problems which China must confront and eliminate 'opacity and resistance' without leaving hundreds of millions of impoverished Chinese by the wayside, it will be necessary to support the devleopment of a broad democracy (*une large democratie*). This cannot happen unless the sad tale of the 'correct line' of the single party, which silences justifiable criticisms if they do not 'conform to the line', is ended. Although the student demonstrations at the end of 1986 were short-lived, as were the youth demonstrations of 1978–79, they pose the real problem: that of a democracy which can make economy and society capable of rising to the challenge of history. State action is obviously indispensable for the solution of long-run problems, but without democracy this action is blind and paralytic, particularly when those who hold state power believe themselves to be all-powerful, clearsighted and possessors of the greatest wisdom.

One more question remains to be answered: what is the role of Marxism in the Chinese polical economy?

After a number of years, the Chinese Communist Party seems to wish to break with the pseudo-Marxist dogmatism before it leads to even worse catastrophies. This is the meaning of Deng's frequently repeated phrase 'One must argue from the facts'. The *People's Daily* of 7 December 1984 put it thus: 'There are many situations which Marx and Engels did not experience, nor Lenin . . . . Thus problems cannot be solved simply by referring to texts they wrote in another age.' It is true that the CPC still claims to be 'Marxist-

Leninist' and uses this label to attempt to silence those who do not agree with the Party, but this did not prevent Zhao Ziyang from saying since 1965 that it is necessary to know 'the truth through facts',[109] nor from the *Red Flag* from stating (on 1st May 1986) that: 'Marxism is not an immutable dogma' [a sentiment to which Marx, who did not wish to be considered a 'Marxist' himself, would certainly have subscribed – C.B.] . . . 'no area should be closed to academic research.' Only a little earlier Su Shaozhi, the director of the Marxist-Leninist Institute, had traced a parallel between 'modernisation' and 'democratisation',[110] a concept which had cost Wei Jingsheng dear in 1979.[111]

Many more statements such as these could be quoted to the effect that a number of influential theoreticians argue that the pretense of 'Marxist legitimacy' should be abandoned.[112] This renunciation could lend authority to the regime, when it regains a degree of legitimacy from the expectations raised from the reforms, by permitting decisions to be taken without having to worry whether they are consistent with a 'theory' which at best can only be indirectly useful in the resolution of entirely new problems. However, this 'authority' will not be sufficient to successfully tackle the difficulties China must face. Real debates are necessary, but they are incompatible in the long run with the temptation for the political leadership to hide behind their own 'political authority' and to try to exercise 'rule over thought' (*gouvernement de la pensée*).

That all these questions should arise now and that the issue of separating the powers of the Party from those of government should be raised[113] demonstrates that the transformation of political and ideological relationships go together with economic reforms. A really new China, even if not socialist, is probably emerging from the matrix of change already under way – a transformation which is sufficiently deep-rooted to be difficult to reverse.

NOTES

Abbreviations

BI	*Beijing Information*
BR	*Beijing Review*
CEMI	Centre d'Etudes des Modes d'Industrialisation
CESRRI	China Economic System Reform Research Institute
CPE	Courrier des Pays de l'Est
EHESS	Ecole des Hautes Etudes en Sciences Sociales
JCE	*Journal of Comparative Economics*
PCC	Parti communiste chinois
PCUS	Parti communiste del'Union Sovietique
PME	Petites et moyennes entreprises
RMRB	*Renmin Ribao* (Quotidien du Peuple)
RPC	République populaire de Chine

1. See list of abbreviations above.
2. The 'great leap forward' disorganised production and transport and, after the experience of rapid growth between 1957 and 1959, national income did not return to its 1960 level until 1965. The 'cultural revolution' was accompanied by falling national income in 1967 and 1968. See Shigeru Ishikawa, 'China's Economic Growth since 1949 – An Assessment', *China Quarterly,* June 1983, pp.242–81, Figure 1, p.247.
3. K.C. Yeh, 'Macroeconomic Changes in the Chinese Economy during the Readjustment', *China Quarterly,* Dec. 1984, pp.691–716, Table 1, p.700. Note that the 2.5 per cent growth is

calculated in 1980 prices and based on national income per head, not consumption. According to S.L. Travers ('Getting Rich through Diligence', in E.J. Parry and C. Wong (eds.), *Reform in Post- Mao China,* Cambridge, MA: Harvard University Press, 1985, p.111) peasant consumption has risen by 0.5 per cent a year over the past twenty years, although urban incomes have risen somewhat faster (ibid., pp.111–12).

4. Calculated from official figures and those given in T. Pairault, '1952–84: Quelle croissance? Quel developpement?', *Revue Tiers Monde* (Oct.–Dec. 1986, pp.952–4).

5. Yeh, op. cit., p.702.

6. Ibid., p.706.

7. These figures are calculated at 1980 prices, from the same source as Note 5.

8. The history of the formation of the 'Maoist development model' has often been described; this is not the place to repeat it. I will simply recall that the organisation of the state sector under Mao was very similar to the Soviet model, even though the collective sector, with its rural popular communes and its collective neighbourhood enterprises, was specifically Chinese. The principles of economic policy were also formally different from those of the USSR, particularly because of the adoption of the principle of 'agriculture as the base and industry as the leader' and the stress, above all at the local level, of that other principle of 'development by one's own efforts'. The general principles of 'imperative planning' were very close to those of the USSR, although in theory a greater scope was allowed to enterprise initiative. In my book, *La construction du socialisme en Chine* (Paris: Maspero, 1965 – in collaboration with J. Charrière and H. Marchisio) there is a description of the 'Chinese model' on the eve of the Cultural Revolution. In *Mao Tsé-toung et la construction du socialisme en Chine* (Paris: Hachette, 1974) are to be found unpublished texts (translated by Hu Chi-hsi) which state Mao's basic ideas on these problems, particularly critical notes on Stalin's *Problèmes économiques du socialisme en URSS.*

9. On these points, see Xue Muqiao *Chinese Socialist Economy* (Beijing: The Foreign Language Press, 1986), and the analysis of Chinese statistics in *China's Economy Looks Towards the Year 2000,* Vol.I, 'The Four Modernisations' R.F. Dernberger, above all 'Economic Policy and Performance' (JCE, Washington: 1986, pp.15–48) and R.F. Field, 'China: The Changing Structure of Industry' (pp.505–47).

10. On living standards, Liang Wensen and Tian Liangshia ('Final Products: A New Departure', *Social Sciences in China,* No.4, 1980) state that between 1957 and 1977, despite an increase of 10.7 per cent in the average nominal wage, the real wage declined and the real income per head of the peasantry only rose marginally.

11. R.M. Field (op. cit., p.506) suggests that during the two years after 1966 the Central Bureau of Statistics could hardly function because its staff had been reduced to 14! This drastic reduction in the number of professionals and specialists in the enterprises and public administration was due principally to their not being trusted by the Revolutionary Committees.

12. During the Cultural Revolution the universities, engineering schools and other similar institutions only functioned at low levels (at least between 1966 and 1974), while reading foreign publications – even technical ones – was regarded with suspicion.

13a. Since the 1960s, I have insisted on the need to avoid becoming trapped within the constraints of highly centralised imperative planning and to take mercantile relationships into account. The main elements of my argument then can be found in two books: *La transition vers l'économie socialiste* (Paris: Maspero, 1968) and *Calcul économique et formes de propiété* (Paris: Maspero, 1970).

13b. W. Brus *Histoire économique de l'Europe de l'Est 1945–85* (Paris: Ed. La Decouverte, 1986).

14. See Xue Muqiao, 'The Two Roads Struggle in the Economic Field during the Transition Period' (*BR,* 1977, 49–52; 2, 9, 16 and 16 Dec.), and more generally C. Riskin *China's Political Economy – the Quest for Development since 1949* (Oxford: Oxford University Press, 1987).

15. In Sichuan, this movement enjoyed the support of provincial party leader Zhao Ziyang, the future prime minister, although this fact should not obscure its mass support among the population. See A.R. Khan and L. Eddy *Agrarian Politics and Institutions in China after Mao* (Bangkok: ILO, 1983), particularly pp.14–15.

16. Some biographical points about Deng Xiaoping might be useful, as he is the true leader of the Chinese People's Republic. Born in Sichuan in 1904, Deng did political work in France in the early 1920s with Zhou Enlai, the future prime minister of China from the establishment of the

new regime until his death in 1976. On returning to China, Deng took part in the guerrilla war and was on Mao's side in the conflict within the leadership about the strategy to be adopted against Chian Kai-shek. He was a leader in the armed struggles between 1934 and 1949. He is, therefore, one of the 'founding fathers' of the People's Republic.

Initially one of the leading administrators in south-east China, he soon moved to high office at the centre of power: he was deputy prime minister under Zhou Enlai in 1952 and became a member of the Permanent Committee of the Politburo and Secretary of the Central Committee in 1956. The Great Leap Forward of 1958 was the start of his disagreement with Mao, and Deng was one of the main architects of the pragmatic policies applied between 1960 and 1962, but which subsequently became one of the principle targets of the Cultural Revolution after 1966. He was 'rehabilitated' in 1973 and appointed deputy prime minister and party vice-president in 1975. However, after the death of Zhou he was once again forced out of power in April 1977.

Shortly after the death of Mao and the arrest of the 'Gang of Four' in October 1976, Deng appeared again and was restored to his posts in 1977. He then supported a process of 'de-Maoisation' and modernisation. In the Twelfth Congress of September 1982, he became chairman of the advisory commission to the Central Committee, created on his initiative, while keeping his seat on the permanent committee of the Politburo and his membership of the powerful Military Commission.

17. On the notion of the 'effective political line' see my *Questions sur la Chine apres la mort de Mao* (Paris: Maspero, 1978, pp.70 *et seq.*)

18. See the four volumes of my *Les lutes de classes en URSS* (Paris: Seuil/Maspero, 1974–83). This study is complemented by two articles published by the *Monthly Review* in Sept. 1985 and Dec. 1986.

19. *Les luttes* ... Vol.III, t.1, pp.9–17, pp.41–64, pp.167–204, pp.305–6; and Vol.III, t.2, pp.157–223.

20. Among these, I will only mention some of the better-known ones: Riskin op. cit.; Perry and Wong, op. cit.; M. Chossudovsky, *Towards Capitalist Restoration? Chinese Socialism after Mao* (London: Macmillan, 1986); F. Lemoine, *L'économie chinoise* (Paris: La Decouverte, 1986); M.C. Bergère *La Republique Populaire de Chine de 1949 a nos jours* (Paris: Colin, 1986); C. Aubert (ed.), 'Les réformes en Chine' (special issue of the *Revue Tiers Monde*, Oct.–Dec. 1986); and R. Dumont *La Chine décollectivisée* (Paris: Seuil, 1984).

21. One possible answer to the question is given by Bergère (op. cit., p.160) who argues that China still has to undergo its own 'Meiji revolution'. For my part, I believe that the specificity of China's history and conditions is such that no foreign 'model' can be applied to it.

22. Bergère, op. cit., p.159.

23. According to Ma Hong, the president of the Social Science Academy.

24. This expression has been employed by C. Aubert 'Rural China: The Silent Revolution' (*Projet*, July 1982).

25. See the project 'Une Chine rurale "responsabilisée" ' carried out jointly by the Laboratoire d'Anthropologie et de Sociologie de Tours, the Institut National d'Economie Rurale (Montpellier) and the Amitiés Franco-Chinoises. They published a report in 1985, in which H. Marchisio participated as author and editor.

26a. These prices are fixed at a level between the former obligatory devilery price and that of the market. On this point see Riskin (op. cit., pp.284–302) who describes well the process of privatisation of peasant plots and the successive directives designed to halt the peasant movement, which was going further than the Party leadership seemed to want. On the problems of agricultural prices and incomes during this period, see also T.B. Wiens, 'Issues in the Structural Reform of Chinese Agriculture' *Journal of Comparative Economics,* Vol.11, pp.373–84 (1987) which shows the narrowing gap between market prices and the higher prices paid by the state.

26b. It should be clearly stated that in general Chinese statistics are particularly unreliable. This holds true in all fields including demography, industry, employment, etc. The original sources themselves admit distorted declarations and the statistical services do not have the means to undertake serious checking. None the less these statistics reflect the direction of change and its approximate extent.

27. A rough estimate from the figures given in Wiens op. cit., p.379.

28. Statement by the director of the Rural Research and Development Centre (*Le Monde*, 10 Sept. 1987).

29. See Lemoine, op. cit.; *Agence Xinhua (XH)* of 13 Jan. 1985; and *Quotidien du Peuple (RMBR)* of 10 Oct. 1985; all cited by W. Zafanolli, 'De la transition socialiste a la transicion capitaliste?' *Est–Oest*, No.4, 1985, p.11.
30. F. Lemoine, 'Les cahots de la Chine', *Le Monde,* 29 April 1986.
31. Figures given by Professor Xun Dazhui to a group of Indian economists and reproduced in the mission report by K.S. Krishnaswamy, *Economic Change in China* (Bangalore, Aug. 1987) p.18.
31b. 28 Sept. 1987, p.5.
32. It is known that employment in non-state industry and commerce reached 7.5 million in 1983, of which 5.2 millions were in rural areas, which was 16 times higher than in 1978 (Riskin, op. cit., p.382).
33. See the political report by Zhao in *BI*, 9 Nov. 1987, p.19.
34. Ibid., pp.22–3.
35. Lemoine op. cit., pp.81 and 84.
36. Weins op. cit., p.382.
37. Ibid., p.374.
38. Lemoine op. cit., p.85.
39. See C.P.W. Wong, 'Between Plan and Market – The Role of the Local Sector in Post-Mao China', *JCE* 11 (1987), p.391.
40. Zhao Ziyang *BI*, 9 Nov. 1987, pp.28–9.
41. Enterprise management (private, collective or state) was from now on judged essentially by profitability and quality control was poor. Sales of low quality products multiplied, as the result of the lack of information on the part of the purchaser, of the absence of administrative control, or of collusion with the distributors. In this way on the Guangxi 50,000 hectares of rice were destroyed by bad fertilisers imported from another province; while in Hubei hundreds of hectares have been made unsuitable for cultivation by the excessive application of insecticides under the distributor's advice. Unsafe practices also occur in consumer goods, as in the sale of 'reconditioned' industrial oil as 'salad oil', poisoned cottonseed oil, or adulterated alcohol. Many thousands of people are victims of these sharp practices, of which state enterprises are also guilty; they also demonstrate the collapse of regulatory mechanisms and the corruption of both managers and civil servants. According to *Le Monde* (20 Aug. 1987) one-and-a-half million manufacturers and merchants of perished foodstuffs were punished between 1984 and 1987.
42. The *personal relationships* between peasant families and the administrative cadres responsible for the distribution of land, with the bank staff responsible for the distribution of the means of production (part of which was allocated adminstratively rather than being sold at market prices) played an important role here, as in other areas of the economy.
43. See *BR* (21 June 1982) and Riskin, op. cit., p.307.
44. W. Hinton, 'A Trip to Fenyang County', *Monthly Review*, Nov. 1983, pp.24–6.
45. K. Leiberthal, 'The Political Implications of Document No. 1', *China Quarterly* (March 1985), pp.109–10.
46. Wan Li, 'Developing Rural Commodity Production', *BR* (27 Feb. 1984).
47. Lu Yun, 'Specialised Households Emerge', *BR* (3 Dec. 1984), pp.26–7.
48. B. Chavance, 'L'économie politique des réformes chinoises', forthcoming in *Revue d'Etudes Comparatives Est*–Oest.
49. J. Oi, 'Commercialising China's Rural Cadres', *Problems of Communism* (Sept.–Oct. 1986).
50. Bergère, op. cit., p.183.
51. J. Crall, 'L'obsession du grain', *Le Monde* (8 Sept. 1987), p.40.
52. Riskin, op. cit., p.308.
53. Bergère, op. cit., p.133.
54. Zhao Ziyang, *BI* (7 Dec. 1987), p.25.
55. *BI* (9 Nov. 1987), p.22 *et seq.*
56. According to W. Zafonelli, 'De la transition socialiste a la transition capitaliste' (*Est–Ouest*, No.4, 1985, pp.33–4) in 1984 70,000 state PMEs had already been privatised.
57. Ibid., p.34.
58. This transformation has a symbolic nature, for two reasons: first, imperative planning was considered to be indissolubly linked to socialism as such; and second, this change would overthrow the formal rules by which the economy functioned. In fact, production and investment by enterprises were already quite distinct from the forecasts and orders of the

plan, as is the case in all other socialist countries.

59. Lemoine, op. cit., p.32.
60. These estimates seem to be confirmed by local data: see, for instance Wong, op. cit., pp.385–98.
61. Ibid., p.389.
62. Lemoine, op. cit., p.29. There are many reasons for this exceptionally acute separation between the facade of planning and reality. They range from the upheavals the country suffered between the late 1950s and 1978, to the rudimentary state of the statistical services and the planning apparatus itself. The Chinese statistical service had only 16,000 staff on the eve of the reforms, compared to 220,000 in the USSR (ibid., p.29). To these must be added the size of the population, the extent of the country itself, and the weakness of the data collection and communications systems.
63. For example, I use here the results of the surveys carried out in 1984 and 1985 by the Chinese Economic System Reform Research Institute (CESRRI). These surveys cover 429 enterprises in 27 towns and are complemented by two opinion polls (with a sample of 76,000) on the public reaction to the price reforms of May 1985, on the attitudes of young people to the reforms, and on socio-economic conditions. A summary of these surveys has been published by Chen Yizi, Wang Xiaoqiang and their colleagues from the CESRRI as 'Reform: resultats et lecons de l'enquete de 1985 du CESRRI' (*CJE*, Sept. 1987, pp.462–78).
64. On these points see B. Chavance, 'La nouvelle strategie de developpement en Chine'(*Cahiers du GERRTTD*, Serie Developpement, U. Paris 7, Jan. 1986), Lemoine, op. cit. and Zafanolli, op. cit. For the changes in state enterprise operations up to 1984, see also R.M. Field, 'Changes in Chinese Industry since 1978' (*China Quarterly*, Dec. 1984, p.742 *et seq*).
65. *Quotidien de l'economie*, 25 Jan. 1986.
66. *Quotidien du Peuple*, 14 Jan. 1986.
67. Chen Yizi *et al.* op. cit., p.464.
68. Ibid., p.465.
69. Between June 1983 and June 1985, the proportion of bad debts to construction banks rose from 24 per cent to 52 per cent of their outstanding loans (ibid., p.465).
70a. The press only rarely publicises these bankruptcies, but see the *Quotidien des Travailleurs* (16 July 1986) on the case of a Shenyang factory. A law of 2 Dec. 1986 regulates bankruptcy in state enterprises. This law is only to be applied gradually and on an experimental basis. The refloating or the restructuring of a loss-making enterprise can be attempted by an administrator nominated by the supervisory authority. When such operations require additional financial resources, it is possible to have recourse to a share issue, of which a proportion should be taken up by the employees of the enterprise themselves (*Le Monde*, 30 Dec. 1986).
70b. According to Liu Guoguang, 'La planification combinee avec le marche' (*BI*, 2 Nov. 1987, pp.15–18), who attempts to systematise the experience of the economic reform decisions of the Third Plenum as a consequence of the Twelfth Congress.
71. Since 1984, the purchasing power of the urban and rural population rose by 200 billion yuan, equivalent to 60 per cent of their monetary income; in 1985, consumer demand increased by 80 billion yuan (Chen and Wang op. cit., p.471).
72. Zhou Xiapchuan and Zhu Li, 'China's Banking System: Current Status, Perspective on Reform' (*CJE*, Vol.11, 1987, pp.399–409).
73. B. Naughton, 'Macroeconomic Policy and Response in the Chinese Economy: the Impact of the Reform Process' (*CJE*, Vol.11, 1987, pp.334–53).
74. Between 1982 and 1986, aggregate investment (in the state sector and other sectors) rose from 120 to 297 billion yuan, an annual rate of growth of over 25 per cent. Between 1982 and 1985, investment tripled in the private sector and doubled in the state sector. Pairault, who gives these figures, observes that in 1986 one-third of investment was outside the state sector, and that its growth was particularly rapid: about 31 per cent per annum between 1982 and 1986. He also points out that the banks have become a very important financial instrument; since 1979 their role has been transformed: 'from simple cashiers distributing government investment allocations [they] have . . . recovered their function as sources of credit on their own account – and even as creators of money – and have thus contributed to the expansion of extra-budgetary funds' (T. Pairault, 'Investissement et fonds extra-budgetaires en Chine', *Le Courrier des Pays de l'Est*, June 1987, pp.25–31).
75. Chavance, op. cit.

76. In the model that Zhou Xiaochuan and Zhu Li constructed in order to simulate the banking system, they demonstrate that under the current Chinese conditions 'the banking system will characteristically generate a monetary policy cycle – cycling between tight and easy money' (op. cit., p.405).

77. *Le Monde* (12 Aug. 1986), *BI* (7 Sept. 1987, p.5; 14 Sept. 1987, p.17). It is extremely difficult to construct an all-China price index because price controls are exercised by the state, by provinces, and by municipalities. The proportion of prices fixed by the state fell from 98 per cent in 1978 to 20 per cent in 1986, but that of locally fixed prices (albeit only 'indicatively') was still 30 per cent in Guangzhou (a town in Guandong). The situation differs from one town to another. 'Indicative' prices allow sales organisations to adjust their prices within certain limits according to quality and market fluctuations.

In early 1987, 50 per cent of retail prices were entirely free in Guangzhou as opposed to two per cent in 1978. According to the Guandong Price Bureau, retail prices and wages have changed as follows in Guangzou:

	1979	1980	1981	1982	1983	1984	1985	1986
Retail Prices (annual change)	4.5	12.9	5.9	0.3	0.6	1.2	22.5	3.3
Annual Income of employees (yuan)	824	931	1008	1083	1144	1318	1596	1759

The policy of reducing the number of categories of subsidised goods reduced them from 26 in 1979 to 12 in 1985. This eliminated the losses on the sales of certain goods and reduced the dispersion of profit rates (Li Rongxia, 'La réforme des prix au Guandong', *BI*, 14 Sept. 1987 pp.13–18).

78. The yuan depreciated 47 per cent against the US dollar between December 1984 and December 1986, and 62 per cent aainst the deutschmark (*CPE*, June 1987, p.3).

79. It is not feasible to examine the important topic of Chinese international economic relations within the space of this article. It should be recalled that China has 'opened' here economic policy in this respect, creating 'economic zones' which are really free trade areas where foreign investments receive particularly advantageous conditions – at least in principle, because reality is more complex. This policy has also led to the creation of joint ventures and foreign borrowing. These forms of 'opening', if taken to their logical conclusion, might justify alarm as to increased external dependence; which explains why in March 1985 Zhao Ziyang, in his report on government activities, recalled a principle that had seemed somewhat forgotton, that of 'counting on one's own strength'.

Chussudovsky, op. cit., discusses this 'policy of opening' and some of its consequences, with a wide bibliography. See also Wang Niang, 'La reforme bancaire en Chine' (*CPE*, June 1987 pp.41–55).

80. For example, the optimal size of a washing machine plant is some 200,000 units per annum, but of the 130 factories of this kind in China in 1984, only 9 had this capacity (Chen and Wang, op. cit., p.475).

81. Ibid., p.474. The rapid growth of real estate investment is revealed for 1979–84) in *BI* (28 Sept. 1987). This growth is partly explained by the twenty-year lag in housing construction.

82. Pairault, op. cit., p.39.

84. Naughton, op. cit., p.349. Wang Niang op. cit. also gives some data on share issues and the creation of stock markets in China (pp.49–50). Yue Haitao, 'Emission d'actionns a Shanghai' (*BI*, 5 Oct. 1987, pp.24–9) explains the conditions under which state enterprises may issue shares to the public (for up to 30 per cent of their capital), the limited rights of shareholders, and the guarantees in case of bankruptcy.

85. In 1985 the subsidies and indirect benefits received by state employees were worth 526 yuan per head, equivalent to 82 per cent of the average wage (N. Lardy, 'Consumption and Living Standards in China', *CC*, No.100, Dec. 1984, p.854). At this time total wages, including social services, of a permanent state employee were six times the income of a peasant (ibid., p.851). On the system of permanent employment and the attempts to reform it, see White (op. cit. pp.368 *et seq.*).

86. R. Lew, 'Chine: un Etat-ouvrier? Le monde ouvrier sous le "socialisme reel" ' in C. Aubert *et al., La société chinoise après Mao* (Paris: Fayard, 1986), pp.43–89.

87. Ibid., pp.66–7.
88. It should be added that since then they have been free to leave their employment.
89. Between 1978 and 1981 worker productivity grew hardly at all, and in fact fell between 1980 and 1981. After 1982 there was a notable improvement. Productivity increased eight per cent between 1980 and 1984 (White, op. cit., p.373) but this is undoubtedly due mostly to the reduction of ineffective workers in industry and the onset of 'modernisation'.
90. Ibid., p.378.
91. See the political report mentioned above, *BI* (4 Nov. 1987), p.34.
91b. According to the Chinese statistical yearbook for 1986.
91c. *BI*, 2 Nov. 1987.
92. At the official exchange rate, the yuan was worth 2.35Frs. in February 1986; but this rate overestimates the purchasing power of the Chinese because traditional consumer goods are very cheap if translated into francs; this is also true of services such as rents and canteens, for example. On urban incomes, see also note 77 above. Peasant income per head estimated for 1987 in *BI* (14 Sept. 1987) p.7; the same source indicates that in 1987 that incomes will be 16 per cent higher than in 1986 for peasants, as opposed to 13 per cent for urban dwellers, at current prices.
93. The government is trying to stop the acceleration in retail inflation without abandoning price 'liberalisation' by also exercising stricter controls.
94. Tian Jiyuan was speaking as a member of the Politburo and as Deputy Prime Minister for economic affairs; see P. de Beer, 'La Chine au grand vent des réformes économiques', *Le Mond Diplomatique* (July 1986), pp.1 and 7.
94b. The foreign trade situation has improved in 1987 due to the measures taken to reduce the deficit. During the first nine months of the year, exports rose 24 per cent (reaching US\$ 26.5 billion) and imports fell by four per cent (to US\$ 29.2 billion), so that the trade deficit fell to US\$ 2.7 billion as against 9.0 a year earlier (*BI*, 2 Nov. 1987, p.10).
95. See X. Luccioni, 'Vers le "troisième pas historique" de la Chine', *Le Monde Diplomatique* (Dec. 1987), p.3.

    The composition of the standing committee of the Politburo as well as Zhao's report and what is known of the debates, all confirm that the Thirteenth Congress saw the victory of the reformers. Hu Yaobang, the former general secretary, remains in the Politburo and in the standing committee there are two of his political allies, Hu Qili and Qiao Shi. Zhao, the present general secretary, is one of the instigators of the reforms, and enjoys a noticeable popularity – particularly among the peasants. See P. Sabatier, 'Zhao Ziyang – The Reformist Wave', *Liberation* (3 Nov. 1987), p.18. The influence of the 'hardline planners' such as Li Peng and Yao Yilin has been reduced, and they no longer represent a strong current of opinion. A small sign of democracy was that there were more candidates than places for the central committee: after a secret ballot Deng Liqun, one of the adversaries of the 'liberal intellectuals', was excluded.

    The majority of the amendments proposed by those at the Congress to the Zhao report were in the sense on a 'gradual but real liberalisation'. One such amendment spoke openly of 'violations of rights and liberties'. See F. Deron, 'Passionants amendements' *Le Monde* (9 Nov. 1987).
96. *BI* (9 Nov. 1987) and Luccioni, op. cit.
97. *BI* (9 Nov. 1987), pp.30–35.
98. This slogan had been one of the 'great orientations' launched by Mao during the Cultural Revolution. It had favoured the multiplication of the *dazibao,* and made possible the publication of small uncensored journals, the right to strike and the election of really representative Revolutionary Committees. The 'great democracy' had attracted the support of those who saw in it a means of fighting the party bureaucracy. In fact, after a brief initial impulse from May 1966 until February 1967, the Cultural Revolution movement came more and more under the control of Mao's followers. On these little known events, it is indispensable to read the book by Hua Linshan, *Les années rouges* (Paris: Seuil, 1987). Denguist policy has been to condemn the 'great democracy', including the right to strike, separating in this way economic liberalisation from political freedom.
99. The minor parties, including a local remnant of the Cuomindang under the control of the CPC, are only memories and their existence does not imply in any way an officially recognised 'pluralism'.
100. *BI* (9 Nov. 1987), p.35.

101. More than 2,000 cases of this kind occurred between January and June of 1987 (*Chronique d'Amnesty International,* Nov. 1987, pp.8–9). A reading of the press shows that these practices continue despite the apparent desire of the authorities. Torture is an ancient and deep-rooted habit in China, sometimes leading to the death of the victim. Here again the weakness of a supposedly 'strong power' when facing solid institutions is apparent.

102. Notably the emission of bonds by the Bank of China (not to be confused with the People's Bank of China to which it is subordinated), which have a face value of 10,000 yuan and cannot yield more than savings accounts. Enterprises are authorised to subscribe to these bonds and to rediscount them to other firms (within the state sector) or to issue their own. On share issues and bearer bonds see *Le Monde* (7 May and 2 Sept. 1987); at present domestic issues of bonds and shares are reserved to Chinese nationals.

103. Many authors speak of the reforms as a 'transition from socialism to capitalism'. As well as Chossudovski, op. cit., there is J. Decornoy 'Socialisme . . . ou tentation capitaliste' (*Le Monde Diplomatique,* Dec. 1987) and a small number of Chinese opposed to the actual course of events: Zhao Ziyang made an indirect reference to them in his report to the Thirteenth Congress (*BI,* loc. cit., p.23). Many others speak of a 'bureaucratic class' which holds power above all in 'the administration of the means of production and in its role as mediator in class conflicts'; see, for example, C. Durand, 'Toward a Theory of the State in Socialism', *Monthly Review* (June 1984).

104. This is an approximation. Not all births are registered, especially in the villages. Moreover, it is also the consequence of the infanticide of new-born girls, according to custom. However, if the birth rate does not fall in the near future, the population growth rate may exceed 1.5 per cent because for a number of years after 1987 the number of fertile women will rise rapidly (this figure rose by 7.3 million in 1987) as a result of the 'baby boom' of the 1960s (*BI,* 7 Sept. 1987, p.31).

105. F. Crouigneau, 'Dérapage des prix et des investissements' (*Le Monde,* 6 Oct. 1987).

106. Thirteen million a year by 1990, and nine million from 1990 to the year 2000 (Lemoine, op. cit., p.80). See also the changes in the balance of payments and the reserves between 1982 and 1986 (*BI,* 7 Sept. 1987, p.32).

107. A return of 'imperative planning' seems very improbable. Its shortcomings are still obvious: for example, it encouraged the construction of factories (above all steel mills) supplying products so defective that they could not be sold; the state continued to extend orders to them so that they would not close down.

108. I refer here to the appearance in Peking on 15 November 1978 of the 'democratic wall' in which young people took the initiative. On this wall among others, thousands of citizens pasted posters written by themselves which raised questions previously stifled by official thought. They began to get answers. This experience began to spread, but in March of 1979 on the orders of Deng Xiaoping it was crushed and one of its leaders Wei Jinsheng was arrested. Wei was sentenced to a long prison term and after some years all trace of him was lost because international solidarity did not pursue the case; about which the Chinese leadership was pleased, demonstrating thereby their sensitivity on the issue.

109. Luccioni, op. cit.

110. *Le Mond* (6 June 1986).

111. At the end of 1987, Su was relieved of his post as Director, which seems to indicate that he was considered to be too supportive of 'democratisation'.

112. It is proposed to abandon 'pseudo-Marxist legitimacy' but not the study of Marx's thought in depth to make it more relevant to contemporary reality. On the contrary, an unprecedented effort is being made in this direction, according to G.H. Chang in an interview with Su Shaozhi, Director of the Institute of Marxism-Leninism (*Monthly Review,* June 1986, pp.14–28).

113. This is confirmed in the speech by Zhao Ziyang to the Thirteenth Congress (*BI* 9 Nov. 1987, p.37).

State Accumulation and Market Equilibria: An Application of Kalecki–Kornai Analysis to Planned Economies in the Third World

by E.V.K. FitzGerald*

This article contains an analysis of macroeconomics and inter-sectoral disequilibria in peripheral socialist economies, based on an adaptation of the theories of Kornai and Kalecki to the planned primary-export economy with a large peasant/artisan sector. The origins of excess state accumulation in such economies is identified, and consequences of system reforms for economic management discussed. It is argued that macroeconomic policy should take into account heterogeneous production forms, severe external resource constraints and social pressure for basic needs satisfaction.

I. SYSTEMIC IMBALANCES IN THE PERIPHERAL SOCIALIST ECONOMY

Those poor and underdeveloped countries of the Third World which have embarked upon the construction of socialism in the post-war decades appear to encounter a number of characteristic economic problems that might be expected to have been overcome by central planning.[1] Among these problems are the recurrence of food shortages and parallel markets, budget deficits and excessive state investment, balance of payments difficulties and underutilised manufacturing capacity, and even declining real wages and conflicts with the peasantry.

These imbalances might be attributed to the very real exogenous difficulties faced by any underdeveloped country, such as hostile world trade conditions and inherited production structures; and indeed their governments often justify poor plan results in this way. Alternatively it might be suggested, as multilateral financial institutions are prone to do, that such disequilibria are the result of ill-conceived (or 'ideological') expansion of the state sector and public expenditure. The former explanation, however, denies any specificity to the socialist experience, and thus gives little scope for rational improvement of development strategy. The latter, of course, argues that these problems can be simply resolved by minimising the state sector and relying upon market forces to organise an efficient economy.

It is the purpose of this article to contribute to the analysis of macroeconomic and inter-sectoral disequilibria in these 'peripheral socialist economies' in the light of current debates among economic theorists on similar phenomena in the more industrialised socialist economies of Eastern Europe, on the one hand, and in that of the structural characteristics of

*Institute of Social Studies, The Hague.

primary exporters with a large peasant/artisan sector, on the other. It is my general contention that the two lines of argument indicated in the previous paragraph are incorrect because they neglect the systemic forces arising from the heterogeneity of production organisation in these economies, which require a redefinition of national economic management in order to ensure balanced development.

Those Third World nations explicitly adopting a socialist development strategy generally inherit an underdeveloped economy based upon a primary export sector providing foreign exchange with which to purchase producer goods, while a large proportion of the population is still engaged in small-scale production activities organised around the household. None the less, the new regime is immediately faced by greatly increased economic responsibilities, to be carried out largely by the state.[2] Investment must be raised so as to appropriately industrialise the economy and overcome underdevelopment in the long run; much of the population requires (and demands) considerable improvements in nutrition, education, health and housing to bring them up to minimal levels of basic needs satisfaction in the medium term; while military and security strength must be established almost immediately in order to defend national sovereignty and the new social order.

Such an inevitable expansion of activities usually requires vastly more resources than those already at the disposal of the state as tax income or public enterprise profits, even allowing for external assistance. In consequence, some way of mobilising resources from the domestic economy must be worked out, by design or by default. What is more, the state is responsible for redistributing income between classes and sectors in the economy as a whole. Any planned economy will logically have a 'socialist mode of surplus appropriation' because the immediate economic interests of enterprises and households cannot be expected to coincide with those of the economy as a whole.[3] Our problem arises from the fact that such a 'mode of appropriation' appears in practice to have such a disequilibrating effect upon the economy that the original strategic social objective itself becomes even more difficult to attain.

Elsewhere, I have attempted to deal with some of the more technical issues involved in the analysis of this problematic, by adapting the Kaleckian framework for industrialised socialist economies and developing mixed economies, to the case of the planned peripheral economy. Specifically, FitzGerald [1985] explores the general issues involved in establishing a sectoral balance for those economics where the export sector effectively takes the place of the classical 'Department One' while 'Department Two' can be seen as basic needs provision; in a poor economy both may well be centred on the agricultural sector. Taking this argument further, FitzGerald [1988] analyses the internal terms of trade in an expanded Kaleckian model of investment finance; and FitzGerald [1987] examines the constraints on industrial growth imposed by food agriculture the one hand and foreign trade on the other. These technical exercises indicate very clearly the material constraints faced by 'forced growth' concentrated upon the state sector, and the disequilibrating effects on income distribution and non-state output of attempts to reach plan targets outside those limits. However, they do not indicate why such imbalances should recur so frequently. What is more, such exercises tend to imply that the problem is one of 'policy error' which could be rectified with relative ease – requiring only a greater command of economics and more political foresight on behalf of planners.

It is necessary, therefore, to explore those aspects of the institutional aspects of the socialist developing economy which might lead to disequilibrating state accumulation. In this article, we shall proceed as follows. First, we shall examine the theoretical debate on the institutional origins of the disequilibria in decentralised socialist economies, particularly the theories of Kalecki and Kornai on the relationship between plans and market forces. Second, we shall attempt to define the essential differences between accumulation in industrial and less-developed socialist economies so as to modify the Kalecki–Kornai model appropriately. This enables us to take the third step of identifying the origins of excess state accumulation in such economies, and its limitations, particularly the reaction of various economic groups to the extent and manner of resource mobilisation. Finally, the consequences for economic management of undertaking the reforms necessary to overcome this systematic distortion are discussed.

I shall argue throughout that there exist systematic insitutional characteristics in the socialist developing economy which arise from a combination of heterogeneous enterprise forms, severe resource constraints, and social pressure for basic needs satisfaction, and that macroeconomic policy analysis should be based on a proper understanding of those factors.

II. MACROECONOMIC IMBALANCE IN INDUSTRIALISED SOCIALIST ECONOMIES

The combination of excessively high levels of accumulation, chronic shortages of producer and consumer goods, low labour productivity and enterprise inefficiency is hardly a new subject of debate in Eastern Europe. Indeed, it is central to the discussions of 'reform' which have been flourishing for over two decades. However, in the light of the difficulties encountered in introducing market forces into a planned economy, a number of different interpretations have emerged in recent years, which attempt to identify the source of such endemic difficulties as a prelude to their solution.

One approach is to conceive of the problem in terms of the aggregate balance between investment and consumption, and as subject to central strategic policy decisions. Kalecki[4] gives the classic analysis of the consequences of over-accumulation for both industrial and non-industrial planned economics; in terms of inflation, deteriorating income distribution, balance of payments deficits and production inefficiency. However, he sees the decision on the rate of accumulation as an essentially cabinet-level one: choosing a point on what he calls the 'government decision curve' which represents trade-off between present and future consumption by the population. The implicit solution is more clear-sightedness in the cabinet, or perhaps a change in its composition. The countervailing power of workers' councils that he proposes is to be exercised at a sectoral level within the vertically integrated production combines.[5]

This approach is not dissimilar in essence from that of those authors[6] who would argue that these problems are essentially Keynesian in nature, in the sense of being the result of excess demand generated by high budget expenditures in an economy already operating at full capacity. Here, the implicit solution is less ambitious growth targets, but it is not clear why such problems should be endemic to planned economies and so difficult to solve because, in Eastern Europe, the degree of social hegemony is such as to permit quite radical changes in expenditure patterns when required. In any case, socialist financial practice is marked by extreme monetary caution and strict control over consumer demand aggregates.

Another approach is to see the problem of 'accumulation bias' as not so much one of policy error, but rather as one of vested interests.[7] It is suggested that state managers (that is, senior bureaucrats, enterprise directors, engineers, etc.) have a joint interest in high rates of state accumulation and the suppression of small enterprise because their own advancement depends upon managing larger production complexes, new technologies and so on. Their own income levels do not derive from production efficiency, nor do their consumption levels reflect those of the population as a whole, but rather upon their privileged access to goods and services to which their position in the state apparatus entitles them. This situation not only leads to what might be called 'class conflict' between state managers and workers (and, by implication, with peasants and artisans, too) and severe political consequences, but also to state enterprise inefficiency because of extreme bureaucratisation under the central planning system. Decentralising reform measures introduced from above in order to increase efficiency and raise consumption logically meet over-whelming resistance from state managers.

'Feasible socialism'[8] would involve, therefore, a considerable degree of reform in enterprise organisation, particularly the expansion of small enterprise to create competition, and the extension of consumer choice to make enterprises responsive to demand. The social phenomenon identified is a very real one, but the motivations attributed to state managers do not seem to be so very different from those of administrators in capitalist economies, so there must be some further systemic institutional root to the problem, other than vested interest.

A better starting point for such an analysis would be the model of socialist state enterprise proposed by Kornai,[9] which is in essence a development of the Kaleckian approach to oligopolistic behaviour. Kalecki had argued that 'market socialism'[10] of the type propounded by Lange, Sik and Horvat, was based upon an illusory optimism about enterprise behaviour in markets, for 'the concept of free competition in the classic form in which it is treated in the political economy textbooks never existed in capitalist economies'.[11] In an industrialised socialist economy, full decentralisation (even without private property) would lead to price collusion between firms, and leave no means of adequately adjusting to infrastructural bottlenecks. Kalecki stresses that whereas the capitalist economy is demand-constrained (ensuring productivity by bankruptcy and unemployment), the socialist economy is supply-constrained and, as it can be planned, is potentially a superior insitutional system. Kornai takes this as his point of departure to build up a picture of oligopolistic state enterprise behaviour under conditions of shortage, where firms are no longer price responsive.

This situation of endemic shortage is not due, in Kornai's view, to Keynesian excess consumer demand, but rather to the 'soft' budget constraint on state firms. In essence, the concept contains three central propositions: first, that enterprises can undertake new investment and expand production without limits of profitability or own saving, because their access to funds (from banks or budgets) is unconstrained economically, and limited only by bureaucratic delay. *Ex ante* planning is the main allocation system, but *ex post* adjustments are always needed due to uncertainty, which justifies the soft budget but does not release the corresponding goods. Second, that enterprises cannot go bankrupt even if they suffer financial losses or have productivity levels far below domestic or international standards, revealing the primacy of gross output and employment over efficiency or financial criteria. Third, that prices are based on average costs for the branch in question. The soft budget constraint is quite compatible with overall budgetary equilibrium because *ex post* savings are brought up to *ex ante* investment through the centralisation of profits. Monetary policy is passive in such a system, adjusting automatically to transactions demand.

The heart of Kornai's contribution, however, is enterprise behaviour and its effect upon other sectors of the economy, particularly households. The demand for *producer* goods (that is, the output of 'Department I' in the classical scheme) does not depend upon income or price, but rather upon the autonomous expansion programmes of firms themselves, supported by their respective ministries. Households, in contrast, have a 'hard budget' based on salary income, but must suffer from the continuous 'suction' of consumer goods and services (that is, Department II output) from distribution channels by enterprises and government entities for 'on site' consumption by their own workforces and, in the last resort, for special commissariats, etc. Thus there is a double conflict over resources: between Departments I and II for inputs, on the one hand, and between enterprises and households for Department II output, on the other. Similarly, it is the pressure to import producer goods by enterprises (and not exchange rate distortions or consumer demand) and the ease of selling exportable goods on the home market, which lead to balance of payments difficulties.

This form of behaviour is not accidental; it arises from the logic of the planned economy itself. The distribution of a great part of consumer goods and services according to need rather than market demand (that is, ability to pay) creates a continuous expansion of planned output growth; while the strategy commitment to full employment lowers the efficiency of labour and creates skill shortages. The 'paternalism' of the state towards its enterprises in terms of finance and subsidies allows investment demand to rise unchecked (particularly in Department I itself) because the objective of state enterprise is to produce, not to make profits. The input shortages permit Department II producers to neglect quality control and technical progress, thus reducing living standards. Production in a socialist economy is not coordinated through the 'law of value' with its demand constraints, unemployment and bankruptcies as disciplinary instruments that make the market 'work'. Planning provides the output targets and fixes prices *ex ante*, but cannot enforce productivity norms *ex post*; unless they are adopted voluntarily.

The labour market in socialist economies has characteristic features, according to Kornai. Whereas in the capitalist economy, employment is constrained by aggregate demand in a Keynesian fashion (and indeed, wage control and job flexibility are explicitly maintained via unemployment), full employment is a fundamental feature of the socialist economy and is indeed a constitutional right. The result is what Kornai calls 'internal labour slack' within enterprises because of lowered worker discipline, reinforced by the tendency for firms to hoard labour. This concept is similar to that of 'internal labour makets' identified within the stable workforce of large capitalist firms. This slack is effectively only available for individual mobilisation in the 'second economy' (that is, black market), which also makes use of materials obtained from the enterprise. He argues that this labour shortage arises not from the achievement of a high stage of economic development, but rather from the institutional characteristics of the system itself.

Wage scales are set centrally so as to preserve macroeconomic balances; and although labour can move between firms and branches, it does so more in response to job conditions than to wage differentials as such, although wage-drift is observed for skilled workers. Capital-intensive investments are made, not in order to save on expensive labour, but rather in order to economise on employment and improve conditions for the existing enterprise workforce – not least the managers and engineers. The institutional conditions are such, therefore, that the labour market (as in the case of goods markets) cannot be analysed in neo-classical terms, even if 'distortions' are invoked to explain inability to clear via price. Firms are not responsive to input prices and workers enter the labour market through institutional channels; so even if wage controls and job security conditions were to be relaxed, the Marshallian equilibrium would not be achieved.

Unfortunately, Kornai does not deal with the influence of foreign trade upon enterprise efficiency, nor with the interaction of the state sector with small producers; which is surprising in the current East European context. None the less, his model does provide a microeconomic view of enterprise organisation in the planned economy, as a complement to Kalecki's macroeconomics.

III. THE ORGANISATION OF PRODUCTION AND EXCHANGE IN PERIPHERAL SOCIALISM

We cannot proceed to transpose the Kalecki–Kornai framework directly to our situation of socialist underdevelopment, without first defining the institutional structure within production and exchange take place, and the resource constraints involved. To do this clearly implies an enormous degree of generalisation, so the following paragraphs should be regarded as 'stylised facts' rather than a universally valid description.[12]

The central feature of such economies (which is clearly derived from their pre-revolutionary history as subordinate sources of cheap raw materials for industrialised countries) is the combination of very diverse enterprise forms and production systems, within a heterogeneous social structure. The economy is integrated into the world market primarily as a raw materials exporter, in exchange for which a substantial part of the producer goods necessary for the economy to function are obtained. This implies that production decisions respond to a considerable extent to world market demand at international prices. There also exists a very extensive petty commodity production sector, comprising both peasants and artisans, which plays a large part in the supply of consumer goods and services. The state sector as such is confined to 'modern' corporate enterprises and governmental entities, and directly controls foreign trade, banking, wholesale commerce, factory industry and the like. The degree of significance of this foreign trade dependency and the 'mixed' ownership depends not so much on strategic choice as upon the size of the economy and its degree of industrialisation.

In terms of the classical production departments, the role of Department I in supplying producer goods may be largely taken over by foreign trade, so that it is the *export* sector which provides the growth dynamic. This is not an exclusive substitution, of course, because the domestic construction sector accounts for up to half of fixed investment in developing countries,[13] while local supplies of energy, chemicals, agricultural machinery, etc. may be quite advanced. What is more, lack of skilled labour is often a constraint on investment capacity – that is, the ability to translate mobilised resources into increased production. None the less, many spare parts and new machines necessary for the expansion of state enterprises are imported; and must be purchased with processed raw materials, at terms of trade which are not under the planners' control. It is one of the objectives of industrialisation strategy, of course, to overcome this technological dependency; but it remains a central characteristic of such economies for a long period.[14]

The consequences of Department I having this characteristic is that the expansion of the state enterprise sector in particular requires greater amounts of foreign exchange, and not just labour (plus the corresponding wagegoods) for heavy industry as in the classical socialist growth model. This expansion generates pressure to reallocate domestic resources away from consumption into exports, or for state enterprises to direct imports to the rest of the economy towards their own requirements. The 'suction effect' identified by Kornai exists, therefore, but in rather a different form; while the constraint on Department I expansion is more severe than in his model, because it is imposed exogenously by the balance of payments.

Consumer goods and services (Department II) in contrast, are increasingly supplied from domestic sources in the transition to socialism; both because the luxuries consumed in the pre-revolutionary period are no longer imported, and because of the conscious effort to satisfy the basic needs of the population using local resources and labour as part of 'self-reliance'. The product compositon of Department II is also transformed by the rapid expansion of social services, particularly in rural areas. The production of these basic needs becomes increasingly socialised; due not only to state involvement in social services, but also to widespread 'popular mobilisation' in housing, basic education, primary health care, etc. When combined with food rationing and subsidised public transport as means of direct poverty alleviation on the one hand, and limited supply of consumer durables on the other, those characteristics lead to the distribution of Department II output being based on citizen entitlement derived from 'need' (albeit mediated by the political process) rather than commercial criteria as such. This popular mobilisation involves systems of self-financing to obtain necessary inputs or skills (for example, teachers) and not just labour-accumulation; such financing implies in turn appropriate forms of local administration.

The expansion of Department II is thus not constrained by market demand; rather it is driven by the considerable social pressures from below exercised by the newly enfranchised population and the strategic desire of the new state managers to overcome basic needs deficiencies as a prelude to modernisation, as well as obvious political and ethical considerations. To the extent that the population will mobilise itself on a community basis to provide extra labour power, then there will be less constraint on supply but in practice increased government budgets, inputs of producer goods and wagegoods and imported equipment become necessary to complement labour accumulation; although 'self-provisioning' can be obtained by *exchange* with the state sector. This is particularly so where the expansion of labour-intensive primary services (for example, rural health clinics) generate institutionally supported demands upon secondary services (for example, regional hospitals) which are themselves capital-intensive. In contrast to Kornai's model of Eastern Europe therefore, consumption demand is less subject to central control; and while Department II does compete with Department I for resources, it is somewhat less disadvantaged in the contest, although this depends upon the development strategy and its underlying politics of class alliance.

State enterprises and government entities in our case do seem to behave in a similar fashion to that described by Kornai, although again with significant differences. State enterprises do have 'soft budgets' in terms of local currency resources, derived from cost-plus pricing policies, subsidies on basic services, and virtually unlimited credit from state banks. They are not allowed to go bankrupt, however inefficient (although directors may, of course, be moved) nor can they lay off labour easily. On the contrary, labour is hoarded because not only are skilled workers in very short supply nationally and employment projection legislation enforced, but also because it is difficult to find labour at all when it is needed because of the other alternatives available in a mixed economy, particularly where agriculture is seasonal.

These factors make state enterprises in Third World socialism largely unresponsive to the prices of inputs and outputs, while the motivations for expansion and the soft budget to acquire local resources are as in Kornai's model. Labour is attracted by employment conditions as much as by wage levels (leading firms to introduce extensive welfare services) but its intensity of effort does not respond to bonus payments. The difference lies in the hard *foreign* currency budget that enterprises face, as production cannot be maintained nor expansion take place without access to imports. Foreign exchange is strictly rationed by the central authorities and, although this may not be allocated on strict profitability criteria, it certainly will not be freely available to any enterprise. This, in turn, makes preferential access to foreign credits crucial to state enterprises because they tend to be branch-specific and thus 'softer'.

Government institutions in industrialised socialist countries come under strict budgetary control, and are fully financed by turnover taxes. In our case, as we have seen, the social pressure for basic social services and military exigencies are quite independent of the natural expansionary proclivities of bureaucracy or of limits of a narrow tax base. Once quantitative targets are set, ministries feel entitled to spend any sum required in order to meet them, as long as it is in domestic currency. Thus the only effective control open to the financial authorities is to limit public sector wages, leading to an unmotivated civil sevice and to restrict imports, leading to underutilised hospitals, etc. Local purchasing of goods and services by government puts particular pressure on Department II markets, in contrast to state enterprises, which tends to squeeze Department I more.

The motivation for state expansion is also somewhat different in our case to that described by Kornai. He sees this as the result of the natural but unconstrained ambitions of state managers under soft budget constraints, combined with the growth ideology of national leadership, implicitly concerned in both cases to 'catch up with capitalism'. He contrasts this with demand-constrained oligopolistic capitalist firms, for whom uncompetitive expansion would spell ruin. In the case of the Third World, both the motivations and the comparison are different. As far as state managers are concerned, the ideology of modernisation is more concerned with 'overcoming backwardness': a combination of a moral reaction against absolute poverty and the nationalist assertion of economic sovreignty. This seems to require the construction of a strong state sector as a vehicle for rapid economic transformation; strong in terms of both resources and political support.

Two further factors of a non-economic nature are probably relevant. First, the military nature of many revolutionary movements and the subsequent need to rebuild national defence capacity, lead by extension to a heirarchical perception of economic organisation. The provisioning of the armed forces themselves, and the mobilisation of sufficient skilled manpower, also require greater resource centralisation in the state. Second, the somewhat rigid and outdated notions of both Marxist-Leninist theory and planning practice that are transmitted from the industrialised socialist countries[15] give the impression that state ownership is both a necessary and sufficient condition for building socialism.

The relevant comparison with capitalist enterprise is also distinct. Large private firms in developing countries (including transnational corporations) benefit from considerable state protection in the form of tariff barriers, price regulation, market shares, infrastructure provision and so on. They also benefit from preferential access to bank credit and natural resources. In this sense, corporations in capitalist developing countries may well have 'soft budgets' and not be truly constrained by demand or finance or efficiency. Private exporters must, of course, face international competition, but then the same may be said of state enterprises selling on world markets. The main difference between private and state enterprise (apart from the obvious subjection of the latter to greater ministerial control than the former) is the fact that private entrepreneurs can move their capital to more profitable branches (including speculation), indulge in luxury consumption, or shift their financial assets overseas. State managers cannot do this on any considerable scale, and can only accumulate by expanding production in their own branch or in closely related activities.

Petty commodity production, in both rural and urban areas, is a characteristic feature of poor economies: the relationship between the state sector and the peasantry, of course, has been a central feature of the debates on socialist transition since the NEP.[16] This was so then because practically the entire food supply (considered as equivalent to Department II) was in the hands of peasants. In our case, petty commodity production cannot be simply equated with peasant food producers, despite their evident importance. On the one hand, state enterprises supply a considerable proportion of the wagegoods basket itself (processed foodstuffs, textiles, etc.) as well as the goods required for exchange with the peasants for the food they market. On the other hand, small farmers may well be supplying major export crops (and thus effectively forming part of Department I), while artisans provide essential goods and services (such as footwear). Small traders probably form an essential part of the retail distribution network. Finally, many social services, which are outside commodity production altogether, are organised by local community groups and are consumed directly by their producers. As these groups form part of the market economy themselves, this is a good reason for linking social services provision to collective forms of producing commodities. All of those activities, moreover, require inputs supplied by the state: either in the form of imports and producer goods; or in that of infrastructure such as water, roads or energy.

The nature of petty production is clearly *quantitatively* distinct from the situation in industrialised socialist countries. The proportion of the workforce engaged in such activities is much higher, and its contribution to output in a number of labour-intensive branches much greater. The state is materially constrained by its lack of administrative capacity and the dispersed nature of the production process from directly controlling much of the economy. This is not just a question of the relative efficiency of state farms and peasants, rather that there is no realistic alternative to peasant production. This situation, it should be noted, is independent of the frequent long-term desire on the part of socialist planners to absorb the whole 'informal' sector into the 'modern' sector in a Lewisian fashion over the long run, for this would require an extended period of massive accumulation to provide sufficient wage employment.

The nature of petty commodity production is also *qualitatively* different from the situation in industrialised socialist countries. The commodities produced and sold by peasants and artisans are generally unsophisticated consumer items or raw materials; almost the reverse obtains in advanced socialist economics where petty production is encouraged in areas such as specialised tailoring, quality restaurants, consumer durables repairs or private holiday housebuilding. Of course, in both cases there are 'grey' areas of transactions involving illegal activities and stolen goods, but it is essential to contrast the supplementary nature of petty production in developed socialism with its fundamental role in basic production in developing countries.

The petty production sector requires access to the resources controlled by the state: on the one hand, production inputs to its own production process (barbed wire, fertilisers, cement, cloth, etc.); and on the other, consumer goods to maintain their families. The exchange relationship with the state involves both these categories: the former closely related to credit and extension programmes; the latter to official marketing channels. The internal terms of trade (reflecting the prices of inputs, outputs and consumer goods) are a major determinant of petty producers' disposition to produce for the market and to sell through regulated channels. However, it is the *availability* of exchange-goods as much as their relative prices which will determine this disposition and even the ability to produce at all. Shortages lead not only to parallel markets in produce, but also in inputs themselves.

In Kornai's model, the soft-budgeted state enterprises crowd out (or 'siphon off', in his terminology) the hard-budgeted households. In our economies, state enterprises are soft-budgeted in local currency, but hard-budgeted in foreign exchange, so crowding out takes the form of reducing petty producers' access to productive inputs available on the domestic market using their greater purchasing power and more favoured administrative position. State enterprises and government entities also drain off 'exchange' goods for their own use. This is combined with a logical policy inclination to hold down the official prices of consumer goods (particularly food) in order to sustain the real value of wages in the state sector, in response to demands by organised workers newly enfranchised by the revolution. In sum, the 'siphon effect' operates between the two enterprise forms, rather than betwen enterprises and households, as in Kornai's model.

What is more, while Kornai's households have hard budgets made up of centrally planned wages (and no consumer credit), in our case households are as often as not engaged in small-scale production themselves, which allows them to increase their monetised demand at times of shortage quite independently of wage policies. Indeed, an optimal 'household strategy' may well involve having some members in the state sector (to obtain access to official facilities and even marketable goods) and others in the petty commodity sector in order to augment disposable income.[17] Although such 'multi-modal' households do face a hard-budget constraint (in the sense that they do not generally have access to endless credit nor can they raise their own prices) they do appear to have much more autonomy as economic actors than their counterparts in Eastern Europe, derived from their ability to generate non-wage incomes and to gain access to non-state marketing channels. This enables households to 'compete' much more effectively with state enterprise than in Kornai's model, although the competition is still far from being fair. Moreover, the 'multi-modal' household can constitute a powerful mechanism for petty capitalist accumulation in the rural economy, once family survival has been guaranteed.

Having thus redefined Kornai's institutional structure within a modified Kaleckian macroeconomic framework, we can now turn to the question of accumulation itself.

IV. THE ACCUMULATION PROBLEM

From the discussion so far, it should be clear that the planning of aggregate investment is highly constrained by the institutional framework of the economy. Both the level and composition of capital formation are bound by the inter-sectoral balances required in such a heterogeneous economy, and by the effects of resource mobilisation on non-state sectors.

In perspective planning theory[18] as applied to industrialised socialist countries, the long-term consumption levels set for the population permit production output targets to be derived for final and intermediate goods, capacity expansions estimated, and the corresponding investment to be programmed subject, of course, to short-term consumption requirements and trade balances. It is assumed in such theory that the state controls all those variables directly, but in our case this is not true. Quite apart from exogenous shocks (such as the weather or insurgency), the state does not directly manage either the conditions of world trade or the petty commodity production: its relationship with those two sectors, which determine to a great extent what happens in the plan period, is essentially one of exchange rather than control. The state is confined, so to speak, between the internal and external terms of trade.

The composition of investment will first depend upon the balance chosen as between export production and supply for the domestic market, as those two generally involve different products or branches. Any long-run growth target will (for a given forecast of the external terms of trade) require a specific export level to finance sufficient imports, thus determining by iteration the correct sectoral balance.[19] Too low an assignment to exports leads to subsequent exchange crises, depressed growth and underutilised capacity; too high an assignment, to excessive consumption repression and declining labour productivity.

The choice of export branches themselves will depend not only upon anticipated world price levels (forecast or directly negotiated) but also upon the capacity to penetrate overseas markets, implying in turn both geopolitical relationships and specific processing technologies. In contrast, investment for domestic supply can rely upon planned domestic consumption requirements, which in the case of poor countries is undoubtedly simpler to ascertain, being essentially a question of basic needs satisfaction, rather than the variegated and mutating consumer demand of Europe. The expansion of producer-goods supply in existing branches can then be derived from the export and consumer-goods programmes, although the creation of new branches, particularly in capital goods, will require strategic technology decisions.[20]

The supply plans for export commodities, inputs, and consumer goods cannot have a mechanical 'input–output' relationship to one another. On the one hand, the essentially *exchange* relationship between petty producers and the state means that both inputs specific to their technology and appropriate consumer goods should be programmed in proportion to expected deliveries to official marketing channels, which in turn implies specific investments or import categories. On the other hand, the establishment of wage incentives for productivity in the state sector implies that (on the assumption that basic needs are covered by the base-wage and social provision) specific 'incentive' goods should be available in order to make such incentives meaningful. Again, specific investment or trade decisions will have to be made accordingly. Planners seem to overlook the fact that such consumption is directly productive,[21] and that if those supply categories are neglected, labour productivity throughout the economy will decline, despite rising investment.

The choice of technique in investment projects and the nature of technology imported will also be conditioned by the balance between forms of production. It is not logical to adopt labour-intensive methods in the state sector in order to generate employment in a socialist economy where access to basic necessities is met socially, and in any case labour is scarce. None the less, such entitlement must be explicitly linked to the place of employment or community where people live, which will have an obvious effect on the supply of labour between sectors. Moreover, in sectors such as export processing, industrial import-substitution, communications, or banking, reasonable international standard of technology is necessary to maintain competitive. The petty production sector, however, can operate effectively at much lower levels of capital intensity even while undergoing the technological transformation necessary for its voluntary collectivisation around common production facilities.

Thus balanced growth requires that specific accumulation targets be set for the petty production sector and the appropriate machinery, training and inputs be supplied: this technological diffusion is best carried out from the state sector itself, rather than in competition with it.[22] If the whole growth burden is born by state industry, not only will production suffer, but the capital investment requirements will drain off resources from the rest of the economy and place great pressure on the balance of payments.

Industrialisation is clearly necessary in order to raise and sustain the per capita productivity of the population, but this need not take place exclusively in manufacturing, nor in state enterprises. Indeed it may well be that in small economies without large domestic markets, higher education and research geared to the adaptation of international technology (particularly in the export sector) on the one hand, and the development of domestic technical capacity in branches such as construction, export inputs, food production, energy and transport on the other, would be a more viable nursery for infant industry. Progress in industrialisation then affects the appropriate balance between forms of production, as greater division of labour permits further socialisation.

Turning to the problem of resource mobilisation to support the industrialisation process (as well as that needed for economic and social infrastructure, defense, etc.) we can identify two immediate sources characteristic of developing socialist economies: foreign exchange generated in the export sector (particularly to import machinery), and the use of surplus labour (particularly for construction). In the former case, the economic surplus available in the foreign trade sector is the difference between export receipts and costs, which can be expressed as direct or indirect imports, including the cost of wagegoods for the labour force. Export prices for raw materials are exogenous, and ultimately determined by the marginal production cost in competing capitalist export economies, which rely upon very low wages and limited social services. Socialist economies necessarily have higher costs of reproduction for their labour force so productivity must be higher in order to compete internationally, requiring modernisation and further investment.

None the less, a good part of the surplus generated will in fact be *rent*, in the sense of taking advantage of a particular natural resource endowment or geographical location. The value to the economy of this rent depends upon the external terms of trade, of course, and this is reduced by the process of unequal exchange in world trade. This is even true of trade with industrialised socialist countries which use 'world' (that is, capitalist market) prices as the basis for trade agreements.[23]

The economy as a whole, and the state enterprise sector in particular, has access to foreign assistance in the form of loans, donations and technical co-operation.[24] This forms an essential part of accumulation during the transition itself when both production and trade patterns have been distorted by social and institutional transformation; in any case commercial credits (beyond short-term trade liquidity) are not normally available to such countries. In the longer run loans have to be repaid, implying the allocation of a considerable proportion of the producer goods (imported on lines of credit) to the export sector or to effective import-substitution, unless joint ventures are set up repayable in export commodities.

However, such external assitance also strengthens the drive towards state enterprise autonomy. This arises in part from the fact that enterprises (or their sponsoring ministry) can in practice directly negotiate agreements with foreign firms and rely upon the central bank to service them subsequently, independently of the profitability of the plant itself. It also arises because the counterpart agencies tend to support state accumulation in particular branches as a client for their exporters' own technologies.

For our economies with their large investment requirements, the relatively small and inefficient state enterprise sector cannot finance the entire domestic resource programme (or put up matching funds for import credits) out of its own profits. We have already argued that attempts to drive down the internal terms of trade in a Preobrazhensky fashion as a source of surplus (that is, generating large profits out of state sales to the peasantry) are counter-productive. Moreover, state intervention tends to produce what Saith [*1985*] calls 'selective commoditisation', where particular commodities (such as coffee for export) are supported because surplus can be appropriated from them more easily, to the detriment of integral rural development.

Taxation has been recognised from early on[25] as a more stable method of financing state investment but its limitations in our case are many. Direct (income) taxation could be on state enterprise or petty producers. The former has been useful for its administrative consequences (particularly if firms are encouraged to reinvest 'own funds' and grant profit bonuses to the workforce) and permits inter-sectoral profit transfers, but it clearly does not resolve the problem of financing the state. The latter, however, is difficult to collect, particularly because it relates, above all, to rent (in the sense of super-normal profits arising from land tenure, location, etc.) requiring data from cadasters and accounts which, by definition, the sector does not generate normally. It is precisely the fact that the state cannot mobilise funds from petty producers which gives strength to our argument that local basic needs should be financed through territorial forms of collective production and finance. Indirect taxation, if it is not to be a concealed deterioration of the internal terms of trade or a disguised cut in real wages, must take the form of taxation on non-essentials. In socialist economic practice, this takes the form of state appropriation (through marketing companies) of the margin between production costs to the state enterprises and the market clearing price for such commodities or services.[26] This also corresponds to Kalecki's solution for the problem of financing development in mixed economies, not only to generate funds but also to prevent any deterioration in the income distribution.[27]

Taxation does not generate foreign exchange; rather, it gives the state greater (and non-inflationary) command over domestic resources, particularly labour, wagegoods and construction materials. Macroeconomic balance is only maintained if these local resources are what state accumulation requires. Taxation may well be, therefore, a more appropriate source of finance for the government sector. This 'command', of course, is over resources extracted from or denied to the non-state sector, reducing its capacity to produce and accumulate.

The non-state sector does have considerable accumulation potential on the basis of its own resources, which are not available for state appropriation because of the production process involved. Petty producers can mobilise surplus labour within the household or co-operative in order to carry out land improvements, construction, breeding and so on, as long as they are supplied with appropriate tools and goods are available to buy with increased income. Denial of those facilities will reduce national investment without an equivalent investible surplus being released for state enterprises, while the labour surplus is not available on a continuous basis suitable for wage employment. This, in turn, is related to the state's own rural strategy and whether it is based on surplus extraction (by the terms of trade and selective commoditisation) or on broad-based basic needs provisioning and rural accumulation. The social differentiation that might arise from 'private' accumulation can be reduced by a combination of direct taxation, co-operative organisation and restrictions on enterprise size. Such differentiation cannot be a sufficient reason, however, for suppressing this form of accumulation (particularly since it can rapidly alleviate shortages of wagegoods as well as raise the living standard of peasants and artisans themselves)[27] unless it can be shown that it really leads back towards capitalist relations.

Community organisation for local investment projects to satisfy basic needs requirements is a second form of non-state accumulation, which mobilises underutilised labour without payment in dry seasons, weekends, etc. because the resulting facilities (latrines, schools, roads, etc.) have use value for the social group concerned. Again, a certain amount of state inputs are necessary to undertake those projects but the labour mobilised would not be available otherwise, so the net gain for national accumulation is considerable. Moreover, as we have argued above, the state inputs for such accumulation (for example, cement) or services (for example, doctors) can be locally financed with resources (savings, taxation, or sales) not otherwise available to the state for national accumulation. Whereas in a capitalist economy there might be some sense in the radical critique of such self-help schemes[28] as a means of lowering the social costs of labour power and overexploiting the workforce, it would appear that in a socialist society this could be properly regarded as households gaining control over their own welfare as part of a wider process of emancipation.

At the macroeconomic level, even after an appropriate balance has been struck between foreign and domestic production on the one hand, and between enterprise forms on the other, the classic problem of the balance between aggregate consumption and aggregate investment remains to be resolved.[29] As we have seen, this balance takes a particular form in peripheral socialism, but the planners' perception is usually such that there is perceived to exist a considerable range of feasible and administrable rates of state accumulation, with accompanying short-term austerity in return for long-term prosperity. The choice between the two is seen as an essentially *political* one.[30] I wish to argue that in fact there are severe structural constraints on high accumulation rates (although not on large investment *expenditures*) and that the minimum feasible consumption level may itself be relatively high.

To the extent that non-state investment is 'crowded out' by being denied access to means of production or to markets (through planners' design or state enterprise 'suction'), then the labour surplus mobilised used therein is not available to the state, as we have seen. The national rate of accumulation would thus fall as state investment rose if this latter were based on diverting relevant producer goods (such as agricultural inputs, construction materials, and transport equipment) because the marginal productivity of the diverted resources is higher in the non-state sector. The level of aggregate consumption would also decline.[31]

The limits on investment capacity itself in a developing country impose a severe constraint on the rate of accumulation, even if supplies of imported plant and equipment are elastic. This occurs because of the limited state capacity to design, construct and put into operation a large number of substantial projects, particularly when these are 'green field' investments rather than the extension of existing plant. It becomes worse when major infrasructural investments must also be made in order to support the projects. In a soft-budget regime, therefore, there is a marked tendency to initiate more projects than can be realistically implemented during the plan period, leaving many of them uncompleted and creating inflationary pressures on supplies of construction materials and skilled manpower. State managers know from experience that once a project has been initiated, funds will always be available to continue it, and construction will eventually be completed. However, the net effect is to depress the rate of real (that is, completed) investment below what it could have been, while raising the rate of investment expenditure.

Curtailing consumption growth in order to increase investment may well conflict with an egalitarian commitment to meeting the basic needs of the population; if only by requiring that a considerable part of current investment be assigned to supply those needs (that is, expansion of Department II), rather than to a 'growth' sector such as exports (that is, Department I).[32] The minimal commitment that consumption per capita should not actually *fall* implies annual Department II growth of around two to three per cent. In Kalecki's famous formulation of this problem,[32] a rate of growth of the state sector higher than warranted by (peasant) food supply and the wage eleasticity of demand for food leads to structural inflationary pressures and a deteriorating income distribution; which can only be overcome by reducing growth or importing wagegoods. The impact on consumption is even more severe under the foreign-exchange constraint than Kalecki states[34] because state enterprise investments will tend to be far more import-intensive than basic consumption, so that the fall in aggregate consumption required to balance increased investment is disproportionately large.

The level of aggregate consumption is not only constrained by the need to maintain the workforce; both egalitarian principles and practical management will tend to raise it. In the first place, the socialist principle of 'reward according to work' cannot be universally applied because of the initially low productivity of many groups, which would leave them below a socially acceptable poverty line. In other words, during the transition a proportion of the population may well have a consumption level above their marginal productivity, which has to be subsidised. Secondly, we have seen how 'incentive' or 'exchange' goods are necessary to maintain the intensity of effort. Indeed, state investment may even expand productive capacity without raising production if wage goods supply is not raised sufficiently.

V. MACROECONOMIC POLICY IN THE MIXED ECONOMY

We can now turn to the problems of macroeconomic policy in such 'mixed' socialist developing countries, where complete central planning is not feasible. Based on arguments similar to those of Kalecki and Kornai, I have suggested that the origins of macroeconomic imbalance are not to be found in excess demand of a Keynesian kind, but rather in problems of state enterprise behaviour and accumulation bias. In this section we shall address the problems of financial control and pricing criteria within the structural context discussed above.

In the supply-constrained 'shortage economy', there is no lack of effective demand, and greater net expenditure will not lead to an increase in output. Money is passive in such an economy, even though budget deficits are usually scrupulously avoided in industrialised socialist countries,[35] and inflation as such is not a major problem. However, in developing planned econonomies, fiscal deficits and inflation can become quite serious. I have already argued that such deficits tend to arise from the combination of extensive expenditure commitments and a narrow tax base arising from the attempt to accelerate development in a backward economy. This domestic deficit (over and above foreign finance for state imports) is financed by monetary emission because a capital market does not exist and bank savings are unlikely to be large. The general inflation associated with such deficits is none the less a result of excess demand (for example, state employees spending wages on food) and is not a monetary phenomenon as such, while the 'location' of such inflation in queues or flexibility in specified product prices depends on administrative decisions.

These budget deficits might be considered simply as 'forced savings' in the Kaldorian sense.[36] For a given *ex ante* level of domestic investment and foreign credit, increases in government dis-saving are matched automatically by the savings of non-state entities and households *ex post*: either as 'voluntary' savings of unspendable cash balances if prices are fixed, or as involuntary reduction in private consumption if prices are allowed to rise. This latter may well appear to be an attractive equivalent to taxation, falling only upon the non-state sector if state enterprise wages and prices are adjusted accordingly. Both practical experience and relevant theory would tend to indicate otherwise.

At first sight, the social (or even political) implications of inflation in terms of real income decline for wages-earners or other groups might seem to be the most critical of these consequences.[37] However, in a mixed economy inflation will disarticulate markets for the various producers with consequences far more difficult to foresee or control. In the face of excess demand, petty producers are in a position to raise their own prices (possibly even more rapidly than state enterprises) so that the redistributive effect is forced back on wage-earners and the state itself. If the authorities attempt to fix prices, parallel markets will spring up immediately, leading to social conflict if they are repressed administratively.

It is true that the non-state sector will require a certain amount of monetary instruments (particularly cash) to carry on its own production and trade,[38] and that the government can run a small deficit in order to supply this liquidity, for which the petty producers pay, so to speak, seigniorage. Deficits of any size will have the effect of creating a progressively greater mass of cash in the hands of the non-state sector, with two destabilising consequences. First, the sector can more easily escape from credit control, accumulate speculative capital, bribe officials, and so forth. Second, as the national currency ceases to serve as a store of value, other instruments such as foreign currency or even commodites take its place. Formulation of such a parallel economy will require the redefinition of distributional priorities and even class alliances, in favour of larger farmers for example.

The state sector also suffers the disarticulating consequences of inflation. Wage employment becomes relatively unattractive compared to speculative activities (particularly with state property!) in the market sector; and there will be increased difficulty in obtaining labour. Financial control over state enterprises and budgetary institutions becomes almost impossible as accounting categories become increasingly meaningless, and soft budgeting reaches its logical extreme.

Finally, the existence of large cash balances outside the banks in a situation of supply shortages and foreign exchange control increases the pressure on parallel currency markets and encourages smuggling, not only of consumer goods, but also of unobtainable spare parts by state enterprises themselves. Such phenomena are in any case intrinsic to planned economies because *ex hypothesi*, the allocation of foreign exchange according to strategic priorities differs from demand expressed in the market-place (for instance, tractors rather than colour televisions), even if at an aggregate level monetised demand

and supply are in balance.

Inflationary state finance is thus not only an ineffective means of centralising the surplus, but also disarticulates production itself, making macroeconomic management even more difficult than it is already. Reasonable price stability is a necessary condition for effective planning, far more so than for policy-making in a developing capitalist economy, where resource allocation is left to the market, which seeks only to maximise nominal profits.

Effective mangement of the economy implies not only aggregate demand balance, but also effective control over sectoral behaviour. Our argument so far would imply that much depends upon overcoming the problem of the 'soft budgeting' of state enterprise and upon establishng adequate exchange relationships with the non-state sector. It can be assumed that the system of basic needs distribution becomes progressively 'demonetised', in the sense that distibution is according to need and organised on a community basis even though production may not be, so controls are essentially social in nature. General wage rates can only be set centrally because the aggregate wagefund must be matched with the planned supply of wagegoods in a shortage economy.

Given the extent of integration with the world economy, it may well be that the most effective way of implementing a 'hard budget' for state enterprises, concentrated as they are in the modern sector of the economy, is to express this in terms of foreign exchange. Such a procedure employs border prices for traded inputs and outputs (and applies indirect calculation of costs of supplying non-traded items such as electricity) and although developed for investment project evaluation in the public sector, is logically applicable to the whole state sector.[39] This would in fact be very much in line with the price reforms carried out in Eastern Europe, to ensure technological competitiveness with the West.[40] For a developing economy, it reflects the need for efficiency relative to other Third World exporters and the need to set relative prices for traded goods so as to reflect foreign exchange scarcity.

As most state enterprises cannot operate without imports, the linkage of access to foreign exchange to their own 'net balance' does provide a strong incentive for efficiency as export prices cannot be raised, and domestic goods can be constantly compared with import costs. It cannot be objected that adoption of border prices for state enterprise accounting implies blind acceptance of the exiting patterns of comparative advantage (rendering impossible the nurturing of infant industries) because major production or trade projects would still be subject to central evaluation on the basis of the stategic accumulation criteria discussed above.

A hard budget also implies the possibility of bankruptcy, closure or takeover if a firm is consistently unprofitable; a requirement which is related not only to the ultimate sanction for management and workforce, but also to the process of resructuring production as technologies and markets change. This latter is particularly important for peripheral socialist economies, which much necessarily have flexible export systems in order to survive. On the domestic market competition betweeen firms (whether state enterprises, co-operatives or petty producers) is probably most relevant in cases of consumer supply (Department II); for producer goods, being able to match import prices (at reasonable levels of protection) seems a better criterion. However, in all three cases, the organisation of labour transfer, spatial allocation of new plant to replace old, and income support during fractional unemployment are essential to reduce institutional resistance to plant closure, against which price policies alone will not be effective.[41]

Exchange relations with the petty production sector imply that state purchasing prices become a key planning variable. A target may be set for food deliveries by peasant co-operatives based on the physical consumption requirements of the rest of the population, but only if the correct price (taking into account input costs, prices of alternative output, etc.) is set, and supported by credit, will targets be met. In this sense, the position is the inverse of that for foreign trade, where prices are exogenous, but the volume can be planned. For major products, therefore, a constant process of *relative* official price adjustment has to be carried out because given the supply concentration and the composition of market demand in a shortage economy, to deregulate such products would only create distorting 'suction' from the state sector itself.[42] Minor product markets can be deregulated more easily, but only if overall monetised demand in the economy is in equilibrium with such supply, for otherwise 'free' prices will rise disproportionately to regulated ones, distorting delivery patterns away from basic necessities.

At first sight, an alternative might appear to be to simply apply the same border price criteria as we have suggested for state enterprises, but there are good reasons for doubting this. First, one of the long-term strategic objectives of socialist development is the voluntary collectivisation of small-scale production in larger units with higher productivity, which implies technical specialisation, building up co-operatives, social infrastructure, training,etc., all of which require considerable long-term financial stability and state supervision. Second, exogenous prices will not guarantee basic needs targets (for example, food delivery volumes) or support petty producer incomes at low levels of technology, thus making income redistribution strategy much more difficult. Third, households or small co-operatives do not have the capital resources or institutional strength to withstand short-term fluctuations in world prices, unlike state enterprises.

There is no reason to expect the two price systems to be consistent with each other; and there may also be good reasons for having a distinct set of price relatives for consumers, especially necessities such as basic foods. It must be recognised that the conjunction involves a considerable tension between world prices (which the economy must respect due to its openness) related above all to accumulation, and domestic prices (to ensure supply from the small-scale sector) related above all to consumption. This topic requires a lot more analytical elaboration than there is space for here [*FitzGerald; 1987, 1988*] but the conclusions are highly dependent on the interaction between the internal and external terms of trade on the one hand, and the desired rate of growth on the other. Taking border prices as a standard would necessarily entail a 'cross-subsidy' system, but it should be emphasised that this is the logical consequence of adopting a domestic market system distinct from World market 'rules' and cannot be avoided, if only for reasons of income distribution. The question is therefore one of how to minimise the negative impact of relative prices on production efficiency. The planning authorities will be concerned with monitoring prices and costs in some detail, and with ensuring that subsidies support policy objectives in reality.[43]

An economy organised along those lines inevitably relies to a considerable extent on the banking system for operational control of the economy, once a rational pricing system and hard budgeting is introduced. The tendency we have mentioned for socialist banking practice to take a passive position, financing any activity sanctioned in the plan, also requires reconsideration. This cannot be done by simply adopting the position taken by banks in a capitalist economy where credits are granted on the basis of the borrowers' capacity to repay, and underwritten by alienable assets as collateral. In a socialist economy, where state enterprises and co-operatives form part of a larger planned system, loan criteria cannot be based on the profitability of the firm itself (which determines repayment capacity only in a capitalist economy) while property is not alienable to a bank at all. This would appear to imply that banks would have to adopt an active 'planning' role (as management consultants, so to speak) in their relationship with firms, within a broader sectoral and macroeconomic framework set by the planning authorities themselves.

CONCLUSION

Our attempt to apply the Kalecki-Kornai model of the industrialised socialist economy has revealed that once certain (considerable) modifications are made to allow for the existence of a large petty-production sector on the one hand, and a subordinate position in the world economy on the other, such a model does shed light on apparently intractable macroeconomic disequilibria. We have shown how the manifestations of the 'shortage economy' cannot be simply interpreted as inept government expenditure policies or excessive rates of accumulation; they are rooted in intrinsic institutional characteristics of the socialist economy in general, and the dynamic of state enterprise in particular.

That comprehensive social control of production units is not possible in such socialist economies in the transitional stage is undoubtedly true, as Bettelheim prints out, because due to their very underdevelopment decentralised enterprise forms are dominant and this implies the appropriation of surplus by groups or individuals.[44] To the extent that financial profitability or socialist economic accounting (*calcule économique*) is the *only* criterion for state enterprise action, then his conclusion[45] that this makes them equivalent to capitalist firms might seem logical. However, we have tried to show that 'existing' state enterprises do not act like capitalist firms, while decentralisation and better use of market forces does not necessarily imply a return to capitalism either, so long as effective central control over accumulation is maintained. The alternative is almost a council of despair, for it implies that the economies of the Third World must await full capitalist develoment before attempting to build socialism.

Our analysis has emphasised the severe restrictions placed upon balanced state accumulation by basic needs requirements, non-state production forms and world markets. None the less, this cannot be taken to imply that state enterprises are a negative force, and that some sort of petty-production system under central macroeconomic control would be a feasible alternative. The state sector alone has the capacity to transform economic structures, mobilise resources on a large scale, redistribute income and negotiate with the world economy, and is thus inevitably the centre of any socialist accumulation model. The problem is how to make such a model socially and economically efficient; to abandon it, is no solution at all.

Our observations on macroeconomic policy and pricing systems are directed towards this end and suggest that a feasible planning system would be based more on the management of exchange relations between the various institutional sectors of the economy than on direct production control. Such a system requires stricter financial rules and a clearer definition of the role of different sorts of enterprises than are usually to be found, but these do not seem to be unattainable conditions.

NOTES

1. There is insufficient space in this article to give proper coverage of country experiences, which would have to range from Cuba to China passing through the twenty or so Third World economies outside Eastern Europe as such that might be classed as 'socialist'. Comprehensive studies are remarkably few, but the collections of case studies in Saith [1985], Morawetz [1980], Jameson and Wilber [1981] White et al. [1983] and White and Croll [1983] do, with this volume, give some empirical basis for the stylised facts' used here.
2. The introduction to Saith [1985] takes this as an empirical definition, rather than an abstract categorisation of 'transition to socialism' as implied in Bettelheim [1975], and we shall do the same.
3. Hindess, in his *Introduction* to Bettelheim [1976] argues that 'all social formations require the appropriation of surplus labour' as 'an effect of the difference between the condition of reproduction of labour and the conditions of reproduction of the economy as a whole'. At a more concrete level, I am arguing here that planning is 'about reconciling heterogeneous enterprise strategies with overall economic strategy.
4. Kalecki [1986], which should be read in the historical context provided by Nuti [1986].
5. FitzGerald [1987] shows how Kalecki's govenment decision curve might be superimposed on a 'workers' decision curve' also measuring productivity growth (based on work intensity) against consumption (that is wage incentives). These two would have contrary slopes, and thus give determinate equilibrium indicating the maximum feasible growth rate.
6. This is a widespread view at present, as Portes [1979], indicates.
7. Nuti [1979] describes his approach as explicitly Marxian, while Nove [1983] is implicitly non-Marxist, but they come to similar conclusions. Bettelheim's conclusions as to the emergence of a 'state bourgeoisie' points in much the same direction.
8. The phrase comes, of course, from the title of Nove [1983]; although he unfortunately does not tackle the issues raised by Kalecki and Kornai, remaining in the realm of microeconomic efficiency.
9. Kornai [1980] is our main source here. For a critique see Gomulka [1985], and the reply in Kornai [1986a]. Kornai [1986b] contrasts his approach with that of other writers on 'market socialism' in Hungary.
10. Lange [1937] is the prime source; Horvat [1982] gives a recent version of a similar argument.
11. 'Central Price Determination as an essential feature of a Socialist Economy' in Kalecki [1986].
12. This approach is also taken by Kornai and Kalecki.
13. Wells [1986] is the only comprehensive study of this key sector that I am aware of.

14. This should not be read as an argument to the effect that such economies *should* remain raw material exporters; but rather as a statement of fact that they do. The proposals in Thomas [*1974*] for autonomous manufacturing/development in small economies seem very optimistic: current research would indicate that successful small economies advance by industrialising their export base.

15. See, for example, Rumantsiev [*1979*] and Smirnov [*1979*] for recent statements of this as the orthodox socialist view on transition to socialism and development planning, respectively; although this may well be about to change.

16. Harrison [*1980*] gives a useful summary of this hotly debated topic.

17. In which case, the concept of the 'working class' as a homogeneous social category (or even an ideological concept) presumably needs some reconsideration.

18. The theoretical foundations of this approach to perspective planning are to be found in Kalecki (perspective). They are quite distinct from the pretended 'laws of socialist planning' based on the maximisation of the rate of accumulation, propounded in Rumantsiev [*1979*].

19. This model is explored in more depth in FitzGerald [*1987*].

20. Fransman [*1986*] has an excellent analysis of the 'make or buy' decision in the capital goods sector. It is worth noting, in passing, that the CMEA system of aid to developing countries involves a more complete transfer of technology (albeit somewhat dated) than is customary with MNC's; see Cassen [*1985*].

21. Nutrition, health and education obviously raise productivity too by improving the capacity of the workforce itself. Both these points are overlooked by Kalecki and Kornai; which is surprising, given their concern for consumption.

22. Particularly in the agricultural sector: see for example, Hartford [*1985*].

23. Bogolomov [*1983*] gives and orthodox treatment of modern socialist trade theory based on world prices. Unequal exchange would in any case obtain between 'socialist centre' and 'socialist periphery,' if wages and growth rates were autonomously planned in the centre, as FitzGerald [*forthcoming*] argues.

24. We do not have the space here to discuss the problems arising in the transition from 'capitalist aid' to 'socialist aid', but on the latter, see Cassen [*1985*]. Some preliminary notes can be found in FitzGerald [*1986*].

25. Lenin made much of this point, of course.

26. Wilczinsky [*1982*].

27. There are other reasons too. First, small producers are seen as a threat to socialism on *ideological* grounds. This seems to me to require political persuasion, not economic repression. Second, they are administratively complicated to deal with, but this is an argument for co-operativisation. Third, state managers are logically opposed to competition in labour and product markets!

28. See the interesting debate on this issue in *Development and Change*, Vol.18 (1987).

29. Kalecki [*1971*] hold that this is *the* central issue in socialist planning.

30. Who the decision makers are is, of course, another matter; and the *political* consequences of high accumulation rates are profound, as the Polish experience shows. However, both Kornai and Kalecki (as well as other authors such as Nuti) see such rates as feasible, albeit undesirable.

31. National income statistics in socialist developing countries usually record only state investment and neglect household production for consumption, so neither of those phenomena will be recorded in the macroeconomic plan results.

32. This constraint is classified by Talas [*1983*] as a major feature of the transition to socialism in LDC's; arguing that this curtails their capcity to undertake 'primitive accumulation' by curtailing consumption in the non-state sector.

33. See 'Financing Development', Kalecki [*1986*], which is set out in a formal model in FitzGerald [*1987*].

34. Both those phenomena are discussed in depth in FitzGerald [*1988*].

35. See Ellman [*1979*] for this argument as applied to the USSR.

36. Thirlwall [*1972*] develops this point for developing countries along Kaldorian lines.

37. Griffith-Jones [*1981*] has this as a principle conclusion, based on the early transition experience of Russia, Czechoslovakia and Chile.

38. This point is made in Fforde [*1984*] who provides a fascinating microeconomic model of the labour interactions between state enterprises and the 'informal sector' in Vietnam. I would suggest, however, that in quantitative terms the seigniorage to be expected is small: if the non-

state sector is 50 per cent off the GDP and grows at five per cent annum, its demand for money (assuming a velocity of circulation of four) will only support a budget deficit of 0.6 per cent of GDP.

39. The method is set out in Little and Mirrlees [1974]. Although designed for use in OECD aid programmes, and officially adopted by the IBRD and other UN agencies, it is in fact more suitable for application in planned economies. Indeed the technical appendix to the *Manual* is set out explicitly in terms of a Lewis-type dual economy where the 'modern' sector is state enterprise.
40. Kornai [1986b] introduces this factor, which is absent in Kornai [1980].
41. The Yugoslav experience clearly indicates the resistance of local (party) authorities to such restructuring.
42. 'Central Price Determination . . .', in Kalecki [1986].
43. This implies the application of modern 'social accounting matrix' methodology to distinguish between the accumulation balances of different institutional sectors, on which see FitzGerald and Vos [1988].
44. Bettelheim [1975] points this out in his key chapter on 'forms and methods of planning', which was written in the context of his earlier work in Cuba, and economy with a degree of centralisation equalled only by the GDR.
45. Bettelheim [1976] argues, in fact, that the mode of production in the USSR is 'state capitalism'.

REFERENCES

Bettelheim, C.L., 1975, *The Transition to Socialist Economy*, Hassocks, Sussex: Harvester Press (French original published by Maspero in 1968).
Bettelheim, C., 1976, *Economic Calculation and Forms of Property*, London: Routledge & Kegan Paul (French original published by Maspero in 1970).
Bogolomov, O., 1983, *Socialist Countries in the International Division of Labour*, Moscow: Progress Publishers.
Brus, W., 1971, 'Kalecki's Economics of Socialism' *Oxford Bulletin of Economics and Statistics*, Vol.39 No.1.
Casen, R.H. (ed.), 1985, *Soviet Interests in the Third World* London: Sage for the RIIA.
Ellman, M., 1979, *Socialist Planning*, Cambridge: Cambridge University Press.
Fforde, A.J., 1984, 'Macro-economic Adjustment and Structural Change in a Low-Income Socialist Developing Economy – An Analytical Model', *Discussion Paper No.168*, London: Birkbeck College, London University.
FitzGerald, E.V.K., 1985, 'The Problem of Balance in the Peripheral Socialist Economy: Conceptual Note', in white and Croll [1985].
FitzGerald, E.V.K., 1986, 'Notes on the Analysis of the Small Underdeveloped Economy in Transition', in Fagen R.R. (ed.) *Transition and Development: Problems of Third World Socialism*, New York: Monthly Review Press.
FitzGerald, E.V.K., 1987, 'Kalecki on Planned Growth in the Mixed Economy', *Development and Change*, Vol.19, No.1.
FitzGerald, E.V.K., 1988, 'Kalecki on the financing of Development: Elements for a Macroeconomics of the Semi-industrialized Economy', *Cambridge Journal of Economics* (forthcoming).
FitzGerald, E.V.K., forthcoming, 'An Analytical Taxonomy of Unequal Exchange Theories in a Heterogeneous World Economy', *ISS Working Papers Series*, The Hague, Institute of Social Studies.
FitzGerald, E.V.K. and R. Vos, 1988, *Financing Economic Development: A Structuralist Approach to Monetary Policy*, London: Gower.
Fransman, M. (ed.), 1986, *Machinery and Economic Development*, London: Macmillan.
Griffith-Jones, S., 1981, *The Role of Finance in the Transition to Socialism*, London: Pinter.
Griffin, K. and J. James, 1981, *The Transition to Egalitarian Development: Economic Policies for Structural Change in the Third World*, London: Macmillan.
Gomulka, S., 1985, 'Kornai's Soft Budget Constraint and the Shortage Phenomenon: A Criticism and a Restatement', *Economics of Planning*, Vol.19, No.1.
Harrison, M., 1980, 'Why Did NEP Fail? *Economics of Planning*, Vol.16, No.2.

Horvat, B., 1982, *The Political Economy of Socialism*, Oxford: Martin Robertson.

Hartford, K., 1985, 'Hungarian Agriculture: A Model for the Socialist World', in White and Croll [*1985*].

Jameson, K.P. and C.K. Wilber (eds.), 1981, 'Socialist Models of Development', Special Issue *World Development*, Vol.9, Nos.9/10.

Kalecki, M., 1970, 'Theories of Growth in Different Social Systems', *Scientia*, No.5-6.

Kalecki, M., 1986, *Selected Essays on Economic Planning*, Cambridge: Cambridge University Press.

Kornai, J., 1980, *The Economics of Shortage*, Amsterdam: North Holland.

Kornai, J., 1986a, 'The Soft Budget Constraint', *Kyklos*, No.29.

Kornai, J., 1986b, 'The Hungarian Reform Process', *Journal of Economic Literature*, Vol.24, No.4.

Lange, O., 1937, 'On the Economic Theory of Socialism', *Review of Economic Studies* (Feb.).

Little, I.M.D. and J.A. Mirrlees, 1974, *Project Appraisal and Planning for Developing Countries*, London: Heinemann.

Morawetz, D., 1980, 'Economic Lessons from Small Socialist Developing Countries', *World Development*, Vol.8, No.5/6.

Nove, A., 1983, *Feasible Socialism*, London: Allen & Unwin.

Nuti, D.M., 1986, 'Michael Kalecki's Contribution to the Theory and Practice of Socialist Planning', *Cambridge Journal of Economics*, Vol.10, No.4.

Nuti, D.M., 1979, 'The Contraditions of Socialist Economics: a Marxist Interpretation', in R. Miliband and J. Saville (eds.), *The Socialist Register 1979*, London: Merlin.

Preobrazhensky, E., 1965, *The New Economics* Oxford: Oxford University Press (originally published in Moscow, 1926).

Portes, A., 1979, 'Internal and External Balance in a Centrally Planned Economy', *Journal of Comparative Economics*, Vol.3, No.4.

Rumantsiev, A., 1979, *The Political Economy of Socialism* Moscow: Progress Publishers.

Saith, Ashwani (ed.), 1985, *The Agrarian Question in Socialist Transitions*, London: Frank Cass.

Smirnov, G., 1979, *Planning in Developing Countries: Theory and Methodology*, Moscow: Progress Publishers.

Talas, B., 1983, 'Specific Prerequisites for the Transition to Socialism in the Socio-economically Underdeveloped Countries', *Development and Peace*, Vol.4, No.2.

Thirlwall, A.P., 1972, *Growth and Development: With Special Reference to Developing Countries*, London: Macmillan.

Thomas, C.Y., 1974 *Dependence and Transformation: The Economics of the Transition to Socialism*, New York: Monthly Review Press.

Wells, J., 1986, *The Construction Industry in Developing Countries*, Beckenham, Kent: Croom Helm.

Wilczynski, J., 1982, *The Economics of Socialism: Principles Governing the Operation of the Centrally Planned Economics under the New System*, London: Allen & Unwin.

White G. and E. Croll (eds.), 1985, 'Special Issue on Agriculture in Socialist Development', *World Develoment*, Vol.13, No.1.

White G., R. Murray and C. White (eds.), 1983, *Revolutionary Socialist Development in the Third World*, Brighton, Sussex: Harvester.

Wolf, T.A., 1985, 'Economic Stabilization in Planned Economies', *IMF Staff Papers*, Vol.32, No.1.

Central Planning and Market Relations in Socialist Societies

This article examines some problems of central planning in eastern Europe, to see what lessons, if any, may be drawn for developing socialist societies. It is argued that the lessons are not simple ones that can be deduced from directly transposing eastern European problems and solutions to the quite different conditions of developing societies.

I. INTRODUCTION

While political developments in the Western developed countries during the 1980s may make it seem of little immediate interest to discuss issues of socialist planning and economic management, there exists a growing body of experience of such issues in developing societies. This makes it relevant to draw what lessons one can from such attempts at socialist transformation which have usually been conducted in adverse or overtly hostile circumstances. The cost of such attempts has been high, which makes the need for reflection all the greater. In addition, recent developments in the Soviet Union, including at the time of writing the apparent abandoning of annual economic plans [*Walker, 1987*], suggest that there is a place for further consideration on problems of socialist transformation in societies with a developed division of labour.

The problems of 'advanced socialist societies' may yield useful indications of pitfalls and potential solutions for transformation strategies in 'peripheral socialist societies' such as Mozambique.[1] Some of the considerations faced by socialist societies may be of more general applicability, such as relations with neighbouring economies, the advantages and drawbacks of international economic integration, regional diversity within the 'national economy' and so on. However, it is not the intention to provide an analysis of, say, the Soviet Union and 'read off' the lessons to be drawn for societies like Mozambique. Rather, the intention is to use examples from both 'advanced' and 'peripheral' socialist societies to illustrate themes and issues which now seem to merit further discussion. One of the main issues to be addressed is the increased reliance on market forces in both kinds of society, and the extent to which this is related to a possible crisis in traditional central planning.

'Traditional' central planning involves mobilising resources administratively in 'extensive development' through the expansion of the state sector, which tends to monopolise material and human resources, and in which

*School of Social Analysis, University of Bradford. I am grateful to the editors for their helpful comments on an earlier draft.

resource allocation is by administrative means rather than through exchange relations (which only play a subordinate role). The recent attempted shift in eastern Europe to an 'intensive phase' implies a reconsideration of both central planning and market mechanisms. In developing socialist societies, such as Mozambique, central planning has been implemented in a context where (at least in principle) exchange relations with the peasantry are supposed to be maintained while the basis of peasant production is transformed. Central planning tends to deny resources to other non-state sectors, thus producing characteristic problems such as the erosion of official marketing.

Consequently, for the state sector to develop without crowding out the peasantry (and thus retain its support), it must enter the intensive, efficient stage more or less from the outset. This implies the management of market relations as part of a strategy of transormation, rather than just privatising the state or liberalising markets. Rethinking central planning thus entails considering how to handle changing market relations within the state sector, and between that and the rest of the economy.

II. INVESTMENT AND ECONOMIC GROWTH: A CRISIS OF CENTRAL PLANNING?

By the early 1980s, it had become clear that among the European members of the Council for Mutual Economic Assistance (CMEA)[2] there had been a continuing slowdown in the rate of economic growth, coupled with various austerity-based adaptation strategies to deal with international economic relations which had deteriorated in the 1970s. While the causes of and responses to these difficulties were somewhat different in each of the CMEA counties (with the USSR much better placed than the others to absorb these problems), a plausible argument has been mounted that there were nevertheless a series of common features to this crisis. It has been argued that this can be considered a structural crisis of Soviet-type economies, however much the problems are complicated by different policies in each member country, the depression in the capitalist West, or the social and political crisis which occurred in Poland.[3]

Basically the argument is that the reduction in the rate of growth of such economies is due to the over concentration on investment, and poor control of the efficiency of investment. Drach, relying on arguements by Bauer, but with strong supporting evidence,[4] argues that the problem arises from negotiations over investment between the various agents involved (the state planning commission,the branch ministries, and the regional levels). These negotiations privilege a political equilibrium, but result in a cycle of dispersal of investment decisions, leading to over-investment, followed by shortages, restrictions on consumption, re-establishment of strong central control and reduction in investment. This form of control is considered to entail inadequate criteria for investment efficiency, and consequent low productivity of investment, which has effects on economic growth and eventually on investment itself, despite the high priority usually placed on investment in such economies. It is argued that these problems stem from a failure to make the transition from extensive to intensive growth, and/or from the absence of a capital market as a mechanism for investment decision-making.

Drach argues that there are four fundamental reasons why Soviet-type economies have not succeeded in breaking out of a pattern of extensive growth. First, they are hierarchical centralised natural economies (based on use-values) rather than ones in which the microeconomic criteria of demand and profit operate through the market to coordinate the activities of autonomous units. Thus, despite 20 years of debates on investment criteria, investment still functions as a mechanism for distributing resources rather than as a generator of (and reward for) productivity. This means that the 'capital'/output coefficient continues to rise, rather than there being any economising on means of production by more efficient use. Second, the fact that such investment decisions involve the Centre (the central planning agencies) gives rise to a game of manipulating information and goods which in turn fosters a cycle of shortage and stocking up, which undermines effective economic growth. Third, the minor status of consumption goods, especially agricultural ones (with agriculture consequently suffering lack of investment and hoarding too much labour), has made if difficult to use growth of consumer goods to reward growth of labour productivity, which would initiate a virtuous circle. Fourth, partly because of the lack of incentives and the disorganisation of production induced by shortages, such economies have failed to raise labour productivity sufficiently.[5] Because such fundamental inhibitors of intensive growth are related to the system of power, the Centre prefers even stagnation to any reform upsetting the distribution of powers. Hence the failure of almost all the reforms of the 1960s. It is appropriate to use the term 'crisis' where such problems are now affecting political institutions.

Clearly this kind of argument is not new, at least at the level of its theoretical basis.[6] However, its salience is renewed by the evidence that the growth of investment and economic growth are indeed slowing down in such economies, to the point where reform really is on the agenda, even in the USSR which has withstood the effects of this trend better than most of its neighbours. Furthermore, evidence of the effects of this economic deceleration on other aspects of these economies suggests that the effects could be quite serious, both politically and economically, in the short or medium term, in countries other than Poland (where they have already contributed to the overt crisis). As Bastida[7] shows very clearly for the USSR, the growth of other headings in the public budget is suffering disproportionately from the attempt to maintain the *rate* of investment (as opposed to its effectiveness). In general, the growth of socio-cultural measures and science (and, in particular, education and science) has suffered much more. In the case of education and science the slow growth of expenditure has had deleterious effects, judging by public debate in the USSR itself, where claims of chronic lack of resources have been made.[8] This decline scarcely bodes well for attempts to raise the effectiveness of investment, and labour productivity, thus exacerbating the problems of transition to an intensive growth pattern.[9]

The continued prioritisation of the rate of investment in the face of decelerating growth also shows itself with respect to public health expenditure [*Bastida, 1985: 120*-1]. At first sight, such evidence could be used to support the attempt by one commentator to analyse this kind of crisis in terms of a 'legitimation crisis' as described by Habermas.[10] Whatever misgivings one may have about Habermas's position,[11] it is clear from Gorbachev's 1986 criticisms of the ineffectiveness of the Soviet health service that there must be concern in some quarters about the adverse effects of this on the Party's legitimacy. Obviously when confronted with existing budgetary constraints, the proposed reorganisation of the health service and increased responsiveness to patients' demands constitute one strategy to deal with the problem.

In the case of social security and social insurance, there was a big increase between 1966 and 1975, after which their growth rates came much more into line with other headings under the broad heading of socio-cultural measures and science [*Bastida, 1985: 114*–5]. Thus, there is a clear prioritisation of 'economic' as opposed to 'social' needs in the public budget of the USSR, surely an indication of austerity measures associated with an attempt to raise the level of economic growth.

Bastida's figures do not cover Soviet wages, but for the neighbouring CMEA economies, Hungary, Poland and the GDR, Redor provides graphic evidence (literally and metaphorically) of the secular decline in wages as a proportion of national income from 1962 to 1980.[12] Despite fluctuations in investment in these countries (which in itself tends to support Drach's contention that there is a political cycle of investment), Redor seems to have established a strict relationship between the reduction in the proportion of wages in the 1960s and 1970s, on the one hand, and the evolution of the rate of investment, on the other. Redor argues that the example of Poland in 1980 and 1981 shows that any open contestation of the mode of regulating the national income places the very foundations of the economic system in danger [*Redor, 1985: 151*].

Redor complements Drach's and Bastida's arguments, treating the relative decline of wages as a result of poor implementation of investment plans, in terms of both volume and effectiveness, with resulting failures in the growth of labour productivity. In a familiar litany, he cites the following reasons for poor mastery of the effectiveness of investment:

> ... under pressure from enterprises, the plans for investment are often surpassed, but their effectiveness is below the forecasts because of the underutilisation of productive capacity, delays in the construction and putting into service of installations, [and] bottlenecks in production. An indirect proof of this ineffectiveness is given by the fact that during the period of rapid capital accumulation which we have analysed, the rate of growth of national income did not increase [*Redor, 1985: 152*].

It is thus evident that by the early 1980s, CMEA economies all faced a macroeconomic situation in which extensive growth was increasingly ineffective, but the vested institutional interests of those involved in the political bargaining which reproduced this state of affairs were impeding reform. This is not to say that the member countries did not react with various policies and reforms, with varying degress of success. It is to say that reform was not easy, partly for political reasons and partly because there was no serious challenge to the calculations and concepts, on which negotiations between the relevant economic agents were based. The major exception was probably Hungary, where various market based devices were used to promote enterprise efficiency and investment designed to increase exports. Even where official policy was the opposite, as in the USSR in the 1970s, investment priority tended to go to producers' goods, with induced bottleneck effects on the rest of the economy.

However, because of the relative decline in the growth of wages during the 1960s and 1970s, by the early 1980s, most CMEA governments did not wish to restrain personal purchasing power (the exception being Poland following the big wage increases of 1980–81). Consequently, the relative share of investment in national income could not be allowed to grow. This development, when combined with a shortage of labour-power and, in most countries (except the USSR), strong growth in the prices of raw materials, meant that the problems of the 'extensive model' of growth were coming to a head. For Redor [*1985: 156*], this raises the traditional themes of reforms: how to maintain a certain rate of economic growth when an increase in investment and labour-power employed is scarcely possible any longer? Can the centralisation of the economy in relation to investment and regulation of wages be preserved, when this is at the origin of the current crisis? How to pass to a type of growth which is more economical in its use of 'capital', labour and raw materials?

Before assessing this kind of analysis of the crisis of central planning, the use of trade with Western economies as a means of increasing efficiency and thus possibly easing economic problems must be examined. The possible benefits of such trade include (a) the provision of investment funds and goods to ease shorgages, and (b) the provision of 'high technology' investment not readily available within CMEA economies. The problem of quality of production could be at least partly tackled by high technology. The well-known difficulties of technological innovation were not merely a problem for intermediate and consumers' goods in the civilian economy, but were also a problem for defence production, where the arms race made high quality a major political priority. Duchene [*1985: 105–8*] provides evidence suggesting that in the Soviet case, whether or not foreign trade provided high technology to the defence effort, the foreign trade deficit effectively covered defence expenditure from the mid-1970s, allowing it to grow slowly at a time when civilian accumulation was declining. Thus foreign trade did combat the productivity crisis, and ease shortages, at least in the area of defence expenditure. This suggests a continuing importance of foreign trade even to the USSR, as it attempts to maintain the growth of both civilian consumption and military expenditure.

Since economic relations with capitalist economies are almost inevitably market relations, and since fluctuations in the world economy can cause unforeseen perturbations in such market relations, it is evident that international economic relations could cause problems in centrally planned economies, including stimulating the development of (legal or parallel) markets within such economies. The evidence indicates that CMEA countries had growing foreign trade deficits with the rest of the world, from about 1974 to 1978, followed by a slight reduction in such deficits from 1979 to 1981 (apart from Poland) with a return to surplus by 1982 and 1983.[13] Poland was the worst case with 12 years of deficits to 1983, while the USSR had only three such years, two of which were negligible. The six European CMEA members apart from the USSR also had deficits with the USSR itself, which reduced their dependence on convertible foreign currency, but which could lead the USSR to develop its convertible currency exchanges with the west. This in turn could be constraining on the USSR itself in future, especially if Duchene is correct about the additional motive for trade with the west to finance defence expenditure.

The general reaction of the CMEA countries to these developments was first (1976–78) to seek loans. With rising interest rates, this in itself added to the foreign debts, and bankers' worries about CMEA and Third World indebtedness meant that credit to CMEA countries became restricted. Consequently, CMEA countries adopted foreign trade and domestic austerity policies which affected investment much more than consumption [*Andreff and Graziani, 1985: 34*], thus amplifying the 'investment crisis' discussed above. Hence, the recourse to imports (especially of more advanced technology) to generate economic growth by investment proved counter-productive in the six CMEA countries (apart from the USSR). Whereas, in a situation of taut planning, imports of investment goods should have added to disposable resources and raised productivity (making it possible later to pay for the imports by increased exports), the ineffectiveness of management of investment projects (especially in Poland) meant that foreign indebtedness would have occurred even in the absence of world recession.[14] Nevertheless, the world economic recession did increase the extent of the indebtedness, forcing the adjustment of policy within these CMEA countries.

This policy of adjustment involving restriction of investment more than consumption could nevertheless have had an impact on the *efficiency* of investment. Despite problems of managing investment under 'traditional' central planning, some CMEA countries have attempted to use foreign trade pressures to improve the efficiency either of investment or of the management of existing productive capacity. Thus in the German Democratic Republic, one solution attempted has been to force firms to compete in capitalist export markets, and allow a certain degree of import penetration. In Hungary, Richet [*1985: 170*] reports that the 1978 policy to deal with foreign exchange problems and the declining growth rate had two priorities: external equilibrium rather than growth, and maintenance of living standards rather than investment. Control of investment was achieved partly by the government centralising control of a proportion of enterprise investment funds [*Richet, 1985: 171*], but also partly by the imposition of competitive prices on over one third of production [*Richet, 1985: 172*]. This meant that any enterprise exporting at least five per cent of its production could only charge prices on the domestic market which gave it a rate of profit not exceeding that achieved by exports, thereby undercutting demand for investment goods generated by profits based on the former cost-plus formula. Thus in a sense foreign trade has been used to mitigate the investment crisis of 'traditional' central planning. In the case of Hungary, Richet does not see this policy as a response to IMF pressure, but claims that there has been a convergence of points of view [*Richet, 1985: 174*]. The Hungarian policy was developed four years before it joined the IMF and the Hungarians have refused to implement certain IMF policies which would have increased unemployment.

Intensive Growth and Improved Planning

While it is evident that many of the problems highlighted in the preceding section are real enough, the analysis of them is somewhat problematic. The main focus of the critique of CMEA countries seems to be on the centralisation of planning, and on the failure to use the price mechanism as a source of economic information and sanctions (rewards and punishment) on economic agents. Linked to this critique are charges of 'politicisation' of decision-making and the manipulation of investment decisions to affect the distribution of resources (and income) between agents (ministries, enterprises, regional bodies) rather than to increase productivity. The very last point is undoubtedly correct, and reveals the damaging aspects of such institutional negotiations, but the charge carries the implicit assumption that capitalist market decisions on investment are somehow unpolitical, which is surely naive. Competition by states, or by regions or cities within states, for investment by transnational corporations (TNCs) is a well-known political phenomenon, as is the flight of capital from states where political developments do not meet with approval on the international capital markets.

What needs to be questioned is not the politicisation of investment decisions, nor the political nature of enterprise management in socialist countries (as if this were not also true of capitalist management, especially in nationalised industries), but rather the particular politics produced by a complex of institutions, practices and discourses, which has blocked reforms aimed at more effective investment and enterprise management. One could conceivably argue that anything which breaks the log-jam is almost bound to be more effective, even the introduction of market relations. Yet such an approach, if adopted, would require a little more theoretical finesse than the common practice of counterposing 'the plan' and 'the market', or 'centralisation' and 'decentralisation'.[15] There is simply no reason to treat commodity relations as bearing the cloven hoof of capitalism (or as providing the essential basis for rational decentralised decision-making, if one prefers). The assumption that the 'price mechanism' produces essentially the same effects under different circumstances ignores the effects of different forms of organisation (different kinds of economic agent), of varying relations between them (as struggles, negotiations and competition change the practices in which they engage) and of varying discourses which affect the nature of the information and sanctions which prices are thought to generate.

Perhaps the clearest way to illustrate this point is to look at the possibilities for improving the efficiency of investment and enterprise management in the USSR *without* major institutional reforms, even though such reforms are very much on the agenda at the moment. The critiques of inefficiency in the Soviet economy often seem to unconsciously suppress the other side of the coin, namely, that this implies that there is tremendous scope for increasing efficiency. It is usually assumed, rather than argued, that this possibility can only be realised on condition that major reforms occur, and that these reforms include an increased role for market relations. Yet the relative importance of increased market relations may be quite small. For example, in Soviet agriculture, the much publicised 'freeing-up' of the Kolkhoz markets and of sales from the private plots, while certainly producing an impact on retail food trade (and reducing former losses of unsold produce), is unlikely per se to have a substantial impact on agricultural productivity and agricultural investment. It has already led to what is probably a once-for-all increase in activity on and output from personal plots (whether urban allotments or rural family plots). However, in rural areas such plots depend crucially for their inputs (other than unpaid family labour) on the collective and state farms to which they are attached.[16] Without such subsidies, including various kinds of free inputs, their costs of production would be higher and more important, their productivity per hectare would be lower.

It is clear that, even without major reforms, there is considerable scope for increasing agricultural productivity by a variety of measures, many of which are now being taken. Agricultural investment is being made more effective in various ways. Thus, there is currently a huge programme (50,000 million roubles from 1986–90) to irrigate arid areas and to drain swampy areas, which is expected to drastically reduce harvest dependence on what have always been highly erratic rainfall patterns in areas of good soil. This is, of course, an example of extensive growth, but of a kind which could ease or stabilise the problem of agricultural output while 'intensive growth' solutions are developed. In any case, investment is also being made more effective by a pattern of complementary investment to improve the effectiveness of existing facilities. The most notable is the increased use of tarpaulins on trucks used to transport harvested produce to market or to storage and processing facilities. In the past, lack of such tarpaulins contributed to a post-harvest loss of 25 per cent of the crop. This saving alone would eliminate the need to have recourse to world grain markets in the future. Similar investment is being made in storage and processing facilities. In agricultural production, more intensive use is being made of existing machinery by improved availability of spare parts and better repair facilities. Thus, whereas in Kazakhstan in the mid-1970s (as in the rest of the Soviet Union) the proportion of agricultural machinery out of commission was 15 per cent (compared to about three per cent in developed capitalist countries), by the 1980s it had been reduced to about five per cent.[17]

Other less obvious ways to improve agricultural productivity inlude a move to more labour-intensive, high value-added crops in Tadzhikistan,[18] increased regional crop specialisation within and between union republics (based partly on ecological considerations, to combat declining yields), and administrative reforms. The best publicised of the latter has been the creation of Gosagroprom in late 1985.[19] Legally, it is a State Committee, but functions in many respects like a ministry, to integrate various technical agricultural activities and to reduce the 'success indicator' problem whereby, for example, fertiliser suppliers would report success on the basis of their profits, but were not interested in final agricultural production. In other words, Gosagroprom aims to reduce the 'distortion' created by intermediate production in the measurement of plan implementation. This kind of 'distortion' is similar to that produced by an independent capitalist supplier making a profit who has no interest in the efficiency of his customer as long as the latter stays in business. While in the capitalist case the market may pressure the customer to become a more efficient producer, with consequent effects on the supplier, it is interesting to note that a 'central planning' solution to this problem also seems to be an option.

These examples have been chosen to show that in the Soviet Union, which, anyway, has suffered less acutely from the contradictions of extensive growth than its CMEA neighbours, there is considerable scope for easing bottlenecks and increasing the efficiency of investment (and the productivity of existing means of production) without recourse to major reforms, whether political ones or ones giving more free rein to 'the market'. This is not to argue that there is no scope for market incentives. In addition to the recent Kolkhoz market reforms, there is probably a case for market incentives to stimulate marketing by collective farm managers, especially in Soviet Central Asia and Kazakhstan. There, despite republican agricultural surpluses of high quality foods not readily available elsewhere in the USSR (and certainly not so early in the year as March), a sufficiently serious effort is not made to sell these fruits and vegetables into European Russia, the Baltic republics, or Siberia. This is not due to lack of transport, refrigeration or storage facilities; it is simply due to the fact that collective farm managers feel they have done their job if they produce the harvest and sell it to the markets in the same or a nearby republic. Since these republics are net beneficiaries of investment from the All-Union budget, the failure to deliver part of the harvest to other republics to the north evidently reduces the effectiveness of this investment from an All-Union point of view.

Considerations of this kind raise questions about which economic decisions should be made at which level, and by what kinds of economic agents. They are questions about information flows and sanctions, about coordination and autonomy, which tend to crop up in any serious discussion of the division of labour. If it is not enough to refer to 'the market' (either without further specification or else using discredited neoclassical concepts),[20] then it is not enough either to cling to simplistic concepts of central planning. Information flows can be of various kinds, including prices, but can also include democratic pressure exerted by complaints. Gorbachev has rightly tried to mobilise the latter, but it is evident that such information flows can only have limited effects. Moscow consumers can hardly complain about the apparent inertia of collective farm managers in Soviet Central Asia if they don't know about the situation, and the press can only publicise a limited number of problems. Only an appropriate array of information and sanctions can reduce the extent of bottlenecks in any economy, and as the structure of that economy changes, so ought the information and sanctions.

Such changes imply insitutional changes, that is abolition of some agencies, reorganisation of others (involving alterations of objectives, practices and discourses) and changing relations between them, which could lead to transformation of the relations of production. Rather than attempt to suggest how a transfer to intensive growth and greater democracy (both of which imply better education as well as better information flows) could be part of a process of further socialist transformation in CMEA economies,[21] it is more relevant to the concerns of this work to examine the extent to which the problems of policies of extensive growth might also apply to 'peripheral socialist societies'.

III. PERIPHERAL SOCIALIST SOCIETIES

The conditions of 'peripheral' socialist societies differ in many respects from those of 'advanced' ones. One of the most important differences is the way in which markets operate in relation to state planning. Whereas in advanced socialist countries the state is capable of more or less effective plan construction, implementation and monitoring, as a result of various legal and organisational conditions, in peripheral socialist countries such conditions are often absent. The organisational conditions (discourses, practices and resources) of state central planning include regular information flows on the development of the economy, and a capacity to mobilise agencies and resources to effect changes where they are deemed necessary. For state central planning to be effective, the various bodies must be coordinated in a reasonably adequate way to work towards a known set of objectives. The coordination usually takes the form of administrative allocation of resources which are internal to the state, because the state owns an overwhelming proportion of the economy.

In peripheral societies, even apparently extensive nationalisation pro-grammes do not usually give the state the capacity to coordinate its various activities in this manner. Many of the nationalisations can be considered as defensive ones, attempting to maintain minimum conditions for economic activity until some undefined future date at which greater resources for that activity can be supplied. Such practices are often a reaction to a flight of capital and skilled personnel following the achievement of national independence and/or the declaration of some sort of socialist programme. In these circumstances, there may be political competition for investment resources, as in 'advanced' societies, but such resources cannot be so widely spread through the economy, forcing the state to concentrate on a high priority section of even that limited part of the economy which is under its legal control. This can lead to a denationalisation of the lower priority areas as soon as prviate investors can be found to take them over.

The obvious result of this is that markets do not exist within the state sector to the extent that they do in 'advanced' socialist societies, and are hence less susceptible to direct administrative control. Whereas, say, in the USSR, the state bank can in principle withhold credit from an enterprise if the latter cannot produce documents to show that the credit is needed to make specific purchases as part of its plan, such administrative measures are far more difficult to implement against private, especially small scale, enterprises. Even when they are willing to cooperate with state economic policy, small scale private enterprises often lack the record keeping skills which would facilitate the statistical data collection necessary for administrative forms of economic control. The problem is very similar to that faced by small businesses in western Europe when the calculation and recording of VAT was imposed.

Peripheral socialist societies tend to lack the large trained inspectorate capable of enforcing such administrative procedures on private enterprise. Sometimes this applies to state regulation of large private firms and even to state owned enterprises. Thus the way that state economic policy impacts on or influences market relations has to be very different from those traditionally adopted in CMEA economies.

Frequently, this may well mean that the state sector is run on lines influenced by the 'model' of Soviet central planning (even if this is not openly acknowledged) while the organisational conditions for this (especially the administrative resources and management skills) are not present. Among other effects, this can lead to over-investment in the high priority sectors, and inadequate monitoring of the efficiency or effectiveness of this investment, in a manner rather similar to that described above by Drach. However, the belated recognition of this ineffectiveness will not necessarily lead simply to a temporary reduction in investment. It may lead to privatisation of even the formerly high priority state sectors, in despair of adequately managing them.

This outcome may seem like a solution, since privatisation often leads to foreign investment without affecting the central bank's foreign debts. However, private enterprise or 'pure market' solutions do little to affect the structure of dependence inherited by most, if not all, peripheral socialist economies. Indeed, rather than alter such dependent relations, pure market relations may reinforce them. In so far as this occurs, any justification of private enterprise or 'pure market' solutions on the grounds that they 'get the economy moving' has to be balanced against the adverse effects. These may involve not merely a delay in transforming the structure of the economy, but an undermining of the possiblity of such transformation. To prevent such a development, and keep the development of the market within confines which keep open the possibility of later transformation, an attempt may be made to contain the undesired effects of market relations by administrative means. However, the possibilities for the evasion of such 'containment' by the development of parallel markets are very evident, and this is even more true of a situation in which the state sector of the economy has had to contract precisely because of administrative failings.

Apart from breaking with former relations of dependence, there are problems with 'pure market' solutions which would make them unacceptable even if they did not imply such a loss of control over economic policy. First, in agriculture, colonial practices usually involved long-term soil degradation, so that cultivation techniques need to be evolved which combat this problem without incurring the typical problems of dependence on imported hybrid grains and fertiliser associated with the 'Green Revolution'. In any case, the 'Green Revolution' has frequently exacerbated problems of landlessness and other forms of social inequality which peripheral socialist societies are often attempting to resolve. In this respect, the 'Green Revolution' merely amplifies what are general problems of market solutions. Second, to reiterate a classical socialist critique of 'pure market' relations, the pattern of production, both in terms of prices and of the product mix, rarely coincides with what may loosely be termed 'popular needs'. Even if a pure market solution does not entail loss of control over other aspects of economic policy, it is difficult to envisage how it could fail to make it harder to transform the pattern of production in the direction of popular needs, except when it suppies goods which would otherwise not be available at all.

The supply of otherwise unavailable goods is not a valid argument in favour of a 'pure market' solution, however. It is merely an argument in favour of some kind of market relations. If the state or some kind of co-operative agencies are not capable of administrative regulation of the market to secure production for popular needs, then this ought to imply, not a capitulation to private enterprise, but rather a different form of intervention in (or influence upon) the market. The decision as to the forms of intervention clearly depend on the analysis of the markets in question, an analysis which may vary with regional conditions within the society [*Wuyts, 1985: 201*] and which may in part depend on well-informed estimates rather than reliable statistical data. This implies that, rather than a statist approach in which the state sector of the economy takes over and controls an increasing proportion of the rest of the economy, a more viable approach to socialist transformation would be to have a small but efficient state sector concentrating on particular tasks arising out of the differentiated analysis of different markets in the light of conjuncturally defined objectives.

Among these tasks, it is evident that monetary policy (including credit) needs to be directed to securing the development of 'appropriate' forms of organisation to promote the transformation of the economy. In peripheral socialist societies, this implies a policy on credit, pricing and marketing which mobilises resources to foster an articulation of organisational forms (predominantly agricultural ones) which is conducive to the strategic transformations being sought [*FitzGerald, 1985: 224–5*]. The importance of the coexistence and articulation of different organisational forms within such a market-related transformation strategy suggests that the example of the Soviet New Economic Policy (NEP) of the 1920s might be more relevant to peripheral socialist transformation than the current experience of CMEA economies.

As is well known, in that case the fairly small state sector occupying the 'commanding heights' of the economy coexisted with a rural sector dominated by small scale production [*Harrison, 1985: 82*]. While agriculture was the dominant sector of the economy, the state possessed a wide range of instruments to affect the course of economic development. Despite shortcomings, the combination of the use of these instruments, the rapid restoration of industrial production, and the removal of some pre-Revolutionary obstacles to agricultural growth (most notably the abolition of the latifundia) meant that both industrially and agriculturally, the NEP economy was a very dynamic one. In agriculture, the pattern of production was shifting towards mixed farming with more intensive arable crops and livestock [*Harrison, 1985: 84*], reducing the dependence on grain. Although the reduction in grain production worried most sections of the Soviet leadership, grain could not compeltely fulfill its pre-Revolutionary role of paying for imported machinery because the terms of trade were shifting against primary grain producers on the world market [*Harrison, 1985: 85*] and because other producers had replaced Russia as suppliers to the European grain market [*Littlejohn, 1984: 78*]. The overestimation of the importance of grain marketing and the underestimation of the importance of rural industries in contributing to agricultural production [*Harrison, 1985: 94*] both contributed to the policy switch in favour of collectivisation which ended NEP.

Yet while NEP was a viable policy, it is perhaps best to note some points of difference between the NEP period and contemporay peripheral socialist societies. First, the geographical isolation of the Soviet Union made it difficult to destabilise militarily by 'low intensity warfare' or 'pseudo-guerrilla' warfare, and by the time of NEP the western policy of overt invasion, colonisation and dismemberment of the former Russian empire (which underlay the Civil War of 1918–21) had been abandoned. Nevertheless, perceived external military threats in the late 1920s contributed to the abandoning of NEP and the industrialisation drive. Second, the NEP economy was sufficiently large, diverse and dynamic to be able to cope with the loss of export earnings on the grain market, and the loss of foreign investment, albeit with some difficulty [*Harrison, 1985: 85*]. To this extent, the NEP economy was less dependent on the world economy than is now the case for peripheral socialist societies. Third, while the terms of exchange with the peasantry failed to take account of the regionally differentiated class structure of the peasantry (with its implications for regional and class based differences in the composition of demand for industrial products and supply of industrial raw materials), on the whole the problems of managing such exchanges were increasingly well understood, and reasonably well-managed (at least around 1925–27). This was partly achieved by continual reorganisation and policy adjustment in the light of mistakes, but also depended on a reasonable statistical data base and on fairly sophisticated pricing, monetary and fiscal policies. While some peripheral socialist societies may have been able to achieve comparable control of market relations with the peasantry (and with cooperative and state agricultural enterprises), the level of indigenous economic expertise available to the Soviet leadership under NEP must be considered quite rare. This is especially true in respect of the openness of debates over policy which benefitted from this expertise. There was a fairly close relationship between research and policy formulation, even if the latter was naturally also affected by intra-party struggles.

The pertinence of NEP to peripheral socialist societies lies in the attempt to use both the production capacity directly under state control, as well as various stage agencies, to affect the development of market mediated relations with the peasantry in a socialist direction. The policy was abandoned because of a refusal to accept what were thought to be the limits imposed by peasant demand on the increased rate of investment in the state sector, which was apparently required by industrialisation. As Harrison [*1985*] and Smith [*1986b*] indicate, these apparent limits imposed by peasant demand were not so fixed as they appeared. The main investment funds for Soviet industrialisation came from more intensive use of existing means of production, and a considerable increase in urban industrial employment. The political backing for such an option came when it was felt that the central planning agency, Gosplan, had the planning techniques and organisational capacity to handle the possible dislocations engendered by the more rapid industrialisation envisaged. The success of this alternative policy did not mean that NEP was unviable as a strategy [*Harrison, 1985; Littlejohn, 1984*].

Nevertheless, for a NEP type of approach to be successful, various issues have to be resolved. First, while peasant demand is not an absolute constraint on investment policy, the technical conditions of reproduction of various kinds of peasants need to be analysed and met. This includes an analysis of the patterns of social distribution of various kinds of means of production and consumption, access to credit, and various other aspects of peasant markets, such as price structure, crop structure, marketing outlets, and forms of organisation of production (including relation to various labour markets). Second, the relation between the various kinds of peasants (with class structures differentiated regionally, by access to various markets and by forms of organisation of production) and the development of socialist forms of production and distribution needs to be considered. The coexistence of a variety of forms of co-operatives (producers, credit, retailing and so on) with state enterprises and other state agencies (central planning agency, central and other banks, ministries, specialised agencies for the promotion of co-operatives, and so on) means that this aspect of socialist transformation will inevitably be complex and changing. Hence, it needs constant review, which implies constant debate and either routine information flows or regular research. Third, the coherence of objectives and actions of the diverse state agencies themselves must be constantly monitored. The contradictory effects of various state agencies in both containing certain undesired aspects of capitalist development and in fostering other aspects (especially the parallel market) under NEP is well documented, and similar experiences have been reported in contemporary peripheral socialist societies. Fourth, socialist transformation implied reorganisation, not only of forms of production and distribution, but of the relations between various sectors of the economy, whether these sectors are defined as sate/peasant/capitalist, rural/urban/peri-urban, or agricultural/industrial/service. This means that investment has to be made as a function of the calculated requirements of that reorganisation. The possible result may be to prioritise investment in the institutions that mediate relations between sectors, rather than in the sectors themselves. In particular, investment in marketing infrastructure may be more important than, say, investment in productive capacity in the state sector. While investment in state sector productive capacity may be the top priority in certain conditions, the political importance of this sector can easily lead to it being seen as always the top priority, whereas the real priority is socialist transformation. In the light of these rather abstract considerations, it is now appropriate to consider such issues of 'socialist accumulation' in the context of the actual problems faced by a peripheral socialist society.

IV. INVESTMENT PROBLEMS IN MOZAMBIQUE

One of the long-term problems in the Soviet Union has been that of prioritising investment projects in a country with considerable natural resources which had historically suffered from lack of investment. A similar problem confronted Mozambique, albeit on a smaller geographical scale. Mozambique probably had an even lower level of investment before Independence than the Soviet Union had suffered before the Revolution.[22] One of the results of this around 1980 was a stress on 'big projects' as the most effective use of investment funds to develop the economy and transform relations of production. However, as Hanlon points out [*1984: 84–5*] such a strategy of large-scale projects to overcome underdevelopment in ten years depended in part on foreign investment which was unlikely even in the absence of world recession, given the views of international capital on Mozambique's political institutions and economic strategy:

> For its part, Mozambique lacked the planning capacity, trained people and infrastructure to carry out a plan that required building new cities and railways, moving literally millions of peasants, and virtually transforming the contryside in a few years. The big projects which had already started fell further and further behind. And peace was brief: South Africa began its attacks. Finally, despite Frelimo's increasing control over the economy, it failed to rebuild the crucial links between city and country. It proved impossible to plan marketing in the same way as industrial and agricultural projects. So the initial collapse of the trading system was compounded by the lack of consumer goods for peasants, and by war, reducing the flow of food and industrial raw materials to the cities. This was an essential component in a growing economic crisis.

At the Fourth Congress in 1983, Frelimo abandoned this strategy with some self-criticism, but is worth examining the underlying rationale of this approach in more detail. Apart from foreign investment funds, agriculture was expected to provide the main source of investment, partly by deliberately adverse terms of trade with the peasantry to 'squeeze out' a surplus, and partly by the surplus expected to be generated by the large sate farms which were created. To concentrate on the latter aspect of the strategy, the state farms received the overwhelming majority of investment in agriculture, over four-fifths of it consisting of imported machinery and other imports (with consequent effects on foreign exchange). These farms ran at a loss, thereby consuming investment funds instead of generating them. In any case their products were frequently not exported, so that they further exacerbated rather than eased growing foreign exchange difficulties, which became publicly manifest by 1983.

The basic reasons for the state farms running at a loss were associated with the failure to raise labour productivity and productivity per hectare. This failure on productivity was not a failure of central planning *per se* but a failure to find an appropriate form of central planning. Given the huge difficulties of obtaining and transmitting information on the production processes of these farms, an appropriate form of central planning should have included a considerable amount of delegation of decisions to the levels where the information was available (or could reasonably have been acquired). Not only were the connections between state, co-operative and family agriculture ignored, with consequent effects on labour supply, but the very form of planning made it difficult to correct the plans in the light of the information available to the more experienced workers on these farms.

Planning consisted of a series of targets for inputs broken down into ten day periods, three of which would provide the basis for a monthly report to the planning unit (UDA) in the Ministry of Agriculture. Such detailed reporting requirements effectively removed managerial autonomy from the farms (and from their constituent Production Units), and swamped the limited means of communication available, making it difficult to collect and relay what might have been more pertinent information about current production capacity (due to breakdowns or failures of inputs to arrive on time) or about labour supply. Since such a formalistic, input oriented form of planning was not backed by the capacity to deliver the inputs envisaged, managerial autonomy had to be reestablished in informal ways, as one would expect. This was particularly evident in the ad hoc recruitment of casual labour. Labour hoarding in situations of taut planning which engender input shortages is a familiar occurrence with extensive growth strategies fostered by central planning agencies. Usually its extent is known to senior enterprise management, but in the case of Mozambican state farms this was often not the case.[23]

The interplay between the formal organisation envisaged in the plan and the informal one had other serious effects besides loss of control over the size of the labour force. Indeed this loss of control was not simply a response to shortages of inputs. The management and production procedures in the plan were carried out as far as possible, but because they were seen to be ineffective, and hence had little legitimacy, alternative conceptions of how to manage the farms were able to come into play. These were often based on the colonial techniques of managing the settler farms or plantations which had existed on the same sites before Independence. This was particularly true of methods of recruitment and treatment of the labour force, but also included lack of attention to soil conservation and other aspects. In other words, alternative informal management methods often implied, not socialist transformation, but continuity with colonial farming, only on a bigger scale (taking land at the expense of neighbouring peasants, even if it could not be cultivated) and without the need to make a profit.

The consequence was frequently organisational paralysis induced partly by the coexistence of conflicting management practices within the same enterprise, exacerbated by a failure to collect information on those aspects of enterprise performance most closely related to raising the productivity of labour, of machinery and of the land, or to making effective delivery of the harvest to state or private marketing outlets.

Thus the failure of the central planning agencies to establish pertinent forms of information flow, and appropriate forms of decision making at the various organisational levels, led not only to negative economic growth, but also to the blocking of any socialist transformation of the state farms themselves. In addition, the failure to meet their own targets meant that state farms gave little help to co-operatives, and the attempts at extensive growth of surface area cultivated alienated the neighbouring peasantry, many of whom also formed part of the work force of the state farms themselves, where poor working conditions and disregard of their views further alienated them.

Such problems could have been dealt with by a reduction in the size of state farms and by their internal reorganisation, coupled with more investment in rural producer co-operatives, and in marketing infrastructure. The problem of the poor terms of trade for family agriculture (with respect both to prices and to an absolute lack of the producers' and consumer goods demanded by the peasant sector) was partially dealt with after the 1983 Fourth Congress [*Hanlon, 1984: 113*]. However, instead of reducing the state farms in favour of producer co-operatives with more diversified crop cultivation, supported by state investment, the state farms were often simply broken up and handed over to individual peasants and private farmers.[24] This move in favour of the private sector was associated with other measures boosting private agriculture and commerce, apparently as a short term move to foster rapid production and marketing improvements. These changes were partially offset by other Fourth Congress measures to tighten controls on the private sector, but the support for private farmers seems to have been particularly strong since 1983. This fits in well with the conditions set by western donors like the USA and by international agencies like the IMF for giving aid to Mozambique.

One could argue that the recent measures since 1983 to stimulate private agriculture, to free retail food prices (thereby partially undercutting the parallel market), and to move commercial capital into production are an attempt to pause or 'give a breathing space', before a further attempt at state controlled extensive economic development. If this is so, it would be a conception rather similar to the one which prevailed in the USSR in the early 1920s at the start of NEP. As happened with NEP, there seem to be divergent interpretations of the Fourth Congress economic policy among Frelimo leaders, with at least one explicitly disclaiming any interest in new cooperatives and apparently promoting the development of a new group of rich peasants.[25] This promotion of rich peasants could perhaps seem analogous to Bukharin's famous 'Get Rich' slogan of 1925. As in that case, there seems to have been an acceptance of low growth rates in the absence of rapid growth of state farms and industry.[26]

In the case of Mozambique, the support for richer peasants and private farmers seems to be linked with a lack of faith in family farmers (poor and middle peasants) and in rural producer co-operatives.[27] These similarities seem to be related to a statist conception of socialism whose corollary is that market relations are a temporary concession in adverse circumstances (rather than one policy instrument among others to promote socialist transformation inside and outside the 'state sector'). Yet despite these similarities, the analogy with NEP should not be pushed too far. The major difference is the continuation of foreign military intervention in the form of the South African-backed MNR. The economic effects of the destabilisation have been enormous (one estimate putting it at 26 billion dollars between 1980 and 1986, more than all the aid Mozambique has received in that time). This means that expectations of low growth rates have the merit of being realistic, though this in itself does not explain the support for private farmers.

Such support has been justified on the grounds that private farmers can produce rapid results at a time of food shortages, but many of the shortages could have been lessened or avoided (despite the massive drought) if co-operatives and family farmers had been adequately supported in the first place. This would also have avoided the loss of political support for Frelimo in the countryside which led to widespread apathy about the MNR, and which meant that the latter faced less resistance to its destabilisation than would otherwise have been the case. Given the atrocities committed by the MNR, this indifference could never turn into serious support for it, but it made it more difficult for Frelimo to combat the MNR, with serious economic consequences.

Yet the support for private farmers and rich peasants was for reasons other than the ostensible one of rapid results in agriculture. It was based on a misguided conception of the mass of the peasantry as 'subsistence farmers' not involved in marketing (despite a clear refutation of this conception by CEA researchers). This meant that rich peasants and private farmers were seen as the source of the marketed agricultural surplus, while poor peasants were probably seen as potentially or actually involved in wage labour, whereas middle peasants were considered to be self-supporting (and, hence, least involved in market relations).

These misconceptions dovetailed well with pressure from Western donor countries, most notably the USA from 1983 onwards, to direct their aid into stimulating private agriculture. This is another point of difference between the Mozambican experience since 1983 and that of NEP in the USSR: the leverage which foreign indebtedness gave to western governments in directing conditional aid in a manner which affected economic policy. No such policy was followed by Western governments with respect to the USSR during NEP. The carrot of aid and the stick of destabilisation seem to have been used (at least at times) in an attempt to shift Mozambique away from what are considered to be too close relations with CMEA countries, despite Frelimo's commitment to the Non-Aligned Movement on the one hand, and despite repeated attempts since Independence to stimulate private investment in the Mozambican economy, on the other.

While the sheer scale of destabilisation has meant that foreign indebtedness would have occurred anyway, and while the world recession would also have made export led growth difficult for Mozambique, it is clear that the extensive growth strategy of 'big projects' (especially on state farms) exacerbated foreign exchange problems and made the Mozambican economy more vulnerable than it would otherwise have been. Instead of a state pricing policy using the importance of the state sector, both production and marketing agencies, to influence the development of market relations in line with policy objectives such as support for co-operatives and family farms, market relations have increasingly escaped control or even influence by the state.

Perhaps the most graphic recent example of this loss of control under the impact of foreign debt are the two devaluations of 1987 and the associated price increases.[28] The second devaluation follows World Bank credit being granted, agreements being signed with the World Bank and the IMF, and some debt rescheduling. Yet it would be a mistake to treat foreign debt as the only reason for the resurgence of market relations in a way that alters economic policy. As already indicated, if one abstracts from destabilisation and drought (the overwhelming reasons for Mozambique's difficulties), there are reasons for its foreign exchange problems that are the result of its investment priorities (its state sector development strategy). These reasons are also related to a poor control of markets and of price policy, which would have still been present even if the marketing infrastructure had not been so seriously disrupted by the exodus of traders after Independence, and by subsequent sabotage. As indicated earlier, the terms of exchange with the peasantry had been set adversely from their point of view. Marketing prices were sometimes below production price and below world prices, at the official rate of exchange for the metical. In addition, goods for the peasants to purchase were not forthcoming on the whole. Thus it was not until 1983 that sales of hoes, the most vital implement, took place on a large scale.[29] The possibilities in this respect of stimulating peasant marketing can be illustrated from two experiences at which I was privileged to be present. In July 1982, the then Governor of Tete emptied his provincial warehouses of all reserves of goods which could be traded with the peasantry, and had them delivered to Angonia, a food surplus district in the province. The result was a very considerable increase in marketed produce. Similarly, in July 1984, a project funded by the EEC, by Canada and Ireland, to stimulate agricultural marketing by supplying producers' and consumers' goods to the peasantry of Mueda District in Cabo Delgado, resulted in the same amount of produce being marketed to the state purchasing agency, Agricom, in one month, as had been marketed to Agricom in three months in the previous year. This was not simply earlier delivery of produce, since I saw food reserves stored from the previous year. The Mueda food was used to alleviate famine further south in Mozambique that year.

Both these cases refer to food surplus areas, and should not be used to make claims about the total produce of the whole country, but they clearly illustrate the responsiveness of the peasantry to appropriate terms of trade, both in prices and availability. Unfortunately, these cases were exceptions. Thus, apart from general problems of drought, destabilisation and foreign deficits, the very way the state sector impacted on the market generated quite unnecessary problems in a situation where mistakes could not be afforded. Precisely because the major factors were beyond the control of the Mozambican government, it was all the more important to plan market relations well, in those respects which could be influenced by the government.

Central Planning and the International Economy: Integration and Autonomy

There are obvious similarities between the inter-related problems of investment and foreign trade in CMEA economies and the effects of the 'big projects' strategy in Mozambique, which is ironic when one considers that many of these projects were undertaken with aid from various CMEA countries. The fact that these CMEA countries were cushioned to some extent from the full effects of the 1970s developments by their non-transferable rouble debts to the USSR is an interesting aspect of this situation. It raises the question as to whether there is a viable way to cushion countries like Mozambique from the worst effects of foreign deficits, especially from restricting investment which is now so vital. It is possible that the stimulation of greater autonomy for countries like Mozambique by means of their further integration into an international economy of the Southern African Region could be a viable proposition. Not only is it one of the main objectives of SADCC to promote such a policy in various ways, but also there is apparently considerable scope for such a policy in the area of trade. This is beause there is at the moment very little trade between the member countries of SADCC.[30] In 1982, intra-SADCC trade constituted only five per cent of all exports and 4.4 per cent of all imports to the Region. The 1986 SADCC trade study proposes either national revolving funds and/or a Regional revolving fund, to stimulate intra-SADCC trade.[31] However, the promotion of trade within SADCC is unlikely to have any serious short-term effect in reducing the foreign deficits of Mozambique. What then are the other options for peripheral socialist countries to reduce their external indebtedness? One conceivable option might be to increase trade with CMEA countries. In one sense there is plenty of room for such an increase, because whether one examines countries considered by CMEA as being of confirmed socialist orientation [*Don, 1985: 16*] or the countries of sub-Saharan Africa [*Veyrat, 1985*], neither group of countries is a major trading partner of the other. However, both in terms of the composition of such trade and its effects on the external deficits of such countries, trade on existing patterns is unlikely to grow. In general, sub-Saharan African countries export tropical foods and raw materials with little value added, and import from CMEA countries manufactured or semi-finished goods with high value added. The terms of trade are thus unfavourable to African countries and in that respect do not stimulate their development.[32] The effects of this on deficits are easy to guess, and in the case of the five countries of 'confirmed socialist orientation' the deficit on the balance of payments grew roughly thirty-fold between 1975 and 1983.[33]

The effects of the low level of intra-Regional trade within SADCC, and of the low level and adverse terms of trade with the CMEA countries, on a country like Mozambique are readily understood. They mean that the options open for dealing with the problem of foreign exchange deficits (which began in 1977) are fairly limited in the near future. It is probable that the likely implications of the 'big projects' and state sector approach to development on the balance of payments were understood in Mozambique before the deficits appeared publicly. The reliance on imports of machinery, especially from CMEA countries, and the effects of it on the deficits with the CMEA, is probably one of the reasons for Mozambique's application in 1980 to join the CMEA as a full member. This application was turned down in 1981.[34] However, doubtless these deficits were seen by the Mozambican government at the time as temporary ones, which would be eradicated by the exports of the expanded state farm sector. If so, such a strategy looks like an agricultural version of the Polish strategy of the 1970s, but the problems with Poland did not become really obvious until 1980 (although western economists were publicly expressing concern by early 1978).[35] The difficulties of running state farms have already been briefly discussed, but it might be thought that CMEA expertise could have mitigated these problems. At times, this indeed was the case.[36] Yet as Don points out [*1985, 26-7*] co-operation in agriculture has been insufficient and at times poorly adapted to the needs of 'confirmed socialist orientation' countries, which has led to them having recourse to economic relations with capitalist countries and to international agencies for aid.

Aid is thus becoming increasingly important as a means of dealing with economic difficulties. Indeed its importance in comparison with any strategy of promotion of autonomy through trade can be seen from the SADCC trade study finding that development assistance is more than seven times the value of intra-SADCC trade.[37] Thus the foreign exchange deficits and the resulting dependence on aid from and trade with developed capitalist economies (including South Africa) are having important effects on the development of market relations inside Mozambique. It is this which provides the leverage for aid from the USA and the IMF to be conditional on stimulating private agriculture and on ending the policy of state fixed prices in certain markets. As mentioned earlier, this dovetails well with at least some measures in favour of private farmers and rich peasants and with a policy of retail price increases to undercut the parallel market (known as the *candonga*). Given this reorientation by Mozambique and other countries of 'confirmed socialist orientation' towards developed capitalist economies, at least one commentator has argued that the observer status at CMEA enjoyed by such countries is of political rather than economic significance.[38] In my view, however, its economic significance should not be underestimated, not only because CMEA aid is often in vital sectors of the economy, but also because the very fact of such aid gives a bargaining counter against leverage from capitalist economies, and thus helps sustain some economic autonomy under extremely adverse circumstances.

Nevertheless, aid from the CMEA may be a two-edged sword in terms of sustaining economic autonomy. Certainly, the CMEA has recently shown a sympathetic attitude towards Mozambique's indebtedness to the CMEA economies, and this may have facilitated Mozambican rescheduling of debt to western economies. On the other hand, the debts to the CMEA countries arose in the first place because Mozambique bought CMEA machinery which could not readily have been sold elsewhere on the world market. Mozambique financed these purchases by tying the CMEA credit to 'planned delivery contracts'. These contracts guaranteed the supply of tropical fruits and raw materials to the CMEA economies. While the CMEA economies bought these goods at world prices, they would not easily have been able to buy them from other sources, precisely because the other sources might not so readily have bought CMEA machinery. The result was that Mozambique was locked into a pattern of trade. Not only did it encounter adverse terms of trade (which would also have happened with western trading partners) but also it lacked the flexibility to sell its exports to the highest bidder. The resulting deficits with respect to the CMEA were thus virtually inevitable, even if the state sector had been well-managed before 1983.

In such circumstances, unless the CMEA economies ease or write off existing debts, and end the bilateral trade agreements with planned delivery contracts, Mozambican dependence on aid from and trade with developed capitalist economies will continue. Western aid is (openly or surreptitiously) often tied to purchases from the donor country, a fact which often has considerable consequences for the development of market relations within the receiving country. Consequently, a very clear strategy with respect to market relations will be needed simply to retain an acceptable degree of control over the national economy, let alone to sustain a realistic prospect of socialist transformation.

V. CONCLUSION: THE ROLE OF PLANNING AND THE MARKET IN THE ARTICULATION OF ECONOMIC AGENCIES

Several analyses of Mozambique and of 'advanced' socialist economies have tended to distinguish between the state sector (with central planning) and the market (which is thought to be decentralised). In the case of Mozambique, after the Fourth Congress, calls for decentralisation were of a different nature, with proposals to reverse the 'top-down' planning approach associated with the National Planning Commission by District Planning, which would start 'from the bottom'. There is no problem in principle with this, except that it appears to avoid one of the problems of the previous form of planning. This problem was masked by the sheer lack of information [*Egero, 1987: 98–101*], but it was the problem of what kind of information to collect, and the associated forms of intervention in the economy. Clearly forms of intervention need to be related to the actual capacities of the agencies implementing the plan. In the case of Mozambique, the unintended impact of state agencies on the parallel market shows that it can be equally important to avoid certain forms of intervention, in which case planning can quite reasonably consist of coordination of action by state agencies.

The fact that the interaction of stage agencies, including unofficial market competition between them, can produce unintended or contradictory effects on market policy (or other aspects of economic policy) is a clear reason for abandoning a simple sectoral approach in favour of an analysis of agencies. Rather than the 'state sector' and the 'private sector' (or 'family sector'), it is more appropriate to analyse the nature of agencies operating in the economy and their articulation. While it is convenient at times to use the terminology of sectors, it is a mistake to treat them as undifferentiated. This conceptual error is responsible among other things for the conception of socialist trans-formation as the supercession of the private sector (or the peasantry) by the state sector.

It is far more important to examine how agencies condition each other (partly as an effect of their respective internal organisational conditions). This implies a strategy and tactics of socialist transformation of the relations of production which takes account of productive and non-productive agencies, and which examines the various conditions of their transformation, including market conditions. In these circumstances, market relations need not be suppressed by administrative methods, but can be used as part of the strategy. In general one cannot say too much about what such a strategy would look like, since it would need to be tailored to the conjuncture in which it was formulated. However, it would need to deal with the diversity of relevant agencies. It is perhaps worth recalling that these can include various kinds of peasant farms, pastoralist production agencies, settler farms, plantations, producer cooperatives (agricultural or artisanal), state farms, agro-industrial complexes, various kinds of industrial organisation (rural and urban), TNCs, both in industry and agriculture, as well as various government agencies such as ministries, marketing boards, banks and planning agencies.

Since these all condition each other, planning and market relations will need to be judiciously handled in terms of calculating the likely effects of any policy. Yet broadly, any policy ought to be evaluated in terms of its economic effectiveness, its effect on the class structure and its political implications. The latter three aspects of any strategy all affect each other, of course. Nobody said it was easy. Yet the current growth in importance of market relations in both 'advanced' and 'peripheral' socialist societies is not in itself a matter for despair.

If the objective is socialist transformation, rather than simply the expansion of the state sector (and the distinction between nationalisation and socialisation is now well-established), then market relations have a role in attempting to secure the 'intensive' development of the state sector, by providing information and sanctions on the performance of agencies within that sector. In so far as they promote organisational effectiveness and investment efficiency among such agencies, market relations may help prevent the all too common mistake of the state taking control of parts of the economy which it cannot manage, or of individual state enterprises expanding in size beyond the managerial competence of their staff. Thus market relations have a role within the state sector in promoting efficiency, and possibly in forestalling subsequent privatisation. However, this is not an argument for liberalising markets *tout court*. On the contrary, the state sector has a vital role to play in structuring or at least influencing market relations so that they are conducive to (or minimally, not too inconsistent with) the policy objectives of the time.

The first condition for the effective use of the state sector in this way is the recognition that the agencies which compose it have no natural economic (or even political) unity simply because of their legal status. Thus a conscious set of policies and instruments need to be evolved to try and ensure their coordination. It will not come about simply by the establishment of a central planning agency. Rather the practices of such an agency could well be crucial in determining whether the contradictory and potentially incoherent aspects of economic policy are managed in a way which secures the desired changes in the structure of the economy. Precisely because of the limited nature of the state sector in peripheral socialist economies, the management of market relations, using state agencies on the basis of a well defined set of priorities, is of the utmost importance. Even in advanced socialist economies, failure to manage market relations can have serious medium-term consequences.

The management of the market must of course involve political considerations as well as technical economic ones. Investment decisions are frequently subject to political lobbying, in both capitalist and socialist societies. Just as western economists ought to abandon the pretence (even in theory) that market decisions are purely technical and politically neutral, so economists in socialist societies ought to give up the idea that market relations invariably produce effects which are antithetical to politically defined socialist transformation strategies. Markets can be a very useful way of altering the articulation of economic agencies (that is changing the structure of the economy) especially if the markets themselves are articulated in a planned way.

NOTES

1. The author worked in Mozambique in 1982 and 1983, and is consequently particularly concerned with that society. The phrase 'peripheral socialist society' is not meant to imply any lack of intrinsic importance of such societies, but is intended to avoid controversies concerning concepts like 'socialist orientation'. In addition, it is intended to indicate that such societies are not too closely integrated into the metropolitan dominated capitalist 'world economy', which may be considered a positive benefit insofar as they have aspirations to remain non-aligned.
2. The CMEA is otherwise known as Comecon, or by its Russian initials SEV.
3. This argument has been put by several authors in Lavigne and Andreff [1985]. However, the volume presents a variety of contributions from an ongoing seminar, and the views of the contributors are by no means unanimous. See Drach, [1985] for a view that the problems are endemic to Soviet-type economies.
4. Drach, [1985: 56–7.] The statistical evidence concerns declining overall growth rates and investment growth rates, rather than the alleged political cycle of investment.
5. Drach cites a Hungarian joke to the effect that, since the ruling classes have never worked, why should the working class which is in power in the socialist countries be any exception? The joke, of course, tends to blame workers for a situation over which they have little control (that being the real point of the joke). He also argues that there is an incompatibility between party hegemony and effective management. The criticism of party hegemony seems to imply that if one could depoliticise microeconomic management, it would then become more effective. This point will be taken up later.
6. There are considerable similarities with the Austrian school critique of central planning, most notably in the works of Hayek and Von Mises, which were recently summarised by Smith (ed.) [1986a: 2–3]. In other respects, Drach relies heavily on Kornai and Bauer. Drach's conception of 'the Centre' seems similar to that criticised in Ch.3 of Littlejohn [1984].
7. Bastida Vila in Lavigne and Andreff [1985].
8. Television debate seen by the author in March 1986 during a visit to the Soviet Union. I am grateful to the British Academy for supporting this visit to the USSR as part of its exchange agreement with the Academy of Sciences of the USSR. This particular television debate was extremely open concerning the possibility of educational reform in the USSR. There was a 30 per cent increase in teachers' salaries in 1984, noted by Bastida but falling outside the scope of his time series data. It is not clear whether this salary increase has been at the expense of other educational resources, or whether it has helped to reverse the relative decline in the rate of growth of expenditure on education and science. In any case, further criticisms of education have appeared in the Soviet press in 1987.
9. This stagnation of expenditure has produced a recent tendency for the number of pupils to stagnate: Bastida [1985: 120–21].
10. Rogulska in Lavigne and Andreff [1985]. Habermas's position attempts to incorporate theories of 'fiscal crisis' as part of a wider crisis.
11. See, for example, Held, 'Power and legitimacy in contemporary Britain', in McLennan, Held and Hall (eds.) [1984].
12. Redor in Lavigne and Andreff [1985].
13. Andreff and Graziani [1985], in Lavigne and Andreff (eds.) [1985: 21].
14. Lavigne and Andreff (eds.) [1985: 25]. It should be noted that while Poland had a strategy of importing Western technology to later re-export finished goods to the west, no such strategy operated in Bulgaria, Czechloslavakia or the GDR. Thus the main factor in the external deficit of these countries was simply the attempt to overcome the shortages of investment goods. Poland's strategy and poor management of its investment projects simply aggravated a problem it shared with its fellow CMEA members.
15. Such approaches have already been criticised in earlier publications, for example, G. Littlejohn, 'State, Plan and Market . . .' and 'Economic Calculation in the USSR', both reprinted in Smith (ed.) [1986].

16. For more detailed discussion, see Littlejohn [*1984*], and the sources cited there.
17. Personal communication from economists at a meeting in the University of Alma Ata, March 1986. As another example of increased efficiency, improved ecological management is reversing a decline in productivity of sugar beet, according to economists attached to the Kazakhstan Academy of Sciences.
18. Personal communication from economists in Dushanbe, March 1986. These crops are ecologically more suitable, and fit better into the apparent preference in parts of Tadzhikistan for staying in the countryside, rather than migrating to urban employment. It is worth noting that such decisions are taken centrally in Tadzhikistan, based on an overview of the entire republican economy, and are probably associated with more rapid growth than would be the case if the decisions about product mix were taken by individual enterprises. Indeed the overall strategy includes the opening of new state enterprises for broiler ducks and high milk yield dairy cattle farms.
   Yet while this is centralisation at a union republican level, it is decentralisation from the point of view of the All-Union level, and may not be entirely consistent with All-Union investment plans. If it is not consistent with such plans, this implies negotiation, and a 'politicisation' of the investment decisions, and yet may lead to quite a reasonable result in terms of agricultural productivity. Surely this indicates the complexity of coordinating investment decisions in a large and increasingly sophisticated economy, and the weakness of unelaborated critiques of 'hierarchical centralised planning' of 'use values'.
19. Most publicity in the Western press has concerned the failure to implement this reform in the Ukraine, which is said to be associated with possibly corrupt vested interests there. However, despite charges of corruption against the leadership in Kazakhstan, leading to the replacement of the Party leader in late 1986, when I was in Alma Ata in March 1986, the new Gosagroprom had already been established for over a month.
20. See, for example, the critique of such concepts in Cutler, Hindess, Hirst and Hussain [*1977 and 1978*].
21. It is clear that the Soviet policies of *perestroika* and acceleration of the economy, coupled with *glasnost,* are attempts to grapple with such issues, and it is more important at the moment to try to learn from this experience than to predict the likely outcome (or theorise the 'optimal' outcome) of the theoretical debates and political struggles currently taking place.
22. For a discussion of the structure of the colonial Mozambican economy and some post-Independence issues, see Wuyts [*1985*]; First [*1983*]; and Hanlon [*1984*].
23. For a graphic example of this, see the report by the Centre of African Studies (CEA) [*1983*]. In the case of CAIA (Complexo Agro-Industrial de Angonia) the Director in July 1982 believed that his labour force consisted of 3,000 when in fact it was 4,500. The effect of a 50-per cent error in the wages bill on profits is evident.
24. Hanlon [*1984: 118*], where the break-up of CAIL (Complexo Agro-Industrial de Limpopo) is described. CAIA was reorganised and has since been effectively destroyed by the MNR operating out of Malawi.
25. Hanlon [*1984: 209*]. The Minister in question was the Minister of Agriculture, Joao Ferreira. As Wuyts [*1985: 204*] points out, the Fourth Congress left many economic issues vague and thus allowed for further struggle. See also Raikes [*1984*] and Egero [*1987*] for a discussion of the different tendencies on economic policy.
26. See K. Smith's article in Smith (ed.) [*1986*]. The relation between low growth rates and rural differentiation in Bukharin's position at this time is discussed on pp.39–41.
27. Hanlon [*1984: 113 and 183*], on family farming, and [*1984: 103–9*] on co-operatives.
28. Mozambique Information Office [*1987*]. At the beginning of 1987, the exchange rate for the Mozambican currency, the metical (plural meticais), was 39 meticais to the US dollar. At the end of January, it was raised to 200, and on 26 June to 400 meticais to the dollar.
29. Egero [*1987: 97–8*]. This book contains a discussion of central planning of the state sector which complements the concentration on state farms in this article.
30. See page 4 of the Main Report of the study commissioned by SADCC, conducted by a team working under the auspices of the Christian Michelsen Institute (CMI): SADCC [*1986*].
31. SADCC [*1986: Main Report, Ch.6*]. A revolving fund would help make trade flows more regular (which at the moment they are not within SADCC). It could also stimulate the broadening of the composition of such trade. Trade within SADCC is of a different composition than trade between SADCC and the rest of the world, with only a few major commodities making up 40 per cent of intra-SADCC trade. One of the obstacles to intra-

SADCC trade is the apparent lack of complementarity between the economies, but this is partly due to lack of knowledge of each others' markets, and the SADCC trade study proposal of Joint Trade Commissions should ease this problem [*1986: Main Report, 47–8*]. Proposals have been made in the past by SADCC and the UN PTA (The United Nations Preferential Trading Area on Eastern and Southern Africa) to promote trade by tariff reductions, but while there is a place for such measures, they will have little effect on their own on intra-SADCC trade (SADCC [*1986: 20 and passim*]). Improved trade finance and direct measures including countertrade deals are much more likely to be effective.

This is not to say that it will be easy to promote Regional integration and hence relative autonomy from other trade connections. The difficulties of the transport network in the Region, with massive sabotage by the MNR and UNITA, are well known. The SADCC trade study also mentions existing trade connections as a possible obstacle to intra-SADCC trade, including CMEA trade connections, but the latter should not be exaggerated, as will become evident. Yet even in the absence of other problems, bilateral measures, including countertrade deals, will not be easy. They depend on more regular production and delivery, various kinds of government support, and the kind of financing outlined above. Such revolving funds would almost certainly require funding support from donor institutions, and if they are western, then they must be free of the usual ties which pressure SADCC governments to import goods from the donor country. Countertrade deals and mutual clearing facilities would reduce dependence on convertible currency, but would themselves still require such currency to deal with imbalances, and would also require credit on terms which were competitive with those available to traders dealing with developed capitalist economies. Nevertheless, such credit in the form of a revolving fund would not be a panacea, as the pattern of use of CMEA trade credit indicates (D. Don in Lavigne (ed.) [*1985*]). Don argues that although the CMEA provides trade credit in convertible roubles, little use is made of it [*Don, 1985: 46*]. Consequently, even if the measures proposed in the 1986 SADCC trade study are all implemented, then progress will still be slow, and will depend on re-establishment of transport links and the pace of industrialisation, as the study itself indicates.

32. Veyrat [*1985: 225*]. This is not to deny that in other respects economic cooperation with CMEA countries, especially in the field of training, does stimulate their development. Veyrat provides evidence of a considerable increase in the field of technical assistance, including on agricultural investment projects where (apart from Bulgaria and the GDR) there is little direct involvement by CMEA countries.
33. Don [*1985: 16*]. The five countries listed are Afghanistan, Angola, Ethiopia, Mozambique and South Yemen. Don describes this growth in the deficit as dangerous. This deficit of course cushioned the CMEA countries at the time of their deficits with developed capitalist economies: Andreff and Graziani [*1985: 25*]. For a more detailed analysis of the case of Mozambique see Wuyts [*1985: 197*], and Egero [*1987: 90*].
34. Don [*1985: 24*]. This refusal is part of a general policy which has been justified by Soviet commentators on the grounds that 'socialist orientation' is not irreversible, and that the cost of full membership is very high to European CMEA members, as can be seen in the case of Cuba and Vietnam.
35. At the annual conference of the National Association of Soviet and East European Studies, University of Cambridge, March 1978.
36. For example, on CAIA, Bulgarian technicians did an excellent job managing the Production Unit concerned with herding, and of training the Mozambican machinery repair teams, as well as suggesting flexible solutions to unexpected difficulties such as early rainfall which threatened the harvest in 1982.
37. SADCC [*1986: 68*].
38. Don [*1985: 29*]. The example of the accord between CMEA and Mozambique, signed in June 1985, is cited as evidence of this tendency to use relations with the CMEA to 'prove' that economic policy would conform with political orientation, if only conditions permitted.

REFERENCES

Andreff, W. and G. Graziania, 1985, 'Contrainte exterieure et politiques d'adaptation', in Lavigne and Andreff [*1985*].
Bastida, B., 1985, 'Indicateurs de crise a travers le budget de la depense publique en URSS' in

Lavigne and Andreff [*1985*].

Centre of African Studies, 1983, *Organizar os Trabalhadores das Machambas Estatais: o Caso do C.A.I.A.*, Maputo: Centro de Estudos Africanos.

Cutler, A., Hindess, B., Hirst, P. and A. Hussain, 1977 and 1978, *Marx's Capital and Capitalism Today*, Vols.I and II, London: Routledge & Kegan Paul.

Don, D., 1985, 'Les Relations Economiques entre les Pays Socialistes Europeens et les Pays a Orientation Socialistes Observateurs au CAEM', in Lavigne [*1985*].

Drach, M., 1985, 'Les trois crises', in Lavigne (ed.) [*1985*].

Duchene, G., 1985, 'Place de l'effort de defense dans les comptes nationaux de l'URSS', in Lavigne and Andreff [*1985: 83–109*].

Egero, B., 1987, *Mozambique: A Dream Undone: The Political Economy of Democracy 1975–84*, Uppsala: Nordiskaafrikainstitutet.

First, R., 1983, *Black Gold: The Mozambican Miner: Proletarian and Peasant*, Brighton, Sussex: Harvester Press.

FitzGerald, E.V.K., 1985, 'Agrarian Reform as a Model of Accumulation: The Case of Nicaragua since 1979', in *Journal of Development Studies*, (Special Issue on 'The Agrarian Question in Socialist Transitions'), Vol.22, No.1, Oct., pp.208–26.

Hanlon, J., 1984, *Mozambique: The Revolution Under Fire*, London: Zed Books.

Harrison, M., 1985, 'Primary Accumulation in the Soviet Transition', in *The Journal of Development Studies* (Special Issue on 'The Agrarian Question in Socialist Transitions'), Vol.22, No.1, Oct., pp.81–103.

Held, D., 1984, 'Power and legitimacy in contemporary Britain', in G. McLennan, D. Held and S. Hall (eds.) [*1984*].

Lavigne, M. (ed.), 1985, 'Les Relations Est-Sud dans l'Economie Mondiale', Tome II, Paris.

Lavigne, M., and W. Andreff, 1985, *La Realité Socialiste: Crise, Adaptation, Progrès*, Paris: Economica.

Littlejohn, G., 1984, *A Sociology of the Soviet Union*, London: Macmillan.

Littlejohn, G., 1986, 'State, plan and market in the transition to socialism: the legacy of Bukharin', in R. Smith (ed.) [*1986*].

Littlejohn, G., 1986, 'Economic Calculation in the USSR', in K. Smith (ed.) [*1986*].

McLennan, G., Held, D., and S. Hall (eds.), 1984, *State and Society in Contemporary Britain: A Critical Introduction*, Oxford: Polity.

Mozambique Information Office, 1987, *News Review*, No.108, 2 July 1987, London.

Raikes, P., 1984, 'Food Policy and Production in Mozambique since Independence', in *Review of African Political Economy*, No.29, July, pp.95–107.

Redor, D., 1985, 'Regulation de la part salariale et crise en systeme socialiste', in M. Lavigne and W. Andreff [*1985*].

Richet, X., 1985, 'Politiques d'ajustement et reformes institutionelles en Hongrie', in H. Lavigne and W. Andreff [*1985: 169–81*].

Rogulska, B., 1985, 'L'economique, le politique et la crise', in M. Lavigne W. Andreff [*1985: 63–80*].

Smith, K., 1986a, 'Introduction', in K. Smith (ed.) [*1986*].

Smith, K., 1986b, 'Economy theory and the closure of the Soviet industrialisation debate' in K. Smith (ed.), [*1986*].

Smith, K. (ed.), 1986, *Soviet Industrialisation and Soviet Maturity*, London: Routledge & Kegan Paul.

Southern Africa Development Coordinating Conference, (SADCC) 1986, *SADCC Intra-Regional Trade Study: Final Report* (three volumes), Bergen: Christian Michelsen Institute.

Veyrat, B., 1985, 'Les relations economiques entre les pays socialistes europeens et les pays d'Afrique sub-saharienne', in M. Lavigne [*1985*].

Walker, M., 1987, 'Russia drops central planning', *The Guardian*, 30 June 1987.

Wuyts, M., 1985, 'Money, Planning and Rural Transformation in Mozambique', in *The Journal of Development Studies* (Special Issue on The Agrarian Question in Socialist Transitions), Vol.22, No.1, Oct., pp.180–207.

Reforming State Finance in Post-1975 Vietnam

This article analyses the process of transition from a system of state bureaucratic finance to one of socialist economic accounting in the context of the post-1975 economic reforms in Vietnam. Three theoretical issues underlying this reform movement are discussed. First, the tension between the central level and individual enterprises with respect to economic calculus. Second, the conflict between the need to centralise financial resources in the state budget as the most important instrument of economic policy, and the interests and behaviour of state enterprises. Third, direct transfers of enterprise funds to the budget as against a partial decentralisation of resources combined with greater use of financial intermediation. The discussion concludes with the Eighth Plenum of the Party in 1985, which laid the basis for further reforms.

The object of this article is to analyse the transition of a system of 'state bureaucratic finance' to one based on 'socialist economic accounting' in the Socialist Republic of Vietnam (SRV), centred particularly around the important reforms which were announced after the Eighth Plenum of the Central Committee of the Vietnamese Communist Party (VCP) held in June 1985. Reforms which concerned mainly the fields of prices, wages and money.[1]

Following the Vietnamese terminology, the former system of economic and financial management, also known as 'administrative supply management', was inherited from the North (DRV) and has been expanded in the reunified country during the first post-war years with only minor modifications. Debates about its functioning go back to the very beginning of the post-war decade[2], but reforms had to wait until the early 1980s, finally culminating in a major attempt to reform the economic and financial management system, initiated by the Eighth Plenum.

As stated, our concern is with the analysis of a process of transition and, moreover, a process which is as yet unfinished, and as such, the argument will be structured around a periodisation of the main phases of this transitional process. By doing so, an attempt is made to depict the changes within fiscal policy as part and parcel of a broader process of changing the organisation of the economy at large through the introduction of major reforms. The advantage of organising our argument in this way is that it conveys a sense of historical movement: a process of change with multiple complexities which

*The author is currently adviser of the Agricultural Economics Department in the Nacional Autonomous University of Nicaragua in Managua. The research for this article was done at the Institute of Social Studies in The Hague. He would like to thank the *JDS* Editors and the participants at the IDS-seminar 'Post-war Vietnam: Ideology and Action' (1985) for their stimulating remarks on earlier drafts of the article.

inevitably reach well beyond the narrow scope of the article, namely, the specific role of the organisation of state finance within different contexts of overall economic management. The drawback of this form of presenting the analysis is that the major theoretical themes which run through the argument are not always strongly profiled within the analytical account of the major characteristics of each phase within the overall process of change.

For this reason, it may be helpful to put forward the main theoretical preoccupations concerning the role of state finance in relation to the specific organisation of planning and of markets within an overall planning framework. In fact, the article aims to set forth three basic propositions about the role of state finance within socialist development: First, socialist economic calculus takes place both at the level of the economy as a whole, that is, central planning concerned with the production for the social needs of producing classes, and at the level of individual economic units (enterprises) which operate within a relative degree of autonomy, but are subordinated to central planning for overall direction.

There is obviously a certain tension or contradiction between the need for central coordination and direction (an *ex ante* calculus) on the one hand, and the need for initiative and a certain freedom of action at the level of individual enterprises. The issue of centralisation/decentralisation in planning, and related to this, of the use of market mechanisms within a planned context, needs to be understood with respect to this tension between these two levels of economic calculus. Therefore, the concept of 'transition' is used in order to underline that there is no question of a complete dichotomy between 'state bureaucratic finance' and 'socialist economic accounting' but a much more complex problematic of transforming a largely administrative economic and financial management system into a system which is still – at least partly – centrally planned or coordinated but with the integration of financial independence for State enterprises, a certain freedom for market response and operation outside the 'plan', and 'market management' based on 'rational' pricing policies.

Second, there is the issue of the interdependence as well as the contradiction which exists between the finances of the state enterprises and those of the state budget. In general, the better the financial performance of state enterprises (and this depends to a great extent on their productivity and their efficiency in resource use), the greater can be in principle their contribution to the state budget. However, for a given level of financial accumulation of these enterprises, the greater the share transfered to the state budget, the lesser its retained earnings (and hence, its scope for relative autonomous action) [*Minc, 1974: 344*].

As will be shown in subsequent sections, a major concern of the Vietnamese reforms was to end the practice of enterprises offloading their inefficiencies by relying on the state budget to subsidise their losses. The existence of a soft budget constraint [*Kornai, 1979: 801–819*] was seen to be a major impediment to enhancing the discipline of economising on resource use.

The issue of subsidies and transfers between the state budget and individual units became even more complex within the context of a transitional economy which is incompletely socialised. This was definitely the case in Vietnam where the question of taxation of private enterprise and household production, as well as that of subsidies on food played a major role in shaping the character of fiscal reform so as to cut budgetary deficits.

Third, the transition from a more centralised system of bureaucratic finance to that of the socialist economic accounting implies more indirect forms of finance, and a more prominent role for financial mediation. Indeed, the system of bureaucratic finance basically involved the direct centralisation of financial resources in the state budget through taxation and the transfer of surplusses of state enterprises to the budget. Such funds are subsequently directly allocated from the budget to their various uses. Hence, the bureaucratic system of state subsidy is a direct consequence of this process of centralisation of financial accumulation of various enterprises within the economy. A partial decentralisation of the control over financial accumulation involves the need for greater financial intermediation, as well as the need to establish indirect control from the centre over the use of funds within the economy. This poses the issue of the increased reliance on financial discipline – the hardening of the budget constraint as well as the greater importance of the economic return on capital in determining the allocations of loans – but on the other hand, it requires that to make central control operative, it will have to assume more indirect forms which need to be situated in a market context which has to be properly understood.

These premises will be analysed against the background of the changes in economic policy in Vietnam as a result of the reforms. Clearly these concern mainly changes in internal policies, but these changes as well as the debates which accompanied them were not only determined by endogenous factors. The changed international environment with the new tensions at Vietnam's borders and the US-blockade on the one hand, and Vietnam's membership of CMEA (since June 1978) on the other hand – all had their, often, immeasurable influence on the process of change. As far as possible we will try to include at least some of these external influences in our discussion of the reforms with regard to state finance in the SRV.

PERIODISATION

The post-war years until the 1985 reforms will be divided into three periods: The first period runs from 1976–78, in which the economic system of the North (DRV) – with some minor adaptations for the southern zone – was transformed into that of the reunified country. Only by the end of these three years the financial system was a unified one, with one state budget, one currency and one banking system [*Duong, 1978: 30*]. During these first three years of existence of the SRV in general an intensive drive towards socialisation was undertaken. In the second period, from 1979–1981, some reforms (the subcontract system in agriculture, reforms in wages and prices and a devaluation of the national currency, the Dong) were implemented, but still continuous heated debates were raging inside party circles about their possible necessity and value. By the year 1979, economic stagnation in the North, adverse reactions on the pace and the form of socialisation in the South, the destruction caused by the 'Chinese lesson' and Vietnam's intervention in Kampuchea followed by an even greater political isolation, all contributed to a major revision of economic policy, particularly vis-a-vis the agricultural sector. These reforms were made public after the – by now well known – 6th Plenum (Fourth Congress) of the CC/VCP held in August 1979. The third period which we will analyse here runs from 1982–1985, particularly from the Fifth Congress of the VCP in March 1982 to the June 1985 CC Plenum. Because of the length of the debates about the reforms the Congress had been postponed several times, but when it was finally held it expressed generally strong criticisms on the existing economic and financial management system and gave the green light for a fundamental change of the old bureaucratic system of state finance into a system based on principles of economic accounting. The 'drastic changes' announced by the Eighth CC Plenum in 1985 initiated according to the party newspaper *Nhan Dan* 'a new period of leadership and socio-economic management for our party'.[3] These reforms were further extended and confirmed by the 1986 sixth congress of the party. The latter event will not be analysed here as we consider the Eighth Plenum as the crucial historical event, while the following congress showed that this line would be continued and strengthened.

1976–78: BUREAUCRATIC CENTRALISM TAKES OVER

As has been the case in the DRV before, the state budget from the very beginning was the most important instrument in redistributing the national income according to the objectives of government policy. In the three years of this period, domestic revenue on the state budget represented on average 35.7 per cent of national income, while budget expenditure was around 48.6 per cent [*Spoor, 1988*]. During the first two years after the foundation of the SRV the economy operated still in two separated zones, with two budgets, two economic plans, two currencies and – in the early beginning – with two central banks. A unified budget was only introduced by 1977, while the economic plans still remained to have separate parts for the northern and southern zone. In several stages the currencies circulating in both zones were finally unified in the dong with the money reform of May 1978, while the Vietnam State Bank (North) and the National Bank (South) had already merged in the new Vietnam State Bank of the SRV in August 1976.[4]

It seems that during this early period of reunification and economic reconstruction there was a great imbalance between the northern and southern zone. On the one hand the North contributed greatly in the reconstruction of the South, both in manpower and material resources. On the other hand, the South contributed still relatively little to domestic revenue on the state budget as fiscal policies were not yet well developed and the willingness to pay – and government capacity to levy – taxes by the dominating private sectors in the southern economy was not very great.

In the autumn of 1976 the Council of Ministers promulgated new tax regulations for the agricultural sector in the whole country. In comparison with the existing system in the North there was in fact not much change, the principles of farming tax still being based on yearly estimated gross output of the normal average crop.[5] Implementation of this farm tax system in the

whole country gave a sharp rise in tax income. While in 1976 tax had been only
4.2 per cent of gross output, this rose in 1977 to 8.3 per cent in spite of the
sharp decrease in overall paddy output. In the following year when the paddy
harvests were at their lowest point of the whole post-war decade, farm tax still
came to a level of 7.2 per cent [IMF, 1979: 21]. Apart from the farm tax,
particularly for the private sector a number of other taxes existed such as
business tax, income tax, commodity tax and slaughter tax.

Domestic revenue on the state budget increased from 6,322 million dong
($3,090 million) in 1976 to 7,500 million dong ($3,670) in 1978 (see Table 1).
Only 20 per cent of this was provided by taxes [IMF, 1979: 33]. Practically all
other domestic revenue came from state enterprises (industry, agriculture,
transport, domestic and foreign trade – the latter practically a state
monopoly – in the form of turnover tax, profit transfers and depreciations
funds. Turnover tax, a direct transfer of part of the social product to the
budget – well known from other socialist economies – varied between 15 and
50 per cent of the wholesale price of a good. It is paid by the enterprise at
regular intervals in order to provide the budget with a continuous flow of
funds over the fiscal year. Profit transfers, equally important as a source of
income for the state budget, are on the basis of average cost norms and
planned profit margins, to be paid monthly. Finally, depreciation funds had
to be transfered to the budget (as well as included in the production costs)
which were based on original purchasing values, rather than current
replacement costs, a reason why the contribution to domestic revenue of this
item was comparatively low [IMF, 1979: 28–9, 33].

Budget expenditure was 9,275 million dong ($4,540 million) in 1976,
remaining nearly constant in the following year, after which a rather sharp rise
followed to an estimated level of 9,900 million dong ($4,840 million) in 1978
[Spoor, 1988]. While direct reconstruction aid for the South must have been
less by 1978 than in the immediate post-1975 period, there are at least four
other items that account for this increase of budget expenditure (in particular
current expenditure).

TABLE 1

STATE BUDGET SOCIALIST REPUBLIC OF VIET NAM (1976–84)
(Millions of US dollars/$)

	1976	1977	1978	1979	1980	1981	1982	1983	1984
Domestic Revenue	3,090	3,460	3,670	3,580	3,870	3,980	4,120*	4,049	4,909*
%	(68.1)	(77.1)	(75.8)	(70.8)	(72.6)	(73.4)	(74.1)	(70.4)	(72.5)
Expenditure	4,540	4,490	4,840	5,060	5,330	5,420	5,560*	5,754	6,772*
%	(100.0)	(100.0)	(100.0)	(100.0)	(100.0)	(100.0)	(100.0)	(100.0)	(100.0)
Deficit	1,450	1,030	1,170	1,480	1,460	1,440	1,440*	1,705	1,863*
%	(31.9)	(22.9)	(24.2)	(29.2)	(27.4)	(26.6)	(25.9)	(29.6)	(27.5)

Note:* These figures are to be considered as ex ante estimates, presumably indicating
overestimates for at least the domestic revenues.

Source: Adapted from Spoor [1988, forthcoming].

First, the country was struck by a number of natural disasters, like typhoons
and floodings which led to greatly increased emergency aid programmes of the

central government to the affected areas. Second, following the increased tension at its borders with China and Kampuchea, defence expenditure increased. Third, in order to sustain the food distribution programmes to the urban population at low fixed prices (and in view of the very poor production levels of paddy, tax evasion and an increased portion of paddy procurement actually purchased at higher prices) growing subsidies were paid from the budget. Fourth, the government had expanded considerably its social programmes in health, housing, education and social security, mainly financed by the budget. Current budget expenditure therefore increased rapidly. This could partly be realised by a decrease in the capital expenditure directly financed by the budget, while increasing the share of state bank credits as working assets of state enterprises [*IMF, 1979: 29*].

The state budget of the SRV was – from the very beginning – highly unbalanced, with large deficits covered nearly exclusively by foreign aid and for a small share by bank loans to the state [*IMF, 1979: 33*]. The growth of current expenditure in the budget also affected the share of public savings (domestic revenue–current expenditure). As share of national income – according to IMF estimates – public savings were in 1976 no more than 3.4 per cent. Through the increased state control over the economy in the South, this share increased to 4.4 per cent, but it dropped to the level of only 2.9 per cent in 1978. Therefore public savings could only provide a small share of capital expenditure (in 1978 at a level of 20.0 per cent), the rest coming from foreign aid [*IMF, 1979: 31*].

With large deficits on the current account of the balance of payments the SRV received a substantial flow of foreign capital both from the capitalist and socialist world to finance this gap. Still, by receiving government aid and through contracting commercial bank credits the SRV's foreign debt to the convertible currency area was rapidly growing, by 1978 amounting to $1,095 million [*IMF, 1979: 48*].

In general the financial management system of the SRV was still largely administrative, although during 1977 and early 1978 some measures were taken in the direction of greater use of bank credits to finance working capital of state enterprises and towards a stricter adherence to the principles of economic accounting. However, these same state enterprises were probably not very enthusiastic to act according to these principles. The safe system of state supplies at very low prices and the covering of losses at all times by the budget led them – in view of the pressures caused by the plan norms – to overstocking, reselling materials on the free market and other activities 'outside' the plan.

1979–81: FIRST BREACHES IN THE OLD SYSTEM

The Sixth Plenum of the CC of the VCP, held in August/September 1979, introduced economic reforms particularly to overcome the severe problems in the agricultural sector, legalising the subcontracting of land to families and individual peasants, raising purchasing prices (which had been at an extremely low level for many years) for farm products and increasing the freedom to sell their products on the free market. Also in the system of state finance, measures were announced, although they did not have such an impact as the policy changes in the agricultural sector seem to have had. The financial problems were indeed serious. State budgetary revenue decreased in 1979 with 2.5 per cent [*Spoor, 1988*].

An important reason for this fall in income was that particularly in the industrial sector economic activity was decreasing sustantially since 1978. In peacetime conditions the malfunctioning of the state sector was rapidly becoming apparent, leading to stagnation. The 'hasty' take-over of many of the southern industries by the state worsened this situation, while some external factors had a negative influence, for instance, the severe floodings late that year with its effects on the provision of food and raw materials for industry, the Chinese attack on the northern border zone in early 1979, and the outflow of tens of thousands of often skilled workers of ethnic Chinese origin that affected negatively the coal production and the functioning of the Haiphong harbour and, finally, the stop of all remaining Chinese aid in mid-1978. This negative economic trend had direct consequences for the main source of revenue on the state budget, namely, the income from the state enterprises. A further reason for the decrease of budget revenue was the very poor procurement performance of the state in the agricultural sector, particularly in the southern provinces where tax evasion was widespread.[6]

The government tried to overcome part of its financial problems by further adapting and developing new fiscal policies, the system of economic and financial management, and by preparing for a major revision of the wage and price system. In the midst of 1980 several tax regulations were changed. For example, apart from the commercial transaction tax already in existence a new tax 'on major transactions' was introduced. This seems to have been a new step on the road to using fiscal (instead of coercive) instruments to control the private sector, while at the same time gathering extra resources for the budget.

In January 1981 the Council of Ministers adapted regulations for the management of state-run enterprises, in order to increase the financial autonomy of these enterprises and to expand the material incentives for the workers through piece-rates and bonuses. The enterprise production plan would have to consist of three parts, the state-assigned part with state-supplied assets, the part produced with self-procured assets and the part with the production of socalled by-products. From the second part more profits could be held by the enterprise (for the social welfare fund, the bonus fund and the production development fund) than from the first part, while this was the case for all profits from the third part. The by-products could be sold on the free market when a state agency would not want to buy them. Although implementation seems to have brought some improvements in efficiency and output, enterprises also used the 'unclear delineation' between the three parts in order to calculate profits in their favour. Furthermore, there was a 'failure to remit to the state the volume of products assigned under plan and a tendency to retain more products for the plant than allowed by state regulations'.[7]

In the summer of 1981 some drastic measures in the sphere of prices and exchange rates were taken, in line with IMF 'advises' [*Bello, 1983: 12*]. The government raised the prices paid for 40 agricultural products by 400–600 per cent, while the exchange rate to the dollar was changed from just more than two dong to nine dong. Finally, as a further step in rationalisation of the price structure (particularly in its link to world market prices) in the autumn of 1981 a great number of commodities and raw materials – some of them imported ones – rose drastically in price on the domestic market. At the same time – as a form of compensation – wages for state enterprise workers and civil servants were doubled [*FEER Asia Yearbook, 1982: 263*].

During the following two years after 1979 the budget revenue indeed rose, reaching in 1981 a level of 11.1 per cent over 1979 (measured in dollars). Budget expenditure increased by 7.1 per cent over the same period, but in 1979 it had already grown by 4.5 per cent while revenue had decreased as we have seen above [*Spoor, 1988*]. Clearly one important factor in the overall increase in budget expenditure was the rapid increase in defence spending. Another factor causing this increase in particularly current spending was the increasing pressure of subsidies, mainly price subsidies for food. The government was buying more paddy from the peasants against the then higher official purchasing prices or even prices well above that level.

Apart from this rather negative trend in the financial position of the state, the rise in prices of imported goods on the domestic market in late 1981 was a positive step to lessen part of the burden of budget expenditure. Because of the above factors, the government deficit during the years 1979–81 had reached a level that was 32.7 per cent higher than the average for the years 1977–78. Although this deficit was still largely covered by foreign aid, the year 1979 would mean a watershed in the flow of foreign aid and the conditions under which it was extended. Important external influences were of course numerous. First, by mid-1978 all Chinese aid programmes had been stopped overnight which gave a substantial decrease in foreign aid. Second, Vietnam's CMEA membership compensated this loss of aid only partly, although there were perspectives of more aid for the new Five Year Plan starting in 1981. Third, Vietnam's intervention in Kampuchea gave rise to a virtual stop of Western aid, while it also became difficult to obtain commercial credit.

As the gap between foreign aid and government deficit was growing the government took more and more refuge in bank credits, which in fact meant creating more money. The deficit financing rapidly increased money in circulation, contributing to already high inflationary pressures on the free market. Yearly inflation had already reached an average of around 50–60 per cent according to several estimates.[8]

It is important to note that by the end of the years 1979–81 public savings (which had already been relatively small in the previous years) had become negative. Current expenditure had increased over domestic revenue; capital expenditure, therefore, was totally financed through foreign aid programmes.[9] With interest payments and amortisation increasing and the willingness to provide new aid (particularly by Western countries) decreasing Vietnam's deficit on the balance of payments rose. According to the IMF in 1981 the debt service had come to $284 million, 77 per cent of all export earnings and by then 218 per cent of exports to the convertible area [*FEER Asia Yearbook, 1983: 276*]. By then the total foreign debt was estimated at around $3,000 million

($1,400 million in convertible currencies) [*FEER Asia Yearbook, 1983: 263*].
Survival in financial terms was only possible through the increased aid to the
SRV from the CMEA countries. Also, from some of the OPEC countries
loans were obtained, basically to finance fuel imports (Algeria and Libya).

Realising that one of the major problems in the economy had become the
great deficit of the commercial balance, enterprises were in fact urged by the
government to produce more goods for export. Already with the Sixth CC
Plenum of 1979 some measures were introduced to make production for
exports more attractive. Enterprises were allowed to use ten per cent of
foreign currency in their export plan and 50 per cent of their above planned
profits to buy raw materials and spare parts abroad.[10]

On the whole, the years 1979–81 show the intentions of at least a growing
part of the leadership of party and government to achieve important reforms
and improvements in the overall system of economic and financial
management. They show a growing concern for the development of a viable
export sector, improving the organisational structure of foreign trade and
introducing financial incentives to produce directly for exports. The results of
the reforms were still far from positive in terms of the financial problems of the
state, although agricultural production during the 1979–81 years improved
greatly in relation with the forgoing period (1976–1978), and after the deep
depression in 1979–80 the industrial sector recovered also. The rather slow
implementation of reforms in the system of state finance may partly have been
caused by external factors. It was, however, also caused by the lack of clarity
and unity about the way to proceed along the road of economic reform. There
seemed to have been a continuous debate inside the party about important
questions like the 'law of value' within the state sector, state–private sector
relations and market-plan controversies. However, by the end of this
'interregnum' the moderate reformers within the Vietnamese leadership were
certainly stronger than ever before, which would be expressed in the March
1982 Party Congress, not only in the (re)formulation of economic policies, but
also in terms of shifting a number of these leaders to essential positions of
power in the government and the party.

1982–85: DRASTIC CHANGES IN THE MAKING

The third period, 1982–85, starts with the important Fifth Party Congress. It
confirmed clearly the line of economic reform and expressed openly severe
criticisms on previous policies. In its final resolutions emphasis shifted from
the traditional priority on heavy industry to agriculture and light industry,
with particular attention to the development of exports of these sectors. The
Fifth Congress also called for a major review of the system of economic and
financial management. It concluded that 'managerial and planning mechanisms
remain heavily bureaucratic and still rest on budget subsidies' and criticised
the 'insufficient attention to the principle of economic accounting'.[11] The
positive effects of economic liberalisation (as mentioned above) had also been
accompanied by certain important negative ones. The state had a decreasing
grip on the production and circulation of goods, while economic activities
'outside' the plan and the socialised sector increased rapidly, often using (and

tapping) state property and supplies for private benefit and speculation.

In order to improve the financial position of the state by increasing budget revenue, a tax reform was carried out in early 1983. It must equally be seen as an attempt to construct a fiscal system that served to curtail the by now rapidly expanding private commercial sector. Likewise, it promoted co-operative forms of production and distribution through tax exemptions. For the agricultural sector a more fundamental change in fiscal policy followed. Tax rates were now to be fixed during a three-year period according to average yields/hectare and taking into account the geographical situation (delta, midland or mountain village). The general expectation was that the new fiscal policy would improve the budgetary revenue flow.

However, budget expenditure in 1982 had risen more rapidly than revenue giving rise to a deficit considerably higher than the previous year. Again, in particular, current expenditure increased the most due, first, to wages for state enterprise workers and civil servants being doubled at the end of 1981 with substantial costs for the 1982 budget; secondly, state procurement of paddy increased rapidly (including agricultural tax, quota sales at official purchasing prices and above quota sales at 'agreed' or 'encouragement' prices). This meant an even greater burden for the budget.

The policy of cutting capital expenditure financed by the budget was continued. According to one estimate the accumulation rate of national income was down to 14 per cent in 1982 while, according to the author's calculations, the ratio of state investments and national income was no more than 11.4 per cent in 1982 and 11.6 per cent in 1983.[12]

The improvement of the fiscal system, and the rapid growth of the agricultural and industrial sectors finally stabilised the budget deficit somewhat in 1983 but it remained still large by any standard (29.6 per cent of total expenditure, see Table 1). As before it was covered by foreign aid, state bank loans and money issue and, for the first time, also by the issue of govenment bonds. Inflation was estimated to be 80 per cent in 1982 and somewhat tempered to 55 per cent in 1983 on an annual basis [*FEER Asia Yearbook, 1985: 268*].

Exports increased rapidly over 1982, certainly as a result of the improved material incentives. That this development was not seen by all of the party leadership with great enthusiasm became clear from the politburo meeting held in Ho Chi Minh city (the centre of the country's exports) in late 1982, where decisions were taken to restrain the – what was seen as rather uncontrolled – growth of export companies and their range of operation [*FEER Asia Yearbook, 1984: 286*]. These decisions would have a negative impact for the growth of exports in the following year.

Foreign aid that covered most of the deficits, increasingly coming from the Soviet Union, had created by 1982 a foreign debt – using official exchange rates to the dollar – of around $3.5 billion, while by the end of 1984 it was up to about $6.0 billion [*FEER Asia Yearbook, 1984: 9*]. Even while exports had grown substantially in comparison with the years 1979–81 the debt service in foreign currencies continued to be a real problem, leading the government to enter into discussion with several countries and consortia of commercial banks to postpone the repayment of outstanding debts.[13]

The internal financial situation of the state had somewhat improved, but more long-term and fundamental reforms were necessary, particularly within the state sector. The call for a new system of economic and financial management by the Fifth Party Congress was partly concretised in the resolution of the Sixth Plenum of the Party's CC in July 1984 and the decisions of the Council of Ministers on national industry management later that year.[14] The principles of 'economic accounting' for state-run and joint state–private industrial enterprises included more independence in production and business but still under the centralised leadership of the state, the use of enterprise income to cover production costs (calculated on the basis of the full wage fund, current replacement values for capital amortisation) and to secure profits, the use of material incentives and sanctions, and central supervision through financial control. An increasing percentage of profits could be retained by the enterprise for reinvestment and for improving the welfare of the workers.[15] One of the main goals of this reform was to lessen the burden on the budget by making state enterprises more responsible for their expenditures (and losses) while on the other hand material incentives are given to them which will increase production and profitability, ultimately leading to higher budget revenue in the long-run. However, in spite of these considerable changes, it must be noted that the system of administrative supply planning and price subsidisation still largely remained in force. The losses of the state-run distribution sector were still to be covered by the budget. These partial reforms were nothing more than the prelude to the Eighth CC Plenum which announced the end of the state subsidy system and a major reform in the economic and financial system which in practice had still left unchanged the largely administrative character of the economic system.

CONCLUDING NOTES

As the party's daily *Nhan Dan* declared a few days after the closure of the Plenum:[16] 'The system of subsidisation, which was essential during the 30 years of continuous war, has become a habit, a pattern of thinking, a lifestyle and a way of socio-economic management. It has caused negative results that should be quickly overcome.' The final resolution meant a decisive move towards the general implementation of principles of 'economic accounting' with some far-reaching consequences. A process of decentralisation in decision-making and planning is certainly on its way. Experiments of greater autonomy for enterprises were to be generalised instead of remaining isolated initiatives. Clearly 'economic accounting' not only in the merely technical sense of the term but also indicating a greater awareness and responsibility at the level of the enterprise and its management for the first time are seen as important in the system of economic and financial management of the Vietnamese economy. It will be important to see how the horizontal links of an enterprise may develop, with or without knowledge (or control) of the central planning authorities. These links are absolutely necessary if self-procured assets are to become a major source of capital for the enterprise and 'consumer demand' is allowed to influence production and distribution. Tearing down the administrative allocation of state supplies in practice will mean a radical departure from the existing 'habit' within the state sector in which the state receives all profits and covers all losses. The absence of a 'hard budget constraint' and the indefinite covering of losses by the state budget, has given rise to low efficiency, productivity and the misuse of state property for private gains and corruption.

Abolishing the food price subsidies, on the one hand, will certainly improve the current expenditure side of the budget. However, this cheap food ('basic needs') policy enabled the government for many years to guarantee a basic subsistence level for the urban population, in particular for workers in the state sector. If no adequate compensation is given for the loss of these subsidies the nominal income of those who are supposed to be the backbone of the state apparatus (and who need to execute the reforms) will be negatively affected. Wages, although 'adapted' to the new situation, can (and in fact did) prove to be rapidly insufficient if inflation on the expanding free market gets out of control, basically because supply of commodities remains insufficient. Finally, devaluation of the dong, various other monetary stabilisation measures and a much more active fiscal policy were set in with the decisions of the Eighth Plenum. The fundamental changes will need to be accompanied by reforms in the credit policy (and the banking policy), which has been already indicated by the resolution with the remark that 'the economic return of capital must be considered as the most important criterion'.[17]

It would need more detailed study of the most recent developments in the post-Eighth Plenum period to see how the reforms have been implemented, which tensions they encountered or even produced (like the galloping 'open' inflation since price control virtually disappeared), and the development of production and productivity in the enterprise sector.

NOTES

1. Text of the communiqué issued at the end of the Eighth Plenum, in: Vietnam News Agency in English, 21.6.1985: *SWB: FE* 7984/B/7, 22.6.1785.
2. See, for example, several published interventions in *Nhan Dan* of the economist Doan Trong Truyen in 1976.
3. *Nhan Dan,* 21.6.1985, editorial.
4. Ho Chi Minh city, 12.8.1976, *SWB:FE* W891/A/33, 18.8.1976.
5. Ho Chi Minh city, 27–30.10.1976, *SWB:FE* W907/A/30–34, 8.12.76.
6. *Nhan Dan,* 24.6.1980, editorial.
7. *Vietnam Courier,* No. 6 (1982), pp.19–21.
8. *Far Eastern Economic Review* (FEER), 24.5.1984, p.81.
9. *Vietnam Courier,* No.5 (1982), p.6.
10. *Nhan Dan,* 9.10.1979, pp.1–2.
11. *Vietnam Courier,* No.5 (1982), pp.6–7.
12. *Far Eastern Economic Review Asia Yearbook* (1983), p.7 and *CMEA Statistical Yearbook* (1984, Russian edition), pp.37, 133.
13. *Far Eastern Economic Review Asia Yearbook* (1985), p.287 and for example: *Asahi Shimbun,* 21.5.1985, *SWB:FE* 7957/1, 22.5.1985.
14. *Nhan Dan,* 17.12.1984.
15. Hanoi H/S, 17.12.1984, *SWB:FE* 7881/C/11, 21.2.1985.
16. Hanoi H/S, 20.6.1985, *SWB:FE* 7985/B/5, 24.6.1985 (emphasis added).
17. See note 1.

REFERENCES

Bello, W., 1983, 'The IMF and Socialist Construction in Vietnam', *Indochina Chronicle,* No.87.

Duong Dinh Gi, 1978, 'La monnaie vietnamienne depuis la revolucion d'aout', *Courier du Vietnam,* No.73.

Ellman, M., 1979, *Socialist Planning,* Cambridge: Cambridge University Press.

Far Eastern Economic Review Asia Yearbook, 1982–85, Bangkok: FEER.

IMF, 1979, 'Socialist Republic of Vietnam – Recent Economic Developments', New York.

Kornai, J., 1979, *Economics of Shortage,* Amsterdam: North-Holland Publishing, Vol.A, B.

Marr, D., and Chr. White, 1988 (forthcoming), *Post War Vietnam: Dilemmas in Socialist Development,* Ithaca, NY: SEA Program Publications, Cornell University.

Nuti, D.M., 1979, 'The Contradiction of Socialist Economies: A Marxist Interpretation', *Socialist Register*, pp.229–73.

Spoor, Max, 1988, 'State Finance in the Socialist Republic of Vietnam', in D. Marr and Chr. White (eds.), *Post-War Vietnam: Dilemmas in Socialist Development,* Ithaca, NY: SEA Program Publications, Cornell University.

White, Chr., 1982, 'Debates in Vietnamese Development Policy', Sussex, IDS Discussion Paper No.171.

Nicaragua's Experience with Agricultural Planning: From State-Centred Accumulation to the Strategic Alliance with the Peasantry

by David Kaimowitz*

Nicaragua's experience in the agricultural sector between 1979 and 1987 shows using planning to achieve state centered accumulation is inappropriate for peripheral nations in transition. Peasant-based strategies, which make greater use of decentralised market mechanisms are necessary. But these must be used as a tool for social change, not instead of it. Recent Nicaraguan policies seem to be moving in this direction.

I. INTRODUCTION

This article uses the Nicaraguan experience with agricultural planning between 1979 and 1987 to examine the relationship between planning and market mechanisms in peripheral countries in transition to socialism. This relationship, it will be argued, can only be understood in the context of revolutionary governments' specific goals and the unique characteristics of the transition period.

Concretely, the principal problem of economic planning in a peripheral country in transition is how to: (a) alter economic and political structures in favour of a heterogenous combination of previously dispossesed classes and (b) increase the level of economic socialisation, while preventing economic collapse.[1] Moreover, this is to be achieved in the context of widespread difficulties created by imperialist aggression and the disarticulation of the previous institutions and economic balances, at a time when possible alternatives are only beginning to emerge.

To try to use planning in these circumstances, as has been done in a number of countries including Nicaragua, to foster high rates of accumulation concentrated in the state sector is generally unrealistic and often conflicts with the goals presented above. But nor can major economic transformations be achieved if revolutionary governments simply renounce their role in guiding the accumulation process. A better alternative is to use regionally integrated planning to maintain basic consumption and existing productive capacity within an accumulation model in which the peasantry plays an active role.

In examining concrete transitional societies, it is important to acknowledge the specificity and wide variability of possible combinations of planning and

*David Kaimowitz recently received his doctorate from the University of Wisconsin, Madison. He gratefully acknowledges the comments of Arturo Grigsby, Michel Merlet, and the editors.

market mechanisms. The two cannot be artificially juxtaposed, without considering the complex interactions between them and the institutional context in which they operate [*Ruccio, 1987: 6; White, 1984: 103*]. The issue must also be presented historically, since the optimal combination of plan and market mechanisms will vary over time.

Planning should be seen as a multifaceted process through which state economic power is used to effect economic change [*Wuyts, 1985: 180*]; not as an abbreviation for centralised obligatory material balance planning, state production, and direct administrative control over commerce. Furthermore, planning's class content and its relationship with the overall process of social transformation must always be at the forefront of the discussion. Otherwise one is left with few options other than a highly centralised, state-centred inefficient and politically vulnerable planning system or policies which deny the state the capacity to direct the economy or carry out social transformations.

In the Nicaraguan case, a strategy of socialist transition designed to achieve rapid growth in the socialised sector through centralisd material balance planning and state production proved unsustainable, both economically and politically, in the face of massive US intervention. Consequently, the government was forced to change policies and expand the scope of certain market and quasi-market relations. State farms have received greater financial autonomy and portions of their lands have been transferred to agricultural co-operatives and individual small producers.

There has been a trend towards regionalisation and economic decentralisation. Public sector investment is being reduced. Responsibility for agricultural capital goods distribution has been partially shifted from the public sector to producers' co-operatives. Certain agricultural producer price controls have been lifted and consumer price subsidies reduced. More generally, there is increasing sensitivity to the importance of market factors in price determination.

The Nicaraguans, however, have not given up their efforts to direct the process of social transformation. Rather, they have sought to find planning mechanisms with real potential for channelling that process; to replace policies which give apparent control, but which are ill-adjusted to social reality, and inevitably convert planning into a charade, carried out at the margin of an immense unofficial and unplanned economy.

This presents an apparent paradox. More 'market' mechanisms and greater decentralisation may be necessary to achieve more effective social control. More ironic still, the war and US attempts to end Nicaragua's efforts at socialist transition have stimulated the creation of a new model of transition which, it will be argued, is both more viable and has more positive distribution implications than the initial state-centred accumulation model.

The article is divided into five sections. An initial section presents the agrarian structure and planning/market mechanisms which characterised the period prior to the Sandinista Revolution. The Sandinistas' original (implicit) strategy for agricultural transition and the roles anticipated for planning and market mechanisms follow. The early outcomes of that strategy are analysed. The military, political, and economic factors which led to a change in strategy are discussed, as well as recent policy outcomes. Finally, the implications of the Nicaraguan experience for the broader debate regarding planning and the market in peripheral transitional economies are considered.

II. THE HISTORICAL LEGACY

Nicaragua's agrarian structure prior to 1979 was heterogeneous, but relatively well articulated.[2] Different forms of production coexisted in a fashion which allowed a high rate of agricultural export growth, a steady flow of foodstuffs to the urban population, a rapid accumulation of capital, and the reproduction of patterns of social legitimacy and domination over time. Although there were strong underlying tensions and the system led to the impoverishment of the majority of the rural population, there was little evidence of an immediate structural crisis of agriculture.[3]

Monopolised, Paternalistic, and Inter-locking Markets

Central to the system were the patterns of control over land, labour, credit, rural commerce, agro-industrial processing, and political power. By controlling these resources the Somoza regime and those segments of capital closest to it were largely able to determine the composition of output, the internal terms of trade, the allocation of labour, and the rate of investment.

Resource monopolisation ensured that a significant portion of the rural population had to engage in wage labour. This included true agricultural proletarians, semi-proletarians involved in both agricultural production and wage labour, and others who entered the agricultural labour force only on a seasonal basis [FIDA, 1980: 36]. Even so, endemic seasonal labour shortages, particularly for the agro-export harvests, were one of the system's principal tensions.

Monopolisation of finance, trade, and processing facilities made possible the concentration of surplus appropriation and economic decision making, despite the existence of an important group of small and medium-sized commercial producers [Baumeister, 1985: 54-9]. The financial system, oriented by the Somoza controlled Central Bank also played an important role in determining the investment and product mix of the large landowners who financed the bulk of both their working capital and capital expenditures with credit.

The terms of trade for the large export producers followed international market prices. The exchange rate was stable; the cordoba freely convertible; and producer/exporters had direct access to the world market. For smaller producers the terms of trade were defined through a complex network of rural intermediaries who, although exploitative, made available the necessary capital goods and manufactured personal consumption items in exchange for agricultural products. Often the same person purchased and processed the crop; supplied capital and consumer goods, gave technical advice and provided informal credit.

The large landowners (often merchants themselves) also typically operated through a web of paternalistic multi-stranded relationships to obtain the labour, products, and loyalty they required from the surrounding population. Again, the exchanges involved were typically unequal but were the only available source of land, support in times of crisis, and scarce commodities, and were cemented by an elaborate ideological foundation based on kinship, dependence, and shared value systems.

This was particularly true in the country's interior regions. In the Pacific where cotton, sugar cane, sorghum, irrigated rice, and coffee were dominant there was a greater tendency for the direct production of surplus value using more fully proletarianised labour and large quantities of imported capital goods. Market relations tended to be more impersonal.

But in the interior, where coffee, cattle, and basic grain production were prevalent, surplus extraction came largely through the monopolisation of commerce and processing and from land rents. The dominant economic groups often came from peasant backgrounds, were not as assimilated into urban lifestyles, and tended to rely more on personalised and paternalistic relationships.

The Role of the State

The state's economic role under Somoza was limited, but fundamental. Although, of course, if based on the scarce distinction which existed between the Somoza family and the government, Somoza's vast properties are included in the public sector, its role appears much larger. Its key task was to foment a smooth process of capital accumulation favouring the large capitalist landowners associated with the Somoza family. The relation with non-Somocista capital was more contradictory. While these sectors benefitted from many of the government policies they were also in constant conflict with the Somoza group and viewed its control over the state as unfair competition and restricting their possibilities for expansion.

Somoza's National Guard and local authorities were used to support the large landholders' economic and political domination through direct coercion and violence. The public sector provided (and denied) services such as rural road construction, export promotion, agricultural research and technical assistance, rural credit, and marketing facilities to ensure high capitalist earnings and adequate supplies of labour and basic foodstuffs. Likewise, small agricultural colonisation initiatives were carried out in the hopes of increasing basic grain production for the urban market and reducing rural unrest.

While the public sector's overall size and market participation was relatively small, its interventions were strategically chosen to have a significant impact. For example, foreign loans and assistance were effectively channelled to promote export diversification (often in activities owned by Somoza himself). The importation of agricultural machinery and Salvadorean and Honduran labour, combined with direct repression, was sufficient to reduce wage pressures in the cotton harvests. The National Institute of Foreign and Internal Commerce (INCEI) through its marketing facilities and selective commercial activities was able to lower producer grain prices during peak seasons and ensure an adequate flow of foodstuffs to Managua.

Planning in this system was largely organised through the central bank, other public financial institutions, and the national budget. The Ministry of Agriculture and Livestock (MAG) had a planning department, but its activities were largely limited to data collection and the formulation of foreign financed development projects.

III. THE INITIAL SANDINISTA PLANNING PARADIGM: STATE-CENTRED ACCUMULATION

Some elements of the system described above had already collapsed by the time the Sandinistas came to power. The National Guard and the network of rural authorities disintegrated. Somoza and many of the largest landowners fled the country. The private financial sector was bankrupted by the war and had to be nationalised to continue functioning. The historical patterns of ideological domination were weakened.

Other, more global, changes also occured around this time which, themselves, would have probably led the system into crisis. International primary commodity prices fell sharply, dramatically lowering the profitability of traditional agro-export products. Nicaragua's export terms of trade declined 30 per cent between 1978 and 1983 and for key products such as cotton and sugar there were few prospects for long-term improvement [*Collins, 1986: 279, 280*]. Thus, even had they wanted to (which they did not), it would have been exceedingly difficult for the Sandinistas to rearticulate the agrarian system along the old lines.

How exactly the Sandinistas did hope to rearticulate the different forms of production within the agricultural economy was never developed into a clear explicit strategy.[4] But, *ex post,* it is possible to reconstruct an implicit strategy whose key objectives were to: (a) create a strong modern, centrally planned, state sector; (b) maintain production in the other sectors; (c) prolong the wartime political tactical alliance with the non-*Somocista* capitalist producers; (d) guarantee the urban population access to basic foodstuffs at stable prices; and (e) obtain control over the surplus produced in private agriculture through commercial and financial means without having to nationalise production [*Wheelock, 1985*].

Agricultural planning was organised to meet these objectives. It focused on planning state production and creating mechanisms to ensure a transfer of resources to the state farms and the capturing of the marketed surplus of foodstuffs. Institutionally, it was centred in the Ministry of Agriculture (MIDINRA). The National Financial System (FSN) and the Ministries of Planning (MIPLAN), Foreign Commerce (MICE), and Internal Commerce (MICOIN) participated, but, with the exception of the rural credit and basic grains purchasing agencies which were key to the relation with small producers, played a secondary role.

The State Farm Sector

The landholdings of Somoza and his associates (some 20 per cent of total farm lands and half the land in farms larger than 350 hectares) were expropriated and converted to state farms. These farms were given privileged access to credit, foreign exchange, and a wide variety of government services, as well as direct subsidies.

While the state farm enterprises were first being established they were operated under a system of centralised material balance and investment planning and were directly financed out of the national budget. By about 1983, however, as will be discussed below, the state enterprises began to be more financially autonomous.

The sector was promoted as the centre of modernisation and future growth [*MIDINRA, 1983*]. Large, capital-intensive, agro-industrial projects were initiated in the hopes of promoting rapid technological change, improving Nicaragua's market position by exporting semi-processed, rather than raw, materials, and permitting the rapid assimilation of imported capital goods into agriculture [*Wheelock, 1985: 45–64*].

The state farms were also seen as the political vanguard of the revolution in the rural areas. Their workers would be the best organised and most class conscious. The farms were to be symbols of the revolution in the countryside and bases from which its ideological work and political, military, and administrative activities could be organised.

Agricultural Planning and the Non-State Sectors

Direct obligatory material balance planning was not even a possibility for the non-state sectors (which included the large capitalist producers, the small and medium commercial producers, and those semi-proletarianised families who engaged in self-employed agricultural activities). Instead the state relied on indirect controls and incentives.

To give these substance the financial system, agricultural exports and imports, a large portion of industry, and the import of agricultural capital goods were all nationalised. Much of the agro-industrial processing and agricultural machinery capacity also came under state control. Through the creation of two large, highly subsidised, public companies, the National Basic Foodstuff Company (ENABAS) and the Agricultural Products Company (PROAGRO), the government obtained a substantial monopoly position in the domestic commerce of basic foodstuffs and agricultural capital goods. This, along with a series of direct repressive measures (often carried out under the direction of local party secretaries who looked upon commercial activities as inherently exploitative and unproductive) sharply weakened, and in some areas practically eliminated, private rural commerce.

To guide the labour market the government used its regulatory powers, influence over the agricultural workers' unions, and capacity to mobilise voluntary workforces for particular tasks. It also had substantial monopsony power since the state farms employed some 13 per cent of the total economically active population in agriculture, and a much higher percentage of those engaged in wage labour [*CIERA, 1985a: 25*].

The hope was that just as the Somocista state had used its monopoly over these strategic activities and resources to direct the accumulation process and appropriate the surplus generated in agriculture, often without directly managing production itself, the revolutionary state could do likewise. Unlike the previous intermediaries, however, who had simultaneously performed various functions, the government set up a distinct agency for each activity. These agencies extended all the way from the national to the village level, with little prevision for local or regional co-ordination and with the corresponding creation of an enormous number of rural government offices and new jobs for lower-level government officials.

The feasibility of using indirect planning instruments effectively depended greatly on each particular product's market structure. Greater control could be exercised where production was highly vertically integrated and production and/or processing was concentrated in a small number of large and easily supervised units. Such was the case with sugar, irrigated rice, bananas, cigar tobacco, and cotton-seed oil. On the opposite extreme were corn, beans, edible sorghum, and dairy products. These were produced by thousands of small producers, required little processing or capital inputs, and could be made directly available to local consumers. Coffee, cotton, and beef were somewhere in-between.

There were also distinct policies for the different social sectors. Among the non-socialised sectors, the large capitalist export producers (mistakenly believed to have more both economic and politic weight than proved to be the case) received the greatest attention [*Baumeister and Neira, 1986: 175–7*].[5] It was assumed the regime's revolutionary profile would lead these producers to make few new investments and those only with state credit. Thus, the government had an interest in not allowing them to accumulate resources which could be diverted into luxury consumption, parallel markets, or capital flight. On the other hand, the immediate nationalisation of their holdings would have created domestic and international political problems and the state lacked the administrative capacity to manage more enterprises.

Thus, the state sought to capture the surplus generated by these producers through 'cost-plus' pricing. Prices were set through negotiations with producers associations to allow a predetermined profit rate over (government estimated) average production costs with the margin between farm-gate and purchaser prices going to the government. Prices and credit facilities were to be just sufficient to motivate producers to maintain production without allowing them to obtain differential rents.

Policy towards the 'peasantry' also sought to permit simple, but not extended, reproduction. Here, though, the rationale was somewhat different. Prices of basic foodstuffs, produced predominantly by small producers, were kept low to meet the needs of the urban population and (as explained below) avoid labour shortages.[6] The government used its monopsonistic market position, capacity to import grains and, later, state farm basic grain production to this end.

The sector of economically viable small and medium commercial producers was thought to be small and of limited importance. To the extent it existed at all it was associated with both the existence of private commercial monopolies likely to hoard, speculate, and foment parallel markets and the danger of creating a 'kulak' class of rich peasant and rural merchants opposed to the revolutionary project. The 'peasantry' as a social category was considered antithetical to socialism by many middle level functionaries in the key ministries who often tended to view socialism as synonomous with large-scale 'modernised' production.

The smaller producers were believed to have limited technological potential and to face structural constraints which prevented them from responding significantly to price incentives or meeting the country's future agricultural production needs. They were portrayed as semi-proletarian in character and it was felt that their proletarian, rather than peasant attributes should be encouraged; an attitude reinforced by fears that support for their self-employed cultivation activities would lead them to reduce their wage labour participation and aggravate the historical labour shortage problem.

On the issue of co-operativisation the government was ambivalent. Theoretically, it supported the idea both because of an ideological preference for socialised production and the belief that co-operatives would allow greater possibilities for planning peasant production. But there was an underlying concern that fomenting co-operatives would strengthen the peasantry, at the expense of the state farms. Government officials worried that if they provided co-operatives with land or other resources their members would reduce their wage labour participation and shift production from exports to foodstuffs. While the state aggressively supported the creation of credit and service co-operatives (CCS) and convinced a majority of small producers to join, the CCS' economic role was limited by the government's direct administration of most marketing, financing, and processing activities.

Fully socialised production co-operatives, known as Sandinista Agricultural Co-operatives (CAS), where all activities were realised collectively were considered inherently superior to (and thus more important than) the CCSs. But since the Sandinistas were largely unwilling to use land redistribution to stimulate co-operative formation, they could only hope small individual producers would voluntarily join their farms together to create production co-operatives. In reality this almost never happened.

IV. THE INITIAL STRATEGY IN PRACTICE

During the Revolution's first years the strategy outlined above appeared moderately successful. The state sector grew and its participation in agricultural production rose. The Sandinistas succeeded in concentrating investment in this sector. Official statistics showed the ratio of overall agricultural investment to agricultural GDP increasing from eight per cent in 1977 to 25 per cent in 1983 (although some problems with this interpretation will be discussed below) [CIERA, 1985a: 57].

The policy of 'national unity' with the large capitalist growers proved problematic, but not disastrous. An important sector of large producers, organised in the Nicaraguan Union of Agricultural Producers (UPANIC), tried, unsuccessfully, to use their economic power to obtain political concessions. Large producers also often illegally converted government credit to dollars or used it for other improductive purposes. Heterogeneous cost structures and pressure from producer's organisations and the state farms themselves made it difficult to set producer prices which both ensured adequate levels of production and eliminated windfall profits. The Sandinistas did succeed, however, in avoiding the wholesale abandonment of the large private farms or being forced to precipitously nationalise them.

Agricultural production did well, with a few significant exceptions. Basic grains (with the partial exception of corn), coffee, and sugar rapidly regained or surpassed historic production levels. Cotton production lagged, however, as it did throughout Central America in this period [*Deere et al; 1985: 86*]. Similarly, wartime slaughter and illegal exports and subsequent unfavourable government policies led to a decline in livestock production.[7]

TABLE 1
INDICES OF AGRICULTURAL OUTPUT

Product	1977–78	1980–81	1981–82	1982–83	1983–84
Rice	100	133	193	204	202
Beans	100	70	101	115	155
Maize	100	101	107	102	129
Sorghum	100	209	225	124	226
Cotton	100	53	45	55	62
Coffee	100	103	106	125	86
Sugar	100	98	114	112	102
Cattle*	100	83	64	79	81

Note: *Calendar year
Source: Deere *et al.* [*1985: 86*]

The government succeeded in keeping basic foodstuffs generally available to the urban population. A rationing system, which complemented, rather than replaced, the non-rationed market, was created for a limited number of foodstuffs and functioned relatively effectively in the urban areas. The system, combined with consumer price controls and government subsidies, kept price increases for basic foods well below the general level of inflation [*MIDINRA, 1983b: 48–50*]. These apparent successes, however, tended to hide a number of major problems which manifested themselves over time.

Problems with the State Farm Sector

Although state farm production increased rapidly, unit costs were very high. Nor were there strong incentives to reduce them. State farm managers were evaluated principally on production levels, not costs. Besides, with centralised budgetary financing, high levels of long-term capital investment and social infrastructure expenditures, and minimal accounting practices it was nearly impossible to estimate true production costs.

Initially, state farm managers also lacked sufficient authority to reduce costs. Most decisions, including relatively minor ones, were taken in Managua by officials who lacked information on local conditions and the farms' real possibilities.

Once they were consolidated into functioning enterprises the state farms became more financially autonomous. They began to receive funds from the financial system in the form of credits. Greater decision-making powers were given to locally based directors. Most farms, however, due to a combination of poor management, low labour productivity, unfavourable prices, high social overhead, and difficulties obtaining inputs showed consistent losses and were unable to repay their loans. Even when they tried to reduce costs government price policies and, later, defence-related costs and the transfer of some state farm assets to co-operatives ensured that losses continued. When faced with the prospect of either bankrupting the state enterprises or providing new loans the government chose the latter, the result being sharply reduced incentives for cost reduction. State farm directors had greater autonomy, but little to motivate them to make decisions in accord with national priorities.

Finally, since the prices state farms faced often reflected neither world market prices, nor domestic opportunity costs, unit cost reduction did not necessarily imply efficient or optimal solutions. On the other hand, disregard for costs invariably meant considerable waste and inefficiencies.

The large agro-industrial investment projects also proved much less successful than anticipated. Most projects were formulated assuming optimal yields, no unanticipated costs or delays, and high international prices. This was unrealistic for a country undergoing massive social change and a military conflict with the United States and for projects which required completely new technologies and social forms of production. Moreover, world prices remained well below projected levels.

Since these problems were not clearly foreseen, planning targets consistently went unfulfilled. Instead of the state farm sector providing a source of growth and accumulation as anticipated, it became a drain on available resources.

The state farms also created political problems. Many small and medium producers perceived them as poorly managed competitors for resources. Land poor families who expected the Revolution to redistribute land saw them as usurpers and there were numerous conflicts over state lands.

The disappearance of many traditional connections with the local communities aggravated the situation. Former *colonos,* sharecroppers, and farm labour supervisors lost some access to land and other farm resources. Although the disappearance of the large landowners' repressive practices was widely welcomed, there were complaints about the elimination of paternalistic measures such as aiding families in times of distress, providing informal credit, or allowing certain labourers to graze a few head of cattle. These problems were particularly acute in the interior regions where paternalistic practices had been most common. More generally, the state farms operated under standardised bureaucratic norms which provided little flexibility for interacting with local labour and commodity markets. Often they became 'islands' of socialism, connected more closely to Managua than the surrounding communities.

Internally, the state farms also failed to establish a strong base of political support for the revolutionary government. To the contrary, the historic struggles between labour and capital often turned into labour/state conflicts or simply situations of generalised apathy and low labour productivity. The Rural Workers' Association (ATC), the Sandinista sponsored agricultural workers union, found itself squeezed between the workers' immediate concerns and those of the new directors; a situation made worse by the absence of a strong rural trade union tradition.

The 'Peasant Problem'

For the peasantry, both rich and poor, the initial Sandinista strategy had detrimental consequences. As the state sector (and later the military) utilised more resources than anticipated, out of a total production well below planned output, the small and medium producers' access to capital goods, labour and consumer products declined. In addition, rising urban food subsidies increased pressure to lower real farm prices, worsening the basic foodstuff producers' terms of trade. Although a massive influx of foreign savings, mostly loans, equal to some 20 per cent of GDP, kept these problems from reaching critical levels in the first years, with time and the onset of the US war they grew more severe.

Until mid-1981, when they created the National Union of Farmers and Ranchers (UNAG), the Sandinistas had no mass organisation to organise and represent small and medium commercial producers; a group which proved much more important, both economically and politically, than initially anticipated [*Kaimowitz, 1987: 200*]. (See Table 2 for a comparison of the initial view of rural class structure and that which later came to be held.) Even then, government policy remained ambivalent. Many 'medium'-sized producers, particularly the strategically important coffee and cattle producers of the interior, felt threatened by government attempts to limit social differentiation, curtail private rural commerce, and centralise investment and other planning decisions.

TABLE 2

RURAL CLASS STRUCTURE IN NICARAGUA IN 1978 AS
PERCEIVED IN 1979 AND REVISED IN 1985 (%)

Class	Early View	Revised View
Capitalists	9.3	.8
Small and Medium Commercial Producers	12.7	32.2
Semiproletarians or poor peasants	70.4	36.5
Permanent workers or Workers	7.5	30.5
Total	100.0	100.0

Note: *See Kaimowitz [*1987: 36*] for the operational definition given to each class in each period.

Sources: 1980: FIDA [*1980: 28*]; 1985: IHCA [*1985: 5c*].

The strategy also offered little to the poorest peasants. Some obtained full-time employment on the state farms, and a much larger group got small quantities of official credit for the first time. There were also substantial benefits from the 1980 Literacy Crusade and subsequent health and education programs. But for the majority of the rural poor, who continued to depend on agro-export harvest wages and non-agricultural activities, their incomes declined, both absolutely and relative to other groups [*Baumeister and Havens, 1983*]. Real harvest wages fell sharply after 1980 and it became increasingly difficult to obtain raw materials for artisanal activities.

Furthermore, government policies of using confiscated lands for state farms and supporting large private producers' land rights, left them little hope of gaining more access to land. Nor did rural consumers benefit much from cheap food policies. The public distribution system which supplied foodstuffs at official prices worked relatively well in the cities, but not in the rural areas, where little was done to replace the destroyed distribution channels [*Barraclough, 1982: 57*].

Faced with declining terms of trade, the small and medium commercial producers and the poor semiproletarian families reduced their participation in the commodity and labour markets respectively. Commercial producers' marketed output of corn stagnated and investment in livestock and coffee (not adequately measured in national investment statistics) fell sharply. On the labour side, a reduction in supply led to widespread labour shortages in the coffee and cotton harvests.

Economic Imbalances and Plan Enforcement Problems

The monopolisation of the country's foreign exchange and investment capacity by large-scale government investment projects and the use of foreign debt, price manipulations, and government deficits to support the state sector, the military budget, and urban consumer subsidies led to economic disequilibriums which weakened the state's capacity to manage the economy as a whole. High inflation rates resulted, particularly for goods and services not subject to effective price controls. The uneveness in price increases, in turn, generated large relative price distortions.

Under these circumstances petty commerce and other unplanned informal sector activities flourished. This had a negative impact on income distribution, the pattern of growth, and the political strength of different class forces. The creation of a new class of commercial intermediaries was fostered. The wage-earning rural poor, who could not afford the parallel prices but had little access to the official economy, were the hardest hit. Labour and other resources were transferred from productive to improductive and/or unprioritised activities. The combination of urban consumer subsidies for foodstuffs and public services, attractive urban informal sector activities, and declining rural incomes accelerated rural to urban migration. Public sector grain purchases declined, as a growing percentage of grains moved through unofficial channels. Police measures designed to control these channels were, as might be expected, both unpopular among producers and largely ineffective.

A downward spiral began to emerge whereby declining participation in material goods production led to falling output. Goods became scarcer, but the government continued to restrain farm-gate prices. Thus, opportunities for commercial speculation rose, which further accelerated the shift from productive activities.

In this context, policies designed to support state farms and production co-operatives actually weakened them. As part of the official (planned) economy which was under close government control, these enterprises had to sell their produce at official prices. Meanwhile their unorganised private neighbours obtained much higher prices on the parallel markets. Giving the socialised sector privileged access to subsidised capital goods failed to overcome this problem and further distorted relative prices.

Overall, the economy proved much more difficult to centrally plan and administer than anticipated. Under Somoza, planning focused on strategic interventions at key points and its implementation was assisted by a network of localised, multi-faceted agents who were well-informed of regional market conditions and had broad police powers. In comparison, the Sandinista government attempted to directly administer a wide variety of activities, even at the village level. The result was a general decline in effectiveness. Decisions were made at the centre with little knowledge of local conditions or decentralised authority to adjust policies to them, by officials whose assignments were frequently rotated. An amalgam of functionally differentiated and largely uncoordinated agencies replaced the powerful local caciques who were involved in practically everything.

A number of seemingly powerful planning instruments proved weak without the ability to effectively exercise localised supervision and control. Moreover, under the new revolutionary conditions both the rural population and local officials were less willing than before to submit to hierarchical decisions taken from above. Credit, capital goods, and foreign exchange were often diverted from the activities they were allocated for. There was no effective means of regulating the allocation of and intensity of labour – a task previously carried out by a complex system which combined tied labour, repression, subcontracting, and the identification and utilisation of small quantities of available labour. Difficulties in estimating production costs and wide cost variations between regions and types of enterprises made it practically impossible to use 'cost-plus' pricing to determine income distribution, the composition of output, and accumulation levels. High inflation levels also made the financial side of most plans seem practically irrelevant almost as soon as they were printed.

IV. THE 'SURVIVAL' ECONOMY, THE STRATEGIC ALLIANCE WITH THE PEASANTRY, AND THE TERRITORIAL ORGANISATION OF THE ECONOMY

The problems discussed above were made immeasurably worse by the US war of aggression which began in late 1981. Ronald Reagan took office in January 1981 committed to overthrowing the Sandinista government. To this end he created a counter-revolutionary army, whose command structure and initial manpower was recruited from the former *Somocista* National Guard. Between 1982 and 1984 military activities against Nicaragua grew steadily and by 1986 Nicaragua had suffered over $1,000 million in direct material damages, the equivalent of approximately three years worth of total export earnings [*MIDINRA, 1987: 7*]. In addition, there were substantial indirect damages due to lost production, the need to reallocate scarce resources to defense, and the displacement of almost ten per cent of the rural population.

It was also the war, more than any single other factor, which forced a reassessment of state centered accumulation and the planning mechanisms it implied.[8] The Reagan strategy, which came to be associated with the term

Low Intensity Conflict (LIC), stressed the creation and utilisation of rural discontent as a means of subverting the government's control over the rural areas and destabilising the economy. To this end the 'contra' rebels manipulated the rural population's religious sentiments; their limited contact with the government and official communications channels; fears of government land expropriations; and complaints regarding the collapse of rural commerce and the drafting of (already scarce) rural labour for military service.

The war greatly worsened the fiscal deficit and material imbalances which, in turn, dramatically accelerated the disequilibrating consequences of the initial accumulation strategy. The need for a much larger armed forces, the exodus from the zones of military conflict, and war related deaths and injuries further aggravated existing labour shortages.

Initially, the Sandinistas responded with traditional counter-insurgency tactics. As noted above, a military draft was imposed. Families were resettled (often involuntarily) from areas with intense contra activity to large co-operative settlements. Civilian movement and the transport of food supplies were restricted and police measures were taken against contra collaborators.

Over time, however, it became increasingly clear that a principally military approach was both insufficient and often counter-productive. To effectively combat the US sponsored aggression required major efforts to strengthen the revolution's rural political base. This, in turn, demanded both economic and political measures favouring the peasantry; particularly those living in the zones of military conflict. It also required a shift in the government's concerns regarding private agriculture from the agricultural bourgeoise to the peasantry; since the latter became both socially and geographically the key domestic protaganist of the political-military conflict. Shortages of foreign exchange, labour, and construction capacity made it necessary to abandon the emphasis on new, long-term, large-scale, capital-intensive investment projects and stress immediate consumption needs and the maintenance of existing productive capacity. Production and distribution also had to be reorganised to guarantee the entire population access to a limited number of essential goods and services, at the expense of investment and 'non-basic' consumption.

Modifications in agricultural planning instruments followed. Attempts were made to find mechanisms for responding to peasant demands, increasing economic efficiency, and reacting more flexibly to rapidly changing and localised military, political, and economic problems. Planning became more decentralised, producer's organisations were given increased responsibilities and power, and greater attention was given to effectively integrating the different forms of production.

Taken together, these three changes, referred to in Nicaragua as 'the strategic alliance with the peasantry', the 'survival' or 'resistence' economy, and the 'regionalisation and territorial integration' of the economy respectively, constituted a new agricultural planning paradigm. But they did not come about over night. It was only when initial, partial measures failed, that these, more profound, changes began to receive wider acceptance and greater implementation.

Initial Reform Attempts

The first major shift came between 1983 and 1985. The government reallocated land and (to a lesser extent) investment capital from large private and state farms to the agricultural production co-operatives (CAS). Producer organisations were strengthened and certain measures were taken to support the peasantry, particularly in the zones of military conflict.

Although a 1981 Agrarian Reform Law had foreseen the possible transfer of state and expropriated private lands to production co-operatives prior to early 1983 agrarian reform titles were issued almost exclusively for lands already under *de facto* co-operative control or for small, isolated farms which the state could not effectively manage. The tactical political alliance with the agricultural bourgoisie ruled out any large scale redistribution of private landholdings. Only after military activities escalated in 1982, did the government begin widespread redistribution of state lands as a means of seizing the political initiative in the countryside and facilitating participation in the defense of the surrounding territory. Between 1982 and 1984, the percentage of farm land in CAS grew from two per cent to nine per cent [*Deere et al; 1985: 79*]. The percentage in state farms fell from 24 per cent to 19 per cent while that in large private farms went from 17 per cent to 11 per cent. Some 20 per cent of the rural population, principally previously landless semi-proletarianised families, received land as co-operative members [*CIERA, 1985: 26*]. The CAS's share of total agricultural credit went from 1.2 per cent in 1981 to 7.2 per cent in 1983 and increased even further in 1984 [*Enriquez and Spaulding, 1986: 27*].

TABLE 3

EVOLUTION OF THE STRUCTURE OF LAND TENURE BY SECTOR (%)

Type of Property	1978	1981	1982	1983	1984
Private Sector					
350 or more hectares	36	18	14	14	13
140–200	16	13	13	13	13
35–140	30	30	30	30	30
7–35	16	7	7	7	7
less than 7	2	1	1	1	1
Co-operative Sector					
Production Coops (CAS)	0	1	2	5	10
Credit & Service Coops	0	10	10	10	7
State Sector	0	20	23	20	19
Total	100	100	100	100	100

Source: IHCA [*1985: 13c*].

CAS activities were incorporated into the government's material balance plans, but the state had little capacity to enforce these plans. Although each co-operative made an annual production plan, which had to be approved by the financial system to obtain credit and reflected national planning objectives, the actual composition of output and allocation of resources often differed markedly.

Moreover, a difficult balance had to be maintained between ensuring co-operatives' activities corresponded to national priorities and leaving them sufficient autonomy to find innovate solutions to their problems. CIERA found that those co-operatives where direct state participation in decision-making was highest were least successful economically and had poor internal cohesion. Those which received large amounts of resources but little guidance began to act like capitalist enterprises, limiting membership and relying on hired labour. Only relatively autonomous co-operatives which received resources from the state but were constructed on the basis of peasant initiatives, pre-existing social patterns, and an ongoing dialogue with the state and popular organisations were able to consolidate themselves as collective enterprises [*CIERA, 1985b*].

Other important steps favouring the peasantry taken in 1983 and 1984 included: (1) a massive land titling programme designed to give small and medium producers greater tenure security; (2) a sharp increase in real basic grain producer prices; and (3) a cancellation of debts held by 38,000 small and medium basic grain producers. Efforts were made to greatly strengthen the UNAG in its role as representative of the small and medium producers. Eventually, the UNAG became the largest, most influential, and most independent of the Sandinista mass organisations.

Agricultural planning also became more decentralised [*Kaimowitz, 1988*]. A regionalisation programme divided the country into six regions and three special zones. Regional governments were created and encharged, among other things, with developing regional economic plans. Regional cabinets, with significant authority, were formed to ensure better inter-institutional co-ordination. The Ministry of Agriculture's regional offices obtained more resources and greater authority in investment planning, land policies, and the co-ordination of agricultural services. The state's production and distribution activities began to be conceptualised as elements of a process of integrated regional and local development.

Special priority in the decentralisation process was given to areas of military conflict (which were also the areas where small and medium sized commercial holdings were concentrated). Additional financial assistance and more trained personnel were sent to these regions. Attention was given to their consumer-goods shortages, marketing problems, agrarian reform needs, and problems of co-ordinating military and resettlement strategies with economic development policies. Key national leaders were assigned permanently to oversee the affairs of each prioritised region and their presence gave added political weight to regional decisions, allowing them to be made more rapidly and with greater flexibility.

The Reforms Deepen in the Context of a Widening Crisis

Even with the changes enumerated above, however, the basic accumulation model and its accompanying planning paradigm were still largely intact in early 1985. The large agro-industrial investment projects continued with increasingly inflationary consequences. State farm production was still poorly integrated into the regional economies. Price policy and a high proportion of major investment decisions remained highly centralised. Government monopolisation of agricultural commerce and price policies which discriminated against basic foodstuff producers persisted. Co-operatives continued to be treated as if they could be controlled and planned like state farms. Policies promoting a shift from rural/productive/priority activities to urban/speculative/nonprioritised spheres went unabated.

Only in the last few years have stronger measures been taken to deal with these problems. They have been carried out, however, in a context of an increasing economic crisis and imbalances so large they defy any short-term solutions. Nicaragua's GDP declined by 6.2 per cent between 1983 and 1986, while inflation rose from 31 per cent to 62 per cent [*ECLAC, 1987*].

Among the biggest changes has been the official declaration of a new 'strategic' alliance with the peasantry, baptised with that name at the First Congress of the UNAG in May, 1986 [*Carrion, 1986: 4–9*]. The strategic alliance potentially means both greater autonomy and increased resources for the peasantry. Concretely, to date, there has been: a greater willingness to respond to demands for land, even when reform beneficiaries prefer individual holdings over collective production; more flexibility regarding co-operatives, with emphasis on 'intermediate' forms that combine collective and individual production and on co-operative marketing and processing activities; a devolution of certain commercial functions from the state to producers' organisations and a reduction of government controls on grain marketing; improved terms of trade for food producers; and a prioritisation of rural over urban areas for access to scarce goods.

The strategic alliance is simultaneously a military, a political, and an economic strategy. In addition to strengthening the revolution's military defense, the government hopes to reverse the migration from rural production to urban informal sector activities, increase agricultural output, and promote a more solid process of co-operativisation and peasant organisation.

The centre piece of the survival or resistence economy has been a shift away from new large state agro-industrial projects towards the maintenance of current capacity and support for the private and co-operative sectors. Under current circumstances the economy cannot afford to maintain both without creating unsustainable economic disequilibriums. There is increasing (although not unanimous) recognition of this fact, although it has proved difficult to rapidly change investment patterns.

Its second major element is an attempt to give priority to certain products and sectors considered necessary for the revolution's survival. This means concentrating on trying to guarantee basic foodstuffs, a few key manufactured goods and essential services, and the export production needed to import basic goods and a minimal quantity of capital goods. The military, productive wage workers, small and medium commercial producers, and the government bureaucracy are to be given privileged access to the few goods and services available, at the expense of other groups – particularly urban informal sector participants. The two principal instruments for achieving these goals are prices increases for agricultural producers, even at the cost of declining real urban incomes, and the rationing of foreign exchange, public sector industrial output, and the foodstuffs controlled by the government towards the prioritised sectors.

The final key new element of agricultural planning is an effort to rearticulate state production and services with the other sectors on a local and regional basis. The government's idea is to concentrate the socialised sector's efforts on providing the inputs, products, services, processing, and commercial capacity required by the other sectors in an integrated regional framework and to directly barter these services for agricultural products now being channelled through the parallel markets [*IHCA, 1987: 20, 21*]. In each regional context the state has said that it will focus on the most strategic activities, leaving the others to the private sector. Measures are also supposed to be taken to integrate the different state activities on a local level, rather than leaving them in the hands of functionally differentiated agencies managed through vertical chains of command centred in Managua. The pricing policies applicable to such a model have yet to be determined, but it would seem that territorial state enterprises will have to have sufficient flexibility to respond to local market conditions, as well as the rapidly fluctuating international markets.

Within the state itself, there still seem to be two views regarding regional integration. One privileges the need to reorganise the state sector to support the peasant and co-operative sectors. The other continues to seek more effective mechanisms for subordinating the latter to the needs of the state.

VI. NICARAGUA'S SIGNIFICANCE FOR FUTURE ATTEMPTS TO CREATE SOCIALISM IN THE PERIPHERY

One question which remains is to what extent the recent changes reflect a new strategy of socialist transition and how much they are simply tactical retreats in the face of military aggression and political/economic difficulties? Certainly there are many people in Nicaragua today that hold the latter view. For them, in essence, the socialist project has had to be temporarily put in abeyance to guarantee the survival of the revolutionary regime itself.

Others argue, as I would, that these changes have the potential of opening a new approach to the transition to socialism. Admittedly this approach is problematic. It is not clear how a strategic alliance with the peasantry, a survival economy, and localised territorial planning can form the basis for accelerated accumulation or advanced socialism in the future, what the evolution path between the different stages might look like, nor what sort of class alliance and political process are necessary to accompany such an effort. If, however, as will be argued below, peripheral countries in transition have few alternatives to this type of model, these issues cannot be avoided and must form the basis for intensive future research and discussion.

Nor is the dichotomy between tactical and strategic clear cut. Tactical policies may strengthen the peasantry's power and influence within the state itself, thus creating the basis for a strategic alliance in the future. Likewise, to obtain tactical results it may be necessary to treat the policy as if it were a strategic one.

The importance of these issues is that much greater because the problem of state centred accumulation and its implications for agricultural planning are not unique to Nicaragua. Unfortunately, there are strong similarities between

Nicaragua's experience and those of a number of other Third World nations which have attempted to follow a socialist path.

All have begun with an over-optimistic assessment of the possibilities of rapid accumulation and growth based on state production, high levels of investment, and centralised material balance planning. These assessments are based on a supposed superiority of 'socialist' forms of production and are typically buoyed by the relative ease of initially increasing production under conditions of widespread underutilised capacity.

Their high hopes, however, have run aground due to three key problems: (1) the disarticulation of the previous economic and ideological structures brought about in the process of revolutionary transformation has much greater and far-reaching implications than initially realised; (2) it takes more time than generally acknowledged to put new socialist forms of production and distribution into place, and these new forms must allow for substantial innovation and initiative and make greater use of mercantile relations; and (3) imperialist military and economic aggression, with its accompanying dislocation and destruction, is inevitably an endogenous part of the transition process. Therefore, the strategies developed must be explicitly designed to minimise the level of destabilisation it creates, not under the implausible assumption of peacetime conditions.

Given these factors it is unlikely that any peripheral nation in transition will achieve rapid growth rates in the first years. Rather, the problem is one of organising and channelling the process of *disaccumulation* to minimise disruption and affect least those classes which the revolution seeks to benefit. Once the problem is defined in this fashion a quite different set of planning mechanisms is likely to be required. Large-scale state investment projects and planning systems designed more to implement such projects than to incorporate the massive petty production and service sectors are unlikely to achieve the forementioned goals. Moreover, they tend to foment a strong top–down state bureaucracy which, if not checked, may stifle the political participation and mobilisation of the popular classes in whose name socialism is to be built. The hope, yet to be proven, is that a new model of peripheral socialist transition such as that outlined above might be more successful in these regards.

Admittedly, even the new model can make few claims to provide the accelerated growth which has served as a key argument in favour of socialist transition in the periphery in the past. It can be expected though, that it will do somewhat better in this regard than have the state centred accumulation models in actual practice.

These sobering prospects may lead some to question the desirability of the socialist model itself. Nicaragua, however, also provides important lessons in this regard. Despite an undeniable decline in living standards (largely due to US military aggression) for most Nicaraguans, an overwhelming majority of them voted for the Sandinista Party during the country's first free and democratic elections in 1984.

With all its problems and contradictions, the voters reasserted their belief that the revolutionary process they are undergoing offers multiple positive benefits. It has created an important sense of dignity and nationhood for the majority of poor Nicaraguans. It continues to be the only real hope that Nicaragua will ever be a nation which provides its entire population with the basic minimum economic essentials. Above all, it has offered the possibility for Nicaraguans of all classes to consciously participate in the construction of their country's future.

NOTES

1. Socialisation in this context implies a more integrated social division of labour, conscious co-operation in production, and social control over the production process [*Bettelheim, 1975*].
2. For a more complete description of the pre-1979 agrarian system see Kaimowitz [*1987*].
3. It is worth remembering in this regard that the Sandinista revolution, particularly in its final, more generalised, stages, was primarily an urban phenomenon. In recent revisionist history there has been a tendency to locate its immediate origins in some underlying structural crisis inherent in the capitalist agro-export model or widespread rural based class struggle. In my view, neither of these interpretations reflects the true dynamic of the revolutionary process.
4. Many policies discussed here, although referred to as 'Sandinista' policies were actually designed and implemented by middle level functionaries with little direction from the Sandinista Party. Particularly during the revolution's first years the Sandinista national leadership gave relatively little attention to the details of economic policy.
5. The relationship between the Nicaraguan revolution and the agricultural bourgoisie certainly merits a much more detailed discussion than provided here. Due to space limitations and my own limited knowledge of that topic, however, I have concentrated on the state and peasant sectors.
6. The term 'basic foodstuffs' is used to refer to those foodstuffs produced primarily by the peasant sector such as corn, beans, dryland rice, and edible sorghum. Foodstuffs produced mostly on large farms such as irrigated rice, sugar, and cooking oil faced a different situation.
7. Production figures available for Nicaragua tend to better reflect marketed surplus captured by the state and production in the sectors under government control. Available chicken and pork production figures, for example, actually refer to the small percentage of total output produced by large industrialised enterprises. There is a tendency for the statistics (and hence perceptions) to mirror the illusion that the official economy was *the* economy.
8. This is not to say that the war was the only factor in these changes. See Kaimowitz [*1987*] for a discussion of a number of other important determinants.

REFERENCES

Barraclough, Solon, 1982, *A Preliminary Analysis of the Nicaraguan Food System,* Geneva: United Nations Research Institute for Social Development.
Baumeister, Eduardo, 1985, 'Estructuras Productivas y Reforma Agraria en Nicaragua' in Richard Harris (ed.), *La Revolution en Nicaragua,* Mexico DF: Ediciones Era, pp.51–80.
Baumeister, Eduardo and Eugene Havens, 1983, 'Recruitment and Retention of Occasional Workers in the Export Sector of Agriculture in Nicaragua, 1981–1982', mimeo.
Baumeister, Eduardo and Oscar Neira, 1986, 'The Making of a Mixed Economy: Class Struggle and State Policy in the Nicaraguan Transition', in Richard Fagen, Carmen Diana Deere, and José Luis Coraggio (eds.), *Transition and Development: Problems of Third World Socialism,* New York: Monthly Review Press.
Bettelheim, Charles, 1975, *The Transition to Socialist Economy,* Brighton, Sussex Harvester Press.
Carrion, Luis, 1986, 'La Problematica del Campesinado y las Tareas de la UNAG', in Lineas para el Foralecimiento de la Alianza con el Campesinado, Managua: Departamento de Agitacion y Propaganda (DAP).
Centro de Investigaciones y Estudios de la Reforma Agraria (CIERA), 1985a, 'Nicaragua: Estudio sobre Campesinos Pobres', mimeo.

Centro de Investigaciones y Estudios de la Reforma Agraria (CIERA), 1985b, 'Estudio de las co-operativas de produccion de Petacaltepe, Santa Lucia, Los Ebanos, Masaya y Santa Teresa', mimeo.

Collins, Joseph, 1986, *Nicaragua: What Difference can a Revolution Make?*, San Fransisco: Institute for Food and Development Policy, third edition.

Deere, Carmen Diana, Marchetti, Peter and Nola Rheinhart, 'The Peasantry and the Development of Sandinista Agrarian Policy, 1979–1984', *Latin American Research Review*, Vol.20, No.3, pp.75–109.

ECLAC (1987) *Notas para el estudio económico de América Latina y el Caribe, 1986: Nicaragua* Mexico City: UN Economic Commission for Latin America and the Caribbean.

Enriquez, Laura and Rose J. Spaulding, 1986, 'Banking Systems and Revolutionary Change: The Politicals of Agricultural Credit in Revolutionary Nicaragua', in Rose Spaulding (ed.) *The Political Economy of Revolutionary Nicaragua*, Winchester, MA: Allen & Unwin, pp.105–26.

Fitzgerald, E.V.K., 1985, 'The Problem of Balance in the Peripheral Socialist Economy: A Conceptual Note', *World Development*, Vol.13, No.1, Jan., pp.5–14.

Fondo Internacional de Desarrollo Agricola (FIDA), 1980, *Informe de la Mision Especial de Programacion a Nicaragua*, Rome.

Instituto Historico Centroamericano (IHCA), 1987, 'Plan Económico 1987', *Envio*, No.70 (April), pp.14–27.

IHCA, 1985, 'Los Campesinos Nicaraguenses Dan un Nuevo Giro a la Reforma Agraria', *Envio*, No.51 (Sept.), 1c–19c.

Kaimowitz, David, 1988, 'The Role of Decentralization in the Recent Nicaraguan Agrarian Reform', in *Searching for Agrarian Reform in Latin America*, Winchester, MA: William Thiesenhusen (ed.), Allen & Unwin.

Kaimowitz, David, 1987, 'Agrarian Structure in Nicaragua and its Implications for Policies Towards the Rural Poor', unpublished dissertation, University of Wisconsin, Madison.

MIDINRA, 1987, 'Plan de Trabajo 1987: Balance y Perspectivas', Managua: Ministerio de Desarrollo Agropecuario y Reforma Agraria.

MIDINRA, 1983a, 'Marco Estrategico del Desarrollo Agropecuario', Managua: Ministerio de Desarrollo Agropecuario y Reforma Agraria.

MIDINRA, 1983b, 'Informe de Nicaragua a la FAO', Managua: Ministerio de Desarrollo Agropecuario y Reforma Agraria.

Ruccio, David F., 1987, 'The State, Planning and Transition in Nicaragua', *Development and Change*, Vol.18, pp.5–27.

Wheelock Roman, Jaime, 1985, *Entre la Crisis y la Agresion: la Reforma Agraria Sandinista*, Managua: Nueva Nicaragua.

White, Gordon, 1984, 'Developmental States and Socialist Industrialisation in the Third World', *Journal of Development Studies*, Vol.21, No.1, Oct., pp.97–120.

Wuyts, Marc, 1985, 'Money, Planning and Rural Transformation in Mozambique', *Journal of Development Studies*, Vol.22, No.1, Oct. (Special Issue), pp.180–207.

Accumulation, Social Services and Socialist Transition in the Third World: Reflections on Decentralised Planning based on the Mozambican Experience

by Maureen Mackintosh* and Marc Wuyts**

The purpose of this article is to argue for the viability, and the logic, of a distinctive approach to planning economic development and socialist transition in poor economies. The components of this distinctive approach are: more decentralised, and popularly-based, planning and control of accumulation; the close interlinking of investment in social services and in rural production; and an emphasis on intervention in the market as a tool of socialist planning. The article therefore presents an argument about economic planning intended to be relevant to a range of countries with similar general aims and problems. However, the ideas are developed here, as they were in practice, through a reflection on our own understanding of planning and its problems in Mozambique during the first ten years of that country's independence.[1]

In this study we aim to challenge a process of obfuscation and elison of options apparent within the renewed debate on market and plan. Posing the options as plan *or* market, conservative economists in the West have tended to hail all recognition or development of the market, whatever the context, as evidence of the inherent superiority of capitalism, or 'market forces'.[2] In the current context, economic pressures for deregulation become adjuncts of the intense imperialist military pressure on most Third World socialist states, and there is a danger that any detailed criticism of such a country's planning methods can be read as just more grist to the anti-socialist mill.[3] This risk seems worth taking, however, since our aim is to argue that there exist viable socialist planning methods which recognise the market where it exists, and intevene to influence those markets and to incorporate them where appropriate, without capitulating to the class logic of the capitalist market.

It is also our thesis that such planning methods are essential in poor socialist countries with extensive peasant farming sectors, for all such Third World countries contain markets which must be recognised and acted upon, not ignored. And all such countries have conducted rich and interesting debates on the problems of planning in this context. While making no claims to summarise that debate in Mozambique, this article aims to demonstrate some

*Research Fellow of the Development Policy and Practice group at the Open University, Milton Keynes, and Senior Lecturer in Economics at the Kingston Polytechnic, London.
**Senior Lecturer in Economics, Institute of Social Studies, The Hague.

of the complexity of Mozambican efforts to adapt planning methods to their own aims and reality – thereby refuting some of the cruder critiques of that history[4] – and to explain some of the lessons we drew from our experience of those efforts. The Mozambicans are of course in no way responsible for our interpretations and arguments.[5]

The article is organised in two parts. The first section examines the experience of Mozambican planning, with particular reference to the agriculture and social services sectors, exploring particularly the questions of the pattern of accumulation, the role of markets, and the relations between centre and locality in planning. The second section draws from this analysis a general argument for aiming at a more decentralised pattern of accumulation and economic planning in Third World socialist states.

I. ACCUMULATION AND TRANSITION IN MOZAMBIQUE

Mozambique as a Case Study

This section contains a selective analysis of Mozambican planning experience, focused on our central theme of the pattern and location of accumulation, its sources and implications. It is in no way a complete assessment of Mozambican planning – for which the data are in any case lacking – but is intended to explain and illustrate what we believe we learned about the central contradictions involved in planning socialist transition in a country such as Mozambique.

First, a brief discussion of concepts. By the location of accumulation, we mean the question of in whose hands, and within what form of organisation of the social relations of production, accumulation and, hence, development occur. This is a central issue for socialist planning, especially from a starting point at a low level of development because the location of accumulation will determine over time the relative development of the socialist and non-socialist sectors of the economy and, hence, whether a socialist transition occurs at all.[6] We are concerned to analyse in this section the difficulties faced by a socialist state in a poor Third World country in attempting to direct the process of accumulation in ways which support and develop a transition to socialism, in a country where by definition the productive forces are not highly developed, and most enterprise is small scale.

In analysing this question in Mozambique, we shall seek to demonstrate three central points. First, that in such a situation, it is very difficult or impossible for transition to be pursued by means of accumulation solely within the state sector. Planning which, by design or default, tends to concentrate the accumulation effort on the state sector runs into some characteristic problems, identified here through the Mozambican example.

Second, in an economy dominated by peasant producers, this first point implies that the state must be concerned to influence the pattern of accumulation in non-state hands. If it does not direct such accumulation into co-operative forms, it may be faced with an uncontrolled pattern of private accumulation which will actively conflict with state development aims and with the needs of small producers. What is usually called the parallel market, but might be more properly described as the parallel economy, is the manifestation of this conflict.

Third, and most unfamiliar within the existing literature, social services potentially form a crucial link within the economic planning process. Too often, social services have been planned in isolation from the development of production of goods for exchange. However, in Mozambique social services were at times planned and financed in ways which offer lessons for the planning of goods production including agricultural products. Furthermore, this experience suggests possibilities for creating links between social services development and the production of goods. These links might support a more effective planning of transition by encouraging a convergence of production with the needs of the producing classes, and by developing socialised local financing of accumulation to support both social services and goods production.

Generally, we will draw out of the Mozambican experience a theme of interaction between centralised and decentralised accumulation patterns: both under increasing pressure and destruction from an externally-generated war, which we discuss further below, and its disastrous economic consequences.[7] We will then use this discussion as a basis for arguing in the second section that decentralised accumulation, and state planning to support decentralised accumulation, is an essential element in planning socialist transition in economies with a large peasant sector, and that this may be most effectively done by linking social service planning to the planning of goods production.

Accumulation and Reorganisation in Early Mozambican Planning

In the early years after Independence, Mozambican planners placed great emphasis on achieving a rapid rate of development, through a high rate of accumulation and, hence, rising production and productivity. In this effort they were starting from a very low base: at Independence in 1975 Mozambique had a very low standard of living for the black population, and the economy had been further weakened in the short run by the destruction and loss of capital and skills as the settlers, who had monopolised these assets, departed [*Hanlon, 1984: 47–9*]. The economy was dependent on low productivity agriculture, and on labour migration and transit trade payments to and from South Africa and what was then Rhodesia [*Wuyts, 1978: 17–59*].

In 1977 the Third Congress of Frelimo, the first party congress to be held after Independence, adopted a series of Economic and Social Directives [*FRELIMO, 1977*] which set out the main proposed lines of Mozambican economic planning. The aim of planning was to be a rapid growth in production; the means were to be recuperation and reorganisation of existing production, only then followed by development of productive capacity and of the capacity to invest. The Directives emphasise the immediate importance of raising agricultural production, first, to provide food, and then to provide resources for accumulation. Agriculture was to form 'the base' and industry the 'dynamic sector' of the economy: in other words, agriculture was to be developed to provide resources for industrialisation, a common conception in socialist and non-socialist development strategies.

The initial means for recuperating and increasing production in agriculture (as in the rest of the economy) were seen as essentially organisational. The proposals drew heavily on the experience of the liberated areas in the north of the country which were under Frelimo's control before Independence, and which provided experiences of collective production and service provision. Two major new forms of agricultural organisation were to be created, state farms and co-operatives. This decision reflected Frelimo's general approach to the organisation of the economy: 'State ownership and co-operative ownership, which establish new relations of production will form the economic base of Democratic Popular Power' [*FRELIMO, 1977: 23*]. It also recognised the *de facto* result of the necessary take-over of abandoned or sabotaged farms by state or farm workers. In order to promote this transformation, the immediate tasks were 'the political mobilisation and organisation of workers in production units', and an increase in training of managers for these units, and in education and training of the working class as a whole [*FRELIMO, 1977: 21*].

The emphasis on re-organisation and the lessons of the liberated areas were particularly evident in the proposals for communal villages [*FRELIMO, 1977: 117*]. In a country with a majority of peasant producers, Frelimo argued in a review of the policy in 1979:

> The communal villages constitute the basis of rural transformation in Mozambique, – they are the political and economic units by means of which collective life will develop. The fragmented organisation of rural life associated with a low productivity of both land and labour is being transformed into new forms of production, of a superior level of political mobilisation, and with the introduction of education facilities and basic health care at the village level (Provincial seminar on communal villages in Cabo Delgado, quoted in CEA [*1979a: 11*].

The communal villages in other words were conceived, not as a form of production, but as political entities which would enable the organised peasantry to participate in shaping the socialisation of the countryside. They were intended to contain, even to be rooted in, collective production developing over time and co-existing with 'family' farming, as small scale farming was called. And they were intended to provide the organisational framework for social services and collective investment partly financed by collective production.

In this they drew on Frelimo's history. The collective production in the liberated areas had been developed to provide, not only support for the military effort, but also rudimentary health and education [*Munslow, 1983: 141–4*]. These had been essential to the prosecution of the war: under the Portuguese, Mozambique had a quite extraordinary lack of basic services in the countryside or even for the black population in the town [*Marshall, 1985: 158–62; Barker, 1985: 319–21*]. The Frelimo fighters needed people able to undertake first aid and basic medical care, and to read and write. For the population, access to such services provided one major motive for people to join and support the miltary effort.

Partly as a result, Frelimo's initial policies and legislation emphasised the rapid provision of basic social services: 'Our People have a fundamental right to health and education' [*Frelimo, 1977: 26*]. To achieve this, communal villages could help overcome resource constraints: 'counting on their own efforts, and based on collective work, they will mobilise resources to ensure the spreading of social benefits through the community' [*FRELIMO, 1977: 26*]. This link to communal villages was to be the basis for achieving the tasks set out in the Third Congress Directives on health, including spreading health services throughout the country, especially through the establishment of rural health posts, and an emphasis on preventative care and the treatment of the most common endemic diseases [*FRELIMO, 1977: 102–7*].

Through the early discussions of communal villages and co-operatives, therefore, there runs a strong theme of 'self-reliance', and an emphasis on 'the maximal utilisation of the available labour power such that mechanisation is only relied upon if there is an effective shortage of labour' (Eighth Session of the Frelimo Central Committee, February 1976, quoted in CEA [*1979a: 6*]. This reliance on local labour, plus the concept of the collectively-produced social fund to finance a village health worker or other social activities, meant that socialisation of the countryside was understood as the development of collective life, rooted in a surplus from collective production, and requiring the development of the organisational abilities of villagers to manage collective goods and services: a political process rooted in local material developments [*CEA, 1979a: 5–6*].

At the same time as developing these ideas of locally-based rural change, Frelimo also argued that the state must develop its capacity to 'direct, plan and control' the economy. The planners argued that this implied the creation and development of a state-owned productive sector: 'A strong state sector is an objective necessity of this stage of our revolutionary process. It is therefore essential to develop and consolidate a state sector which determines and dominates the economic process' [*FRELIMO, 1977: 28*]. This state sector, created on the basis of abandoned production units, was then to be expanded through new investment.

In these formulations, with their strong emphasis, on the one hand, on a dominant state sector and state planning and, on the other, on local self-reliant initiative, there is a clear embryonic conflict. We would argue, however, that it is wrong to see this as a conflict between two opposed political lines, struggling for dominance within Frelimo. Saul sees such a conflict as the principal contradiction of the Mozambican development process: 'It was precisely this dialectic between leadership and mass action which continued to be at the core of Mozambican politics' [*Saul, 1985: 88*]. Far from this being a resolvable political conflict, however, it is hard to imagine any planning process which could bring about social and economic transformation of the type Frelimo was proposing, which did not contain *both* these elements of central planning and local initiative. The Third Congress documents make this point clearly.

That there was a tension and potential conflict between these elements of planning was, however, inevitable. Problems emerged particularly over the generation and use of investment funds. The conflict arose from the emphasis on the central state role in directing the surpluses of production on the national level; from the emphasis on the expansion of the state sector – reiterated in the Directives in the list of the immediate tasks for the agricultural sector [*FRELIMO, 1977: 34*]; and finally and particularly, from the lack of clarity about the investment needed to support locally-based co-operative production and transformation in the rural areas.

The discussion of self reliant transformation in the countryside appeared to play down the investment required. In both agricultural co-operativisation and in education and health, there was an implicit assumption that rapid expansion could be achieved with minimal reliance on material investment resources provided by the central state. In the Directives, references to essential investment, for co-operatives and for development of education and health services, were couched in terms of the need for credit for local investment. Education and health were indeed distinguished as 'social' rather than 'economic' sectors in the Directives. In the context of proposed central planning of investment resources, this raised by implication the question of whether the material resources, necessary to employ such credit, would be made available, and if so, how. The general lack of clarity about how real investment resources were to be both generated and allocated was storing up problems for the future.

The conception of socialist transformation and economic planning embodied in the Third Congress and other early Frelimo documents, therefore, contains a number of potential contradictions in its approach to accumulation. But the Third Congress documents also contain a potentially creative approach to planning, combining central direction and local initiative. The next few sub-sections discuss how the planning system evolved, and some of the problems which developed, not in order to assign political blame for mistakes, but rather to see what were the central contradictions which produced the problems.

The Development of State-centred Accumulation

After the Third Congress, the Mozambican economy was re-organised, and the structures of the new state were created. In large-scale production and trade, the state sector became dominant: by 1981 it acconted for 65 per cent of total industrial output, 85 per cent of transport and communications activity, 90 per cent of construction and 40 per cent of commerce (mainly the wholesale trade), according to government figures [*FRELIMO, 1983a: 30–48*]. These estimates should be treated with caution, since government data did not include much small-scale transport, construction and, particularly, commerce; similarly, the estimate that in 1981 the state farming sector produced 50 per cent of marketed output in agriculture is likely to be a severe overestimate. Health, education and legal services were wholly nationalised shortly after Independence.

Much of this growth of the state sector was the result of taking over abandoned production units. From the low base of post-Independence economic crisis, the years 1977–81 were years of renewed expansion in the economy, as capacity was recuperated and re-organised; this conclusion is supported by both data and observation [*Wuyts, 1986: 122–34*].

TABLE 1

'GLOBAL SOCIAL PRODUCT' AT CONSTANT 1980 PRICES
('000 MILLION METICAIS)

	1975	1977	1980	1981	1982	1983	1984	% change 1975–7	1977–81	1981–84
Agriculture	26.1	30.6	33.4	33.3	32.5	25.0	25.7	+17.2	+ 8.8	−22.8
Industry	26.4	27.8	30.7	31.6	27.2	22.5	15.5	+ 5.3	+13.7	−50.9
Transport	9.1	7.8	8.1	9.0	8.4	6.7	5.3	−14.3	+15.4	−41.1
Other	9.5	8.8	10.0	9.8	9.8	9.7	9.1	− 7.4	+11.4	− 7.1
GSP	71.1	75.0	82.2	83.7	77.9	63.9	55.6	+ 5.5	+11.6	−33.6

Note: GSP includes commerce and construction, but not 'social service' sectors.
Source: CNP [1985].

As the state sector grew, economic planning was developed. The import–export trade was nationalised, as were the banks, with the exception of one minor bank. The non-state sector – still the overwhelmingly dominant user of labour – included the retail trade (in private hands and, in the town, organised in successful consumer co-operatives), small-scale agriculture, with some scattered agricultural co-operatives and collective fields, and an artisanal sector (including small scale fishing) which was far weaker than in most African countries because of colonial repression and forced labour mobilisation.

Economic planning was organised under a National Planning Commission (NPC). The major ministries, such as Agriculture, Internal Commerce, Transport, were responsible for the relevant parts of the state productive sector, as well as planning non-state production, and were hierarchicially subordinate to the NPC. The effective mechanism of planning was the state budget, which centralised all state financial resources, and provided for their allocation among the ministries in accordance with the central plans drawn up by the NPC. The Bank of Mozambique became the central bank, state financier and major commercial bank, while the People's Development Bank concentrated mainly on agricultural credit [*Wuyts, 1986: 187*].

In the late 1970s, the main constraint on the Mozambican economy was not the balance of payments. Because of the profits on gold sales from payments for Mozambican mine labour up to 1978,[8] the balance of payments remained quite healthy until 1980, despite the loss of transit traffic revenue after Frelimo closed its borders with what was then Rhodesia, in support of the struggle for Zimbabwe.[9]

TABLE 2

BALANCE OF PAYMENTS 1973–84
('000 MILLION METICAIS) CURRENT PRICES

	Balance on Visible Trade	Balance on Invisibles	Current Surplus/ Deficit (b)	% Import Coverage
1973	- 5.9	3	- 2.9	75
1974	- 4.1	4	- 0.1	95
1975	- 5.4	5.4	0	100
1976	- 4.5	4.9	0.4	103
1977	- 5.7	3.6	- 2.1	80
1978	-11.9	2.9	- 7.1	48
1979	-10.3	1.9	- 6.2	55
1980	-16.6	3.3	-11.7	48
1981	-18.4	3.2	-13.1	46
1982	-22.9	3.4	-16.5	38
1983	-20.3	3.5	-13.2	34
(a)1984	-18.8	1.7	-10.0	25

Notes: (a) Provisional figures.
(b) Includes grants.

Import coverage = $\dfrac{\text{Export earnings + balance on invisibles}}{\text{Imports}}$

The profit on gold is *not* included in these figures.

Source: CNP [*1985*].

The initial constraints were low productivity and organisational problems in every sector, compounded by the low levels of literacy and skill of the Mozambican population.[10] Much capital had been destroyed, but the use of remaining capacity was also low, though rising.

In this situation, planning efforts by the government ministries tended to focus on the difficult job of running the state firms, and the rapidly expanding state services, with far too few trained personnel. The state budget was used to allocate recurrent budgets to the state services and ministries, and to distribute investment finance – and the material resources for investment which largely had to be imported – to all sectors of the economy. Material investment planning therefore became a major method by which the state intended to plan the economy as a whole, and to develop the balance between the different sectors.

Government investment therefore constituted virtually all the recorded investment in the economy in the late 1970s and early 1980s. Tables 3 and 4 show its evolution in relation to estimates of GDP, and its breakdown by sectors.

While government revenues continued to cover current spending up to 1984 (the last available figures), there was only a very small surplus for investment. However, as the tables show, investment rates expanded rapidly, implying increasing reliance on foreign funding, and widening deficits on current account. In 1980, the prospective plan for the decade 1980–90 defended this rapid investment drive – investment reached 20 per cent of GDP, in a

TABLE 3

GOVERNMENT INVESTMENT 1978/79–83
(MILLION METICAIS), CURRENT PRICES

	1978/79*	1980	1981	1982	1983
Total investment	8,010	9,916	13,962	14,255	10,197
Of which foreign official assistance	3,689	4,470	6,548	7,796	8,180
GDP	n.a.	66,200	70,400	73,000	68,800
Investment as % of GDP	6 or 7**	11	20	20	15

Note: * 1978/79 figures refer to both years taken together.
　　　** Estimate.
　　　　n.a. (not available)

Source: CNP [*1985*].

desperately poor economy, in 1981 – on the grounds that foreign finance was available to expand the state sector, and that this would accelerate the development process [*Machel, 1979b*].

Foreign finance was indeed available. As investment rose, it became concentrated on the installation of new capacity in the state productive sectors. The area under state farms rose to 100,000 hectares by 1978, and 140,000 by 1982. New industrial units especially for consumer goods production were begun – for example in textiles. State transport capacity grew. Education and health facilities also expanded fast, from a very low base indeed, but as Table 4 shows, the call this made on state investment was relatively small as compared to the main 'economic sectors'.

Agriculture was effectively the priority sector, taking 31 per cent of state investment from 1978–82, and also a substantial share of the infrastructural investment registered under 'construction'. Much of this went on equipping and developing a few major state farms, notably the huge irrigated rice farms in the Limpopo valley, inherited from a major colonial settlement scheme which had already been highly problematic before independence. This scheme – CAIL – took 50 per cent of the agricultural capital budget of the country in 1977; mechanising the state farms, sometimes to try to overcome labour constraints, took 66 per cent of that budget in 1978 [*Hermele, 1986: 13*]. The total effect of this spending should be kept in perspective: in the late 1970s there were no more tractors in Mozambique than in 1969 [*Hermele, 1986*]. Nevertheless, equipping the state farming sector in this way drained the available investment resources from other areas of the economy.

The effects of this investment pattern, as the Fourth Frelimo Congress was

TABLE 4

SECTORAL ALLOCATION OF INVESTMENT 1978–83
(MILLIONS OF METICIAS) CURRENT PRICES

	1978 & 1979	1980	1981	1982	1983
Economic sectors	7,290	8,027	11,827	12,291	14,795
1. Agriculture	1,095	2,271	4,181	4,826	4,345
2. Industry and energy	561	1,227	3,349	3,493	4,332
3. Transport and communications	177	155	345	468	1,203
4. Construction	5,457	3,346	3,270	2,424	4,241
5. Other	-	1,028	682	1,080	674
Social sectors	188	567	458	401	477
State administration	311	660	753	184	100
Local investment	24	127	312	463	600
Other (including military)	197	535	612	916	1,126

Source: CNP [*1985*].

to note in 1983, were particularly dramatic in agriculture. Of agricultural investment 1977–83, 90 per cent went to the state sector, two per cent to co-operatives, and virtually none to the small-scale 'family' farming. And within the state sector, in agriculture and industry, investment was concentrated on what became known as 'big projects', rather than smaller-scale activities.

This concentration of investments in large projects generated problems of management and productivity. Actual investment was invariably below planned investment because the economy could not absorb it at the planned rate. Because of long gestation periods, delays, and organisational and material constraints on using the new investment to capacity once installed, productivity of investment was below plan and, therefore, the weight of the investment on the economy higher than planned.

How did this imbalance of investment develop, given the emphasis in the Third Congress document on a balanced development of state and co-operative sectors? In part, the state sector emphasis resulted from the concentration of the relatively few qualified planners and managers employed by the ministries on trying to get the enterprises for which they were directly responsible to function effectively. This left few cadres for developing the co-operative movement. It also resulted in part from the preference of foreign donors of all political stripes for financing big, visible new projects. It substantially resulted, as we explore below, from a serious under-estimate of the resources necessary for co-operativisation and the maintenance of small-scale production, as well as a misunderstanding of some aspects of the organisation of family farming.

But it also substantially resulted from the fact that many people believed for a few years that it could work: that the big state farms could provide the essential food for the town and cities, as well as some major export crops; that industrial consumer goods production could be expanded fast enough through investment to satisfy demand; that people could be trained and organised fast enough to run the big projects effectively and that a proletariat could be recruited and trained without damaging the rest of the economy. In other words, the essential process was to be one of belt-tightening, substituting investment for consumption, as the Ideological Department of the party explained:

> (The large projects) will involve the expenditure of enormous sums by the State, sums which could have been used instead to buy rice – there is a shortage of rice – sugar, maize flour, meat etc. But here there is a question of choice. If we buy these products which we need (and it is true that we need them) then the money we spend is used up and will not be productive. If on the contrary we make a sacrifice in this phase, so that instead of buying rice, flour, meat, fish we use the money for the construction of factories, then in four or five years the sacrifice we are making today will produce all these goods. We think that to escape from poverty and underdevelopment, this sacrifice is necessary [*FRELIMO, 1982: 31*].

In other words, keep consumption low, and use the saving for import-substituting investment: a very common development prescription from governments of both left and right.

Why this prescription did not work is a complex story which we will explore further. A substantial part of the reason was the development after 1982 – just as the country was emerging from the economic impact of support for the Zimbabwean independence struggle – of the war within Mozambique with the South African-backed MNR. The large projects, like the communal villages, were early targets of destruction, and a very large part of the investment effort has been destroyed.[11] Recurrent drought has also taken a very serious toll. But there were also other reasons for the problems, many of which centre on what was happening in the rest of the economy, outside the centrally-run state sector.

Central and Local Initiative in Agriculture and Health

To return to an earlier theme: Mozambican planning principles emphasised local and popular initiative, as well as central direction. And local initiative was widespread in the early years after Independence. In the main cities, the 'Dynamising Groups' formed the effective local administration for a period, and the consumer co-operative movement grew rapidly and became the backbone of the effective state rationing system. In the countryside, farm workers took over some small abandoned farms as co-operatives, and as Dolny records [*1985: 226*] 'literally thousands' of collective fields were begun in the first two agricultural seasons after Independence. Similarly, a large number of communal villages were set up. In 1981, there were about 350 co-operative and many more collective fields not part of an organised co-operative; the co-operatives involved about 70,000 people, and about one million people were recorded as living in communal villages [*Dolny, 1985: 227, 230*].

There was then a genuine co-operative movement in the early stages of Mozambican Independence, stimulated by the Dynamising Groups and Party organisers in the rural areas, and resulting in a lot of experiments in co-operative production, whereby people began a collective field or fields, while also continuing to cultivate 'family' plots on an individual basis. The nature of the experiments was very varied, from taking over abandoned settler farms, to established peasant farmers within communal villages clearing land together to cultivate a common field. In the south, the co-operatives were often formed largely by women farmers in areas where the men had long been accustomed to seek wage work; in the north, where cash cropping had been established and enforced in colonial times, co-operators were more often men. The class nature of the co-ops also varied: some were groups of relatively successful farmers, seeing a chance to develop co-operative farming on the basis of credit and support from the state; some were groups of impoverished, particularly female, farmers, hoping that co-operative farming would give them a chance to increase their production for sale.[12]

This agricultural co-operative movement ran into substantial problems soon after its inception. A large number of co-operatives failed to produce profitably and ran into debt, unable to repay loans from the People's Development Bank (BPD). The numbers working in co-operatives dropped, and they suffered seriously from organisational problems. The relation between communal village and co-operative became problematic in many villages, because a low proportion of villagers worked on the co-operative fields.

There is no doubt that the low level of spending on investment by co-operatives in the early years – already cited – contributed to these problems. But that low level should be seen more as symptom than cause of the problems. The more fundamental cause of the problems were organisational, technical and economic in a wider sense.

The technical and organisational problems were closely related. Literacy in Mozambique was less than ten per cent of the adult population at Independence (and 300,000 of those literate had been educated by FRELIMO in the liberated areas) [*Marshall, 1985: 166*], and there were two Mozambican agronomists in the whole of the country in 1975 [*Saul, 1985*]. There was virtually no agricultural research available on Mozambican small-scale farming. And there was also no local tradition of self-organisation and co-operation in most rural areas because of the repressive colonial administration.

As a result, the co-operatives had enormous difficulty with the organisational tasks implied by co-operative work: making decisions, registering work inputs, solving problems, distributing returns [*Habermeier,*

1981]. And these problems were sometimes compounded rather than eased in the early years by state intervention. The Ministry of Agriculture allocated only a small proportion of its staff to co-operative support; more important, those who worked with co-ops were often unable to provide what the farmers needed. They were slow to develop assistance with simple accounting and organisational problems; more seriously they were often unwilling or unable to listen closely enough to the farmers, or to help them to draw on their own experience to resolve their problems. And state organisational problems meant inputs were often late, spare parts and repairs unavailable, and payment for crops too long in coming, so debt and demoralisation were reinforced.

Helena Dolny documents the enormous creativity of the co-operative farmers in two areas where she worked, and then describes the problem of technical support as follows:

> One of the romantic notions that dies hard in every revolutionary movement is that getting people to produce collectively will, in itself, generate greater surpluses. What happened in Mozambique shows the opposite to be true: in those co-operatives where basic cultivation methods were the same as on the family farm, the productivity per hectare generally fell. Given existing levels of technology, the gains from a more complex division of labour are offset by the difficulties of initiating collective work [*Dolny, 1985: 238*].

On the other hand, settler technology, based on mechanisation, was too costly to be spread over the country, and was also inappropriate for combining with local small-scale farming: hence, the continuation through colonial times of coerced farm labour under varous guises [*Mackintosh, 1987: Habermeier, 1981*]. The settlers had also been directly subsidised, for strategic reasons, by the Portuguese administration; and without the subsidy, and with fragile technical back-up, it was hard to run the old settler farms at a profit. As a result, state support for the co-operative movement needed a great deal of technical assistance drawing on what is often called adaptive research, involving learning from the farmers and developing appropriate improvements which would help them draw on the advantages of collaboration; exactly the same type of research as is now being widely advocated as a response to the needs of small-scale African farming more generally.[13]

The other main set of problems for the co-operative farmers was marketing problems in the widest sense. The co-ops were sometimes treated in effect as adjuncts of the state farming sector. They were limited in their ability to respond to the market by planting the most profitable crops and, instead, given production plans which suited the government's crop purchase needs. They were more beholden than small-scale or, especially, larger private farmers to sell at official prices, a constraint which became more serious as a rural parallel market developed in a number of areas. As a result, they responded as if part of the state sector: by further running up debt.

Finally, some of the problems with developing a programme for agricultural transformation came from misconceptions by many about the nature of Mozambican peasant farming. The Mozambican agricultural system had been profoundly transformed in colonial times, from a locally-based system of farms, drawing on characteristically African patterns of mutual aid and shifting land use, to a system designed to provide the basis for a labour reserve. From peasant farming, labour was drawn for the South African mines, local estates and settler farms, and for forced cash crop cultivation, especially of cotton. As a result, the farming families came to depend on cash income for their survival, and in many areas, farming also came to depend on cash earned – especially in South Africa – for inputs to the farming cycle. This was especially true in the South, where the heavier soils needed plough cultivation. Conversely, estates and settler farms came to depend on cheap coerced labour [*Wuyts, 1978; O'Laughlin, 1981*].

Frelimo's accession to power broke the cycle of coerced labour, but it was bound to take many years to transform the system it had created. Large farms had to try to increase productivity so as to pay a living wage – and hence attract labour – while the peasant sector had to be developed to provide, also, a living through production and sale of a surplus. Meanwhile, South Africa was reducing its use of Mozambican miners. What was inadequately realised at first was the extent to which the small-scale sector needed material inputs and investment from outside it simply to keep going: it was perceived too often as a self-reliant 'subsistence' agriculture, which it is not.[14] And the scale of transformation required, for non-state farming to support its population, and the investment that would require, was very seriously underestimated. Hence, the imbalance of support between the sectors.

As shown above, far more of the rural population joined communal villages in the early years than ever worked on co-operative farms. In other words, the villages tended to develop independently of collective production, despite the original intentions, becoming rather centres of residence and collective consumption of services. Some were chiefly dormitory villages for state farm workers; many others contained large numbers of individual 'family' farmers continuing to cultivate their own plots.

Furthermore, as Dolny documents, when attempts were made to spread membership of co-operatives to whole villages, that could cause the co-operative organisation to break down, and its purposes to become confused. In practice co-operativisation in Mozambique was being promoted for two entirely separate purposes: first, in order to increase the productivity of agriculture; and second, to provide, through collective labour, a fund which would be expended on social rather than agricultural investment: a school, a clinic, a meeting hut, a health worker. These two aims, which could clearly conflict, were often not clearly distinguished, a fact which could lead to bitterness and division.

Although the data for an accurate calculation are unavailable, the implication of this discussion is that Mozambican co-operatives were the site of very little locally generated accumulation. Only a small proportion of central state resources were re-allocated to co-operatives, and relatively few of the investment resources acquired by co-operatives were backed by real financial surpluses achieved by the co-ops. Indeed, measured in market prices there was probably increasing surplus extraction by the state in the opposite direction, by holding down official prices.

This accumulation pattern interestingly contrasts with the pattern of investment in what we might call social production: that is, the production of social services. Health services are just as much an economic product – using material resources to produce a service which contributed sharply to the standard of living – as are agricultural goods. In the provision of health services, state investment funds and the material resources to back them appear to have been more effectively redistributed from centre to locality, and locally generated investment and funding seems to have been more effectively generated than in agriculture.

This process of decentralisation meant that in health planning and financing, in contrast to agriculture, resources for investment and service provision were shifted in relative, and at some points, in absolute terms, from large to small and from centre to periphery: from central city hospitals towards the provinces; from complex medical intervention to simpler procedures; from doctor's work to that of para-medical staff, and from curative to preventative care. Under the Portuguese, health service resources had been almost wholly concentrated in the cities where the settlers mainly lived [*Walt, 1983: 2*]. By contrast Frelimo before Independence, in the liberated areas of the north, had offered basic preventative care and first aid, and thereby had learned the value of what could be achieved by base-level health workers with minimal training.

Frelimo, furthermore, had learned another lesson: that health service provision was one of the most important ways in which people would judge the revolution Frelimo was seeking, and that involving people in health provision was an effective way of involving them in the development of their society. As the President later argued: 'The hospital is a state institution where Party policy touches the most sensitive points of the population: health, well being and life itself. It is often in the hospital that the people see reflected the organisation of our state' [*Machel, 1979a*]. The effect of this emphasis was that health provision was to become one of the most political areas of Mozambique's economy, one where great efforts were made to reform the internal structures of work and control, and to respond to, and even encourage public pressure on the system.[15]

Health services were nationalised in 1975, and re-organised by the Law on the Socialisation of Medicine in 1976. This made use of the health service virtually free at the point of use, and set out the principles of a referral system based on local health posts and health centres as people's primary contact with the system. An enormous training effort began, and a major political debate on the content of medical and para-medical teaching.[16]

There was from the start an emphasis on training para-medical personnel, and on opening health centres and health posts. The proportion of lower level medical personnel rose, and the proportion of the central health budget going to hospitals fell [*Barker, 1985: 335*]. The pre-liberation experience of base level health workers was developed, and a system was hastily set up whereby the lowest level of health workers, the *agentes polyvalentes elementares,* were to be chosen by the residents of communal villages. These health workers were to concentrate on preventative care and health education, and refer people to health centres as necessary. They were also to be financially supported by the villages – out of co-operative agricultural production to which they would also contribute – after training. Those chosen left the villages for a six-month training course; by 1984, 1,369 such village health workers had been trained [*Cliff et al., 1986: 16*].

These village health workers ran into many problems, and as early as 1980 the Health Ministry estimated the drop out rate at 15 per cent. A number of these problems were those of the communal villages themselves: a number were badly sited and unviable, and as discussed, co-operative production within them was problematic. As a result some health workers could not be financially supported. Also, many found it very difficult to get basic supplies, and discovered that they did not have the minimum curative knowledge to be truly useful to and respected by their communities [*Walt, 1983: 16–17; Barker, 1985: 335–7; Cliff et al., 1986: 16–17*]. Many too resented their dependence on local communities while primary school teachers and agricultural technicians were paid by the central state. And where there were no villages or fairly dense communities, health workers could not be chosen and supported.

On the other hand, many villages put considerable local resources into providing the physical infrastructure and financing their health worker. Like the agricultural co-operatives, the problems of the health workers were the subject of productive debate, and some communities evolved other ways of paying their health workers, some collecting contributions in cash or kind from each local household [*Walt, 1983: 17*].

Furthermore, the health workers provided a link with the discussions of health provision at the district level. (The district is the administrative unit below provincial levels.) The Health Ministry, more than perhaps any other Mozambican Ministry, evolved a pattern of increasing local participation in drawing up annual health spending plans [*Bell, 1983, 88–9*]. While still patchy and insufficient, this did sometimes reach down to district level and provide an input to provincial and national plans [*Barker, 1985: 342*]. Local participation in Mozambique faced, even before the war, huge barriers in the lack of transport and roads, one part of the constraints created by desperate poverty. Despite this, it was in the health sphere, especially in the early years, that local debate and collective investment, and the decentralisation of resources, were most effectively promoted. The health service adapted to people's needs – and encouraged people to define and express those needs – to a greater extent than was achieved in other areas of production. And as a result, it benefited most from an input of locally-generated resources.

All this added up to a partial pattern of genuine decentralisation. It has been destroyed in many areas and very seriously undermined in others because communal villages, health posts and all such collective facilities and their staff (notably including primary school teachers) have been targets for murder and destruction by the South African-backed MNR. The *principle* of health care provision on which this decentralisation is based has also been under attack, especially from aid donors: we return to this issue below.

Markets and the Peasant Economy

We have pointed out above the scale of the Mozambican peasantry's involvement in the cash economy from the colonial period, relying for survival on sale of their labour or in some areas on sale of their crops. The Mozambican peasantry, male and female, had in other words long been compulsorily involved in highly managed markets for their labour and their produce. These markets were not abolished – though they changed somewhat in character – after Independence, and the evolution of rural-based markets came by the early 1980s to pose a very serious set of problems to those seeking to promote co-operative production of goods and services in the Mozambican rural areas.

Mozambican economic planning never sought to abolish private trade, which was always regarded as playing a potentially useful role, especially in rural areas. The Third Congress Directives [*FRELIMO, 1977: 61–5*] emphasised the importance of recreating the trader networks abandoned and destroyed at Independence. The traders, however, were to be regulated through: price setting to control margins; state wholesaling to ensure fair distribution patterns; and monitoring of compliance, with the aim of ensuring that the benefits went to farmers and consumers, not chiefly to traders. A network of state shops was set up to supplement private trading, but these were abolished as inefficient in 1980; the consumer co-operative movement was to be promoted, as it was very effectively in the towns, but much less successfully in most rural areas.

It was thus private traders who were to be the chief intermediaries in buying cash crops from small farmers: a task crucial to Mozambique's capacity to earn foreign exchange and feed the towns. After 1977, the private market re-established itself, though patchily – it never covered the whole country effectively – and a state agricultural wholesaling company, later named Agricom, was established to re-purchase most cash crops from traders and resell to town rationing systems, town traders, and large institutions with a labour force to feed, or to state exporters. One or two of the non-food cash crops – such as cotton – had their own buying system in parallel.

After 1980, this rural marketing system gradually escaped from state monitoring and control as parallel markets for foods developed [*Mackintosh, 1986, 1987*]. Over time, and at very different speeds in different areas, parallel market prices and state-administered prices diverged. Goods produced by small farmers were increasingly sold on to parallel circuits (though not necessarily or even usually by the farmers themselves), while imports and state-produced goods continued to go largely through state channels at official prices. By 1985, a 'two-tier' economy [*Mackintosh, 1986: 564*] was operating, with townspeople and rural farmers alike trying to stay alive by balancing between the two. Worst of all, exchange even in the parallel circuits had broken down in many areas to be replaced with sporadic barter.

The sources of this parallel economy were many. One source was undoubtedly the inflation generated by the financing of the state sector. The pattern of state-centred accumulation traced above had serious internal costs, one of which was the inflationary financing of state enterprise deficits. The financial surplus traced above in the central state's recurrent budget did not reflect the financial position of the state sector as a whole, since this budget centralised actual state enterprise surpluses, but provided finance only for planned enterprise deficits [*Wuyts, 1986: 183–98*]. Unplanned state enterprise deficits were substantial and growing over time (reaching projected levels of 14 million *meticais* in the 1987 state budget), and were financed by credit from the nationalised banks. These unplanned subsidies were financed on demand through credit expansion. As a result, bank credit in the economy, mainly to the state sector, grew well ahead of the Global Social Product, the main measure of the material output of the economy.

TABLE 5

INTERNAL CREDIT AND GLOBAL SOCIAL PRODUCT
('000 MILLION METICAIS) CURRENT PRICES)

	1980	1981	1982	1983
Internal Credit	50	62	73	103
GSP	82	89	91	77

Source: CNP [1985].

The effect of this was to allow the state sector to suck real resources away from the rest of the economy: its command over local resources, already backed by the weight of the state's planning system, was reinforced by easy credit access; its attempts to reach over-optimistic output targets were backed up by priority access to foreign exchange; and the over-tight and over-expansionary planning of the state sector led to inefficiencies which further raised demand on national resources relative to output.

The impact of this financing pattern on rural markets was complex. The problem was not solely the uni-dimensional one of an imbalance between total state-emitted finance and state production of goods at official prices, although this was the way in which the Mozambican authorities initially tended to specify the problem. As the Governor of the Bank of Mozambique pointed out in 1983,[17] the value of money the state was spending on buying cash crops from the peasantry, plus the wage bill, greatly exceeded the value of the commodity supply to wage workers and peasant farmers. This was undoubtedly a problem, and was reinforced by the squeeze just described on the real investment and consumption goods available for rural circulation outside the state sector.

Other factors too were worsening the money-goods imbalance in the early 1980s. The rising financial resources met falling material resources after 1982, reduced by the rapidly growing impact of the war on rural production and the increasingly serious foreign exchange squeeze. A serious drought in the north in 1982 was rapidly followed by a disastrous southern drought. Rural hunger became serious and food speculation rife in the town, fuelling the parallel market.

But all this was reinforced by a problem of economic structure with its roots in the colonial period. This was the nature of the impact, or at times, lack of impact, of these financial resources in rural areas. The money fell in the rural areas into a situation where it could stimulate only very limited increases in local output through the development of intra-rural, extra-state private exchange.

There were two distinct problems.[18] In certain areas the financial resources fuelled a parallel market which benefited traders rather than farmers, and changed the pattern of effective accumulaton in rural areas away from that sought by the government. In others, more widespread over time, the value of cash collapsed completely; far from circulating in rural–rural exchange, it ceased to have exchange value, and farmers and others reverted to barter.

One root of these problems lay in the virtual absence in rural Mozambique of the networks of rural markets and small-scale intra-rural trade so common in other parts of Africa. Far from building up local trade, the Portuguese appear to have suppressed it in favour of a settler-run trading network, focused on extracting crop surpluses and run in settler interests. Artisanal industry was broken up or never allowed to develop. A local trading network which could circulate products of small-scale agricultural and non-agricultural production, and encourage the expansion of such 'small projects', could not be *re*created; it had to be created from scratch, as part of building up and reorganising rural peasant production. This fact was insufficiently realised.

As a result, policies in the early stages were not directed to rural market creation. The goods and information were not available to get local small scale production going, and local markets were not encouraged. Partly as a result, rural commercial policy unintentionally reproduced many of the features of the colonial rural trading structure, designed to create one-dimensional state–farmer exchanges. And financial thinking followed that same track.

This trading structure interacted with rising credit, with the effects of war, drought and a foreign exchange squeeze, and with the organisation of the control of trade, to reduce the power of the state to manage the economy. In the early 1980s, in areas still producing a large food surplus,[19] a parallel market was tending to develop whereby private traders paid farmers at the official price, while selling at higher prices; to some extent the traders' capacity to do that was enhanced by pricing policies which restricted Agricom's ability to compete with other wholesalers, and by a certain state disorganisation which allowed the traders to play state buyers off against each other to their own advantage. In these areas, traders were bringing in consumption goods to trade for agricultural products and were accumulating substantial financial resources in local currency.

These resources were going into private investment in the means of trade and production. Second-hand trucks and maize mills were changing hands at very inflated prices, and warehouses were being built and farm infrastructure set up for larger commercial farms. There was therefore a distinct pattern of private investment challenging the government priorities of co-operative and family farm. Private investment was increasingly the effective competitor with the large-scale state sector for investment resources, co-operatives and small farmers being squeezed from both sides.

Elsewhere, where the agricultural surpluses, especially of food, were not such as to attract such a pattern of trade, the market was breaking down almost completely. Goods were being sucked out of these areas to those just described. The state did not command enough resources, and control, to counter this. Worse, the lack of inputs to family farming, especially hoes and other small implements, and seeds, was threatening to become a binding constraint on production. Farmers stopped producing through lack of incentives in the form of goods to buy, and rural poverty became increasingly serious. Both farmers and the state reverted to barter: the state selling consumer goods only in exchange, at least in part, for agricultural goods; farmers bartering with other producers where they could.

One institution which suffered particularly seriously from both these opposed situations was the co-operatives. Where the parallel market was expanding at the expense of the state, the co-operatives could find themselves constrained to sell at lower prices than particularly the larger 'family' and commercial farmers round about. Frelimo's uncoerced co-operativisation could only be successful as a form of development of farming if the co-operatives were more successful than family farms in the medium term; as the years went by the market became at least as serious a constraint as organisational problems on their development.

In areas where the market had effectively broken down, there was a tendency for people to join production co-operatives particularly to gain access to the consumer co-operatives often attached to them. These co-operatives had some priority of access to valuable state-supplied goods, and therefore helped people to survive; but the weakened state distribution system – weakened by foreign exchange constraints and procurement problems – could not substitute for a thriving local market in providing consumption goods or crop purchase. The co-operative sector became solely an annex of the state sector in this context.

By 1983, when Frelimo's Fourth Congress debated very openly many of these problems, the causes of rural economic crisis had come to be dominated by impact of war and drought. But as the Fourth Congress discussions made clear, many of the underlying economic problems just outlined remained to be solved if the economy was to be re-organised to support the war effort.

At the most general level, many of the policy problems outlined in this section were rooted in a lack of clarity about the relation between market and plan. Planning the market had been seen too much in an administrative framework: laying down a set of rules for traders and policing outlaws. It had been insufficiently realised that the rules laid down gave incentives to market participants which were perverse in relation to government economic objectives and, therefore, almost guaranteed a parallel market development, whatever the financial structure. Such perverse incentives included uniform pricing which encouraged local flour milling, margins too small to allow small traders to survive on the volumes offered to them, and the allocation of monopoly buying areas to private traders, instead of forcing competition. The implication of this analysis was the need to move away from administrative regulation of the market – on a model of an already socialised system – towards a model of more effective market intervention to further the most important government policy aims.

Deregulation, Market Intervention and Decentralised Planning

It is towards a model of market intervention, in association with deregulation and decentralisation of some economic decisions, that the Mozambican government has moved since 1983. It has done this in the context of very strong pressure from foreign multilateral and bilateral agencies to move rapidly away from some established government policy aims, and under pressure from war and economic crisis they have been forced to balance their own internal aims against the external pressures.

In 1983, Frelimo's Fourth Congress, held against considerable odds because of the spread of the war, analysed the country's severe economic problems. The Central Committee's report to this Congress [*FRELIMO, 1983a*] maintained the overall priorities established by the Third Congress, but severely criticised the failures of support for small scale production, describing support for the peasantry as 'almost non-existent'. The market, the report said, must be supported and re-established, a formula which acknowledged the effective breakdown of the market in many rural areas. The Central Committee set out the priority of combatting hunger, the importance of the family sector to this, and the strategy of developing local initiative through decentralising economic planning. Private capital was to be encouraged, especially in import-substituting activities [*FRELIMO, 1983a: 63–8*]. The new Economic and Social Directives [*FRELIMO, 1983b*] stated that (official) prices should provide peasant farmers with reasonable incomes and encourage investment in small-scale enterprises.

Although the Fourth Congress challenged the over-emphasis on state-centred development as an incomplete process of transition, the documents of the Congress remained rather vague with respect to the specific tactics for a socialist strategy based on transforming peasant agriculture. It left room for various interpretations as to what constitutes a policy of aiding small-scale production and of allowing more room for manoeuvre for private enterprise. The depth of the economic crisis made the issue of recuperating production one of paramount importance, and the demand for deregulation in order to allow greater space for the unofficial economy became a powerful position within the economic policy discussions.

Hence, for some, the immediate policy necessity consisted of a tactical retreat from socialist transformation, by allowing production to recover under the impulse of private enterprise within the unofficial economy. In other words, the momentum inherent in the parallel economy as structured by the prior process of state-centred development would be allowed to continue and to gather strength. Opposed to this, however, was also the recognition that the imperatives of the war and of preserving the socialist character of development required the continued intervention of the state within the economy. Both of these themes have been evident in economic policy debates and initiatives since 1983.

Since the Fourth Congress, Mozambican economic policy has seen very substantial changes, along the lines sketched at the Fourth Congress. A number of these changes were crystallised in the Economic Recovery Programme (ERP) presented to the People's Assembly in January 1987 [*Machungo, 1987*]. The central ideas of the programme are the crucial importance of revalorising the metical, ('by making the metical a scarce resource we intend to give our currency value') and developing farm production for sale, including family-sector production. The main methods proposed are price reforms, credit restriction, and reform of state-sector management, including a wage structure allowing productivity bonuses.

In practice, the price reforms and associated partial market liberalisation have had the sharpest immediate impact. The metical has been cumulatively devalued, between January and July 1987, by close to 100 per cent. The prices of most food crops except basic grains had earlier been freed, and the producer and consumer prices of basic grains raised sharply. All other main consumer prices have also been raised.

Meanwhile, state-sector economic management has been reformed substantially. Decentralisation has given ministries more control over their operational budgets, and these have delegated more powers to state farm and enterprise managers, along with more clearly specified duties on accounting and profitability. Some economic decision-making has been decentralised to the provinces, including some price setting, and provincial governments given more influence on economic policy in support of the prosecution of the war. There has been much public discussion of the relation between the economy and defence: the Prime Minister argued, in presenting the ERP, that, 'No war is won just by soldiers on the battlefield, without production. Every country at war finds ways of combining war with production. We cannot separate one from another'.[20]

The effective direction in which these measures take the economy is still at issue, and will depend on the evolution of government thinking, on the continuing devastation caused by the war, and on the pressures from the donors on which Mozambique will continue to rely to support the import programme necessary for the recovery programme, and eventually to service the rescheduled debt.[21]

Not all donor organisations have clearly stated objectives which go well beyond supporting Mozambique in its present crisis of hunger and war. However, some such objectives do exist and pressure is being brought to bear on the Mozambican authorities to effect a basic change in economic and social development. J. Cliff *et al* quote one of USAID's principal stated objectives for aid in Mozambique as that of entering into policy dialogue so as to induce the earlier arrival of a market-based economy and a thriving private sector [*1986: 19*]. Furthermore, they point out that in doing so, USAID relies on and aims to support the leading role of the IMF and the World Bank in setting the tone and the pace of this dialogue [*1986*].

Through its present economic measures, the Mozambican government is seeking to re-establish both the functioning of the economy and its own power to make its economic policies effective. The government has therefore not seen economic liberalisation as an end in itself, but instead has sought to combine market liberalisation with some level of market intervention to ease the impact on standards of living [*Mackintosh, 1986*]. At the same time, it has sought to develop military defence of trade and economic activity, and to use state firms and installations as the basis for support of small-scale production and trade.[22]

The government's capacity to develop and sustain economic recovery will depend centrally on its success in combining military defence with economic rehabilitation. The economic impact of the war has been devastating, and now dominates all other factors in creating the current very severe economic crisis. In 1985 the government calculated that the war had cost the country 132,000 billion mt. (US$3.6 billion at the then rate of exchange) [*CNP, 1985: 96*]. Since then, the destruction has escalated, with virtually all the social and economic infrastructure destroyed in many parts of Zambezia, Mozambique's most populous, and once one of its most productive, provinces.[23] At least 4.5 million people have been threatened by famine.[24] In the 1987 state budget defence forms 35 per cent of recurrent expenditure, but 53 per cent of projected income.

The Mozambican government is therefore faced with difficult choices about how to plan its war economy. From some donors are coming sharp pressures to favour commercial farming and private including foreign investment; others are willing to provide support to the small-scale sector, but refuse to assist co-operatives.[25] The government is seeking ways to assist the small-scale sector effectively, and there are many variations being tried between a 'building on the best' strategy of channelling resources to the more successful, and strategies, including discussion of peasant associations, which seek to channel resources to a wider number of poorer farmers.

Given the pressures of the war, and the resultant impossibility of a full-scale market liberalisation, plus the government's own commitment to a broad-based development benefiting the mass of the population, the government seems like to pursue an economic management policy which is a mixture of selective liberalisation associated with local economic planning and intervention, including continuation of the rationing system and the planned distribution of state-owned goods; state procurement will continued to be essential to feed and support the armed forces and, therefore, a local integration of military and economic planning, including the protection of trade, will continue to be essential.

The government, furthermore, is faced with pressures and choices, not only in economic management, but also in social policies, including health policies. As argued above, health care policies pursued after Independence brought real gains to all Mozambicans – rural and urban – and as such are seen to be one of the major advances of the revolution. A major issue which confronts the Mozambican authorities today is how to preserve the basic objectives of its health policy in the face of escalating war and, also, and significantly so, under pressure of various aid donors – multilateral, governmental or non-governmental alike – to alter its priorities. This is no minor issue: rather, it deeply conditions the credibility of Frelimo and of its policies with the Mozambican people, since the question of health and health care always constituted a central political preoccupation in Mozambique.

The main issue at stake is not merely that of cuts in health expenditures. The escalating cost of maintaining the defence effort as well as the extent of the economic crisis inevitably meant that health expenditures in real terms were bound to fall [*Cliff et al., 1986: 21–2*]. Donor pressures to cut back further on social expenditures may worsen the situation, but the critical issue concerns the actual and potential conflicts over the use of ever scarcer resources allocated to health care. It is at this level that the real impact of the pressures from aid donors needs to be assessed [*Cliff et al., 1986*].

As the funding of health programmes becomes increasingly dependent on donor agencies, health care policies are under pressure to adapt to donor preferences and, hence, to neglect certain sectors which lack donor appeal. It is this trend which progressively erodes the system of central planning in health care, and which undermines the broad-based programmes of locating primary health care within local communities through a system of partially self-financed collective self-provisioning, aided by the state health care services. Two examples can be given of this progressive pressures to undermine official health care policies.

The first concerns drug policies. Post-independence drug policies in Mozambique have been an undoubted success [*Barker, 1985*]. The list of imported drugs was cut down to 300 essential drugs bought on a competitive basis from reputable dealers: as such, the proportion of the health budget spent on drugs was maintained within a range of 10–20 per cent regarded as ideal in international literature compared to 30–40 per cent for most Third World countries [*Cliff et al., 1986: 10*]. However, aid donors increasingly aimed to by-pass the state medicines importer, MEDIMOC, as well as failing to respect the national formulary of acceptable drugs [*Cliff et al: 10–14*]. These measures undermine the Ministry's central planning of health care as well as impose a greater burden on planners since they waste valuable time and effort in trying to convince aid donors to respect the established norms.

A further aspect of donors' interference with the national health policies with respect to pharmaceuticals appears to be the attempt to press for a stratification of the market, allowing essential drugs for the poor through a planned distribution system, but leaving the more affluent sector to be served by a private market [*Cliff et al., 1986: 19–20*].

The second example relates directly to the character of the organisational approach to health care, and particularly to its decentralisation towards local communities. In the Mozambican context, many aid agencies favour selective health care programmes such as those for Immunisation, Essential Drugs, Diarrhoel Disease Control and so on, each with their own separate funding and their own imposed structures [*Cliff et al., 1986: 18*]. Organisationally, the key decisions of such selective programmes are taken by a small central group, usually foreign experts linked with the aid agency [*Open University, 1985: 122*]. This approach, therefore, leaves little or no room for consultation with, or involvement of, the local people in villages and towns and, hence, it raises the question as to who should decide on the priorities of health care: local people, governments, experts or international agencies – each of which would have different opinions based on their particular interest [*Open University, 1985*]. In Mozambique, health policies were made nationally, but – as argued above – involved genuine pressure from below as a result of its integrated approach to health care and the decentralisation of such health care to local communities. The pressures from aid agencies effectively undermine this system, while in practice separate selective health care programmes *de facto* provide for little real integration of the overall effort. There is, therefore, a real danger that if such pressures were effective, health policies would effectively abandon the majority of the people to the *curandeiro* (traditional healer) and a few selective interventions [*Cliff et al., 1986: 22*].

In summary, the implicit thrust of the pressures of many aid agencies is towards the liberalisation of health care policies within the framework of a two-tier health system which cannot but reinforce existing class divisions, as well as aims to play on them. And the same choices between liberalisation and local-based planning re-appear in 'social' policy as in economic management.

II. LESSONS: DECENTRALISED PLANNING AND THE PROVISION OF SOCIAL SERVICES

Accumulation and the Character of Planning

The first section of this article has analysed the interaction within Mozambican planning of central control, local initiative and market activity. The story demonstrates the close inter-relationship between, on the one hand, the character of the planning process and, on the other, the crucial issue of the location of accumulation: in whose hands and to what effect investment effectively occurs. It was argued that in a variety of ways, the pattern of Mozambican planning practice had the effect of undermining the government's planning aims of a broad based development, through co-operativisation and popular initiative, to take place alongside the strengthening of a state sector of large-scale enterprise. The analysis by Frelimo of these conflicts, as a basis of the policy changes after 1983, has also been briefly discussed.

Our purpose in this section is not to draw lessons for Mozambique, but rather to discuss more generally the contradictions just identified, in the context of the broader literature on planning socialist transition. The key problem to which we address ourselves is the nature of the pattern of accumulation outside the state sector proper. In the case study of Mozambique it emerged that such accumulation, in co-operatives and other collective locally based forms, was crucial to rural development of the type sought by the government; it was however undermined by a number of economic processes which tended to squeeze it between state investment on the one hand, and unplanned private investment on the other. How accumulation in semi-autonomous, non-exploitative production units can be encouraged and supported through centrally-managed state planning is the central question this section addresses. This is particularly (but not exclusively) important in a society composed largely of peasant farmers; or of those making at least part of their living through this type of farming.

We address this question by means of a discussion of four inter-related issues. First, we argue that the appropriate relation between plan and market in transition depends crucially on the question of the location of accumulation. Second, we argue that the provision of social services should not be seen as merely wealth-consuming as against the wealth-creating aspect of productive accumulation. This is an unsatisfactory way of posing the opposition between accumulation and consumption, since locally-financed (or partly-financed) social services can constitute a vehicle for accumulation as well as for the provision of basic needs. In other words, the size and nature of the overall accumulation fund, as well as the content of development in terms of the convergence of production and needs, are not independent of the way in which control over resources and over accumulation is socially structured. Indeed, the organisation of social services through the interaction of local collective self-provisioning and central state services allows for the mobilisation of labour power behind such local initiatives which could not be accomplished or financed by the state sector alone.

Third, we argue that finding an appropriate balance between central direction and locally-based initiative and autonomy of action is not merely a question of administrative convenience (that is, of finding the best management system through balancing market and plan), but it also involves a political dimension which is important in its own right. The transition towards a socialist economy involves the progressive convergence of material production with (basic) needs. However, this raises the question as to who should decide on priorities for satisfying human needs – local people, central government, or experts – as each group would have different opinions based on their interests as well as on their perception and knowledge of immediate needs. Hence, planning cannot merely be a question of administering resource use in relation to pre-determined needs, but it also involves the complex process of defining priorities through political processes which in turn react upon the pattern of accumulation. This raises the issue of socialist democracy within the context of a process of transition based on a worker-peasant alliance, and the tensions which may arise from this, as interests may be compatible but are by no means identical.

Finally, we discuss the character of planning in relation to the production and use of information. Decentralised planning within the state apparatus as well as planning within socialised institutions outside the realm of the state sector involve the development of locally-based capabilities to plan (and by implication, to produce and effectively put to use the relevant information needed for such planning) as well as the need to organise the exchange of information.

The Plan-market Dichotomy and the Location of Accumulation

Any transitional economy must be a strongly *managed* economy in which the process of change is subject to direction from the centre. Without this the market will lead a reversion to investment on commercial criteria. Our central question is not what level of 'free' market forces should be allowed, but how markets can be managed so as to allow and even support accumulation in socialised institutions such as co-operatives.

The perception that accumulation within socialist relations of production is the key to socialist transition has a long pedigree in socialist thought. Preobrazhensky famously argued for a concept of primitive socialist accumulation which meant 'the accumulation in the hands of the state of material resources mainly or partly from sources lying outside the complex of the state economy' [*1926 1965: 84*]. Hence, for Preobrazhensky the location of socialist accumulation was set firmly within the confines of the state sector (or state economy as Preobrazhensky referred to it), and the key issue was the ability of the state to alienate 'a certain part of the surplus product of the private economy in all its forms' [*(1926) 1965: 110*].

This conception posed a straightforward opposition between market and state economy. Preobrazhensky stressed the importance of unifying the operation of the state sector, in order to use its strength to create a 'gradual contraction of the field in which "free competition" goes on between the state and private economy' [*(1926) 1965: 128, 130*]. This state strength was created by a fusion of political and economic power. Monopoly control of key sectors of trade, economies of scale, price controls and taxation were all vehicles of the 'power of the proletarian state over the surplus product of private economy' [*(1926) 1965: 130*].

The political implication of this view is that the peasantry is seen to be located outside the realm of the socialist economy (identified with the state economy). In the short run its essential role boils down to that of financing the accumulation of the state economy, while progressively the growth of the state economy will absorb the peasantry within it. In terms of social transformation the role of the peasantry is seen to be rather passive, although it plays a crucial role in determining the rate at which the socialist economy can expand.

Most subsequent discussion of socialist economic strategy has contained as one theme the importance of unifying and extending state economic and political power, and this has implied the importance of state direction of accumulation. Such measures in socialist states as nationalisation of external trade have been designed to reinforce state control of investment through control of physical investment goods. While Cuba continued to focus its economic strategy on accumulation within the state sector [*Meso Lago, 1981*], in most Third World socialist countries, discussion of economic strategy has incorporated an emphasis on a more decentralised pattern of accumulation, within institutions which are not strictly part of the central state structure: either co-operatives or communes. The best-known examples include China, with its development of an explicit theory of labour accumulation within the communes, and its aim of turning the terms of trade in favour of agriculture in order to encourage accumulation at the commune level before 1978 [*Nickum, 1980*]. In Vietnam, likewise, where agriculture is organised chiefly on a co-operative basis, the question of encouraging co-operative accumulation has been an important one in the planning debates [*White, 1983: 251*].

This emphasis in political debates on economic strategy does not imply that these policies can be realised without tensions. Saith [*1985a*] argued that the need for surplus extraction from the rural economy often ran counter to the task of initiating a broadly-based process of rural development through institutional reforms which create socialised institutions located outside the realm of the state sector. This tension – he argued – was specifically noticeable within the context of the Chinese experience where the attempt at propelling rural development based on the interaction of local self-provisioning and state production had been pushed furthest.

The same preoccupation reappears in a different form in Mozambique and Nicaragua: predominantly peasant countries where socialist strategy was not based on forced collectivisation. Here, the discussion of the means and purpose of co-operative development was closely related to the issue of food production and procurement. These countries, where much food production continues to be undertaken within a peasant farm sector, face the problem of maintaining the production of food, and stabilising the exchange relations with the peasant sector, during a prolonged period of transition. In Nicaragua, as in Mozambique, the government has several times re-formulated its policies in an effort to shift more real resources, including investment resources, into the peasant sector [*Kaimovitch, 1988*]. However, the key political issue in this respect is whether such shift in resource allocation is understood as a tactical necessity in order to enlist the support of the peasantry both at the level of the economy and of defence, or whether it forms part of a strategic policy aimed at propelling the transformation of the peasant sector through institutional reform [*Kaimovitch, 1988*].

We are therefore analysing a crucial and an acknowledged problem, but one which has become submerged in the more theoretical literature by the debates on markets *versus* planning. In Ethiopia and Nicaragua as in Mozambique, planning practice was characterised by a tendency for state centred accumulation to become dominant, although with different intensity and in different contexts [*Ghose, 1985; Wuyts, 1985; FitzGerald, 1985*]. In each country a parallel economy has tended to develop, bringing problems for economic planning and control.

It is our thesis that such problems emerge in full seriousness, not from the fact of planning as such, but from the drift to planned accumulation chiefly within the state sector. The Mozambican experience suggests that attempts to plan in such a way as to centralise the investible surplus of the economy in the hands of the state, and to concentrate the whole accumulation effort on the state sector, run into some characteristic problems. The basic assumption that the official economy, organised through state planning and regulation in the manner set forth by Preobrazhensky, can effectively direct the movement of the wider economy and succeed in transferring the surplus of the private economy, is highly problematic. In actual fact, the state's capacity to direct the wider economy tends to be eroded by the development of a parallel economy in competition with the official economy. Furthermore, the productivity of state accumulation itself is thereby undermined, since the state ceases to be able to purchase labour, raw materials and food from the non-state sector. The parallel market blocks the development of the state sector itself: here is the dynamic which has historically sometimes led (but not in Mozambique or Nicaragua) to proposals for forced collectivisation [*Dobb, 1966: 208–29*].

We have shown for the case of Mozambique that the attempt on the part of the state to centralise the investible surplus of the economy both helped to create the parallel economy and, by locking the peasantry into that parallel economy, undermined any attempt to create a broader process of transformation involving socialised institutions outside the realm of the state sector. This same pattern also emerges in other countries [*FitzGerald, 1984; Saith, 1985b*]. This history casts serious doubt on the desirability as well as the feasibility of a concept of transition which – in its dominant aspect – is based on some form of primitive accumulation, whether this in practice runs with or against the grain of the government's expressed intentions.

It follows from this that a socialist government in a largely peasant economy should not attempt to monopolise the investment surplus. Part of the investible surplus of the country is required to sustain and to fuel the transformation of the peasant economy. But this implies in turn the need to ensure that it is indeed to co-operatives, rather than to commercial farmers, that the investment resources go. Lenin put the issue forcefully during the phase of the New Economic Policy: 'A social system emerges only if it has the material backing of a definite class . . . At present we have to realise that the co-operative system is the social system we must now give more than ordinary assistance, and we must actually give that assistance' [*(1923) 1977: 683–4*].

To achieve this aim requires, not less planning but different forms of planning. It is the aim of socialised but non-state accumulation which will determine the structures of planning at different levels of the economy and the role of markets and market intervention within the economy and the planning process.

What are the main characteristics of such a planning process? These would have to follow from the problems to be resolved, and here we sketch some of the central issues. First, since socialist transformation and accumulation would not be confined to the state economy, it follows that the state would be only in part directly responsible for the organisation of production and accumulation within socialised (or better, socialising) institutions. Although the state must assume the task of central direction and co-ordination of the overall process of transition, it has to operate through a variety of indirect mechanisms in order to guide, stimulate and channel the development of non-state socialised accumulation. Some of these indirect mechanisms are political – a point to which we return – while others involve operating through credit and goods markets. A number of pointers to what is involved emerge from the Mozambican example.

It is unlikely that parallel markets can ever be abolished in a transitional situation. By definition, the aim of transition is to produce a future economic structure different to that which the market would create. In such situations which aim to bring about the convergence of demand with (basic) needs the purchasing power of some is to be suppressed in the interests of others [*Griffin and James, 1981: 12–23*]. One aim of both the design of overall economic strategy, and of the local market intervention is, therefore, not to abolish but to control the scope of these markets, and in particular to restrict their capacity to channel private investment. As the Mozambican Prime Minister put it, 'the fight against the illegal market must be waged principally by economic means' [*Machungo, 1987: 4*].

The Mozambican and other experiences suggest that planning with this aim in view implies at least the following. State deficits need to be kept under control, and the availability of *both* finance and material investment goods needs to be ensured for the peasant and co-operative sectors. Market intervention should be aimed, again in the words of Prime Minister Machungo, at avoiding 'the continued accumulation of excess profit in commerce to the detriment of production' [*Machungo, 1987: 3*]. This implies pricing policies adapted to encourage local small scale trade while supporting state purchasing for longer distance wholesaling. Co-operatives in particular should not be restricted from competing and selling at favourable prices; the promotion of co-operative trading as well as production helps to channel goods away from larger scale private hands.[26]

Local goods markets can and should continue to be important in rural areas, even as the participants in the market become increasingly co-operative institutions. There is a great deal that can be done by state institutions operating in local markets to squeeze large traders and favour co-operatives, if co-ordinated marketing can be achieved. Local markets stimulate and provide incentives for investment in small-scale and co-operative production: but the state will need to ensure that the producers' goods necessary for such investment can be obtained.

Second, this need to operate through indirect mechanisms implies a considerable degree of decentralisation of planning within the state sector itself. A process of transition which is in part based on mobilising locally-based initiative and organisational capacities and, hence, which requires a certain degree of autonomy of action on the part of local socialist institutions, necessitates responsiveness and adaptability of the state sector to local needs and conditions. Hence, it would be a specific task of the local state apparatus and the locally-based state sector to be able to plan and organise its interventions at the level of the regional economy.

One level where such local adaptability is required is for the type of market intervention just described. Another is in the area of technical assistance to co-operatives. The Mozambican case study discussed some of the problems of such assistance, which were far from unique to Mozambique: a failure to learn from co-ops and a tendency to give inappropriate instructions; a tendency to inhibit creativity; and a failure to impart skills; in addition to insufficient material support. The effect was to cut off the co-ops from their links to 'family' agriculture and tie them too closely to the state sector, which meant that they could not become successful poles of development for a wider co-operative movement. Locally-based, adaptable support is necessary, though not sufficient condition for overcoming these problems.

Investment finance too needs to be locally-based to be useful. With reference to the Chinese communes, Malima [*1974*] analysed the role of the rural-based branches of the Peoples' Bank of China in providing assistance to agricultural production. Two aspects of his analysis are useful for our discussion. A basic principle of credit provision was that, within an overall objective of self-reliance at the local level,

> credit must be directed at critical links, implying also that it should be used to solve critical bottlenecks. This does not mean that minor requirements should automatically be ignored, but rather to emphasize the need to concentrate loans in a manner which would bring about the greatest impact. What constitutes a critical bottleneck may, of course, vary from one area of a country to another. It is, therefore, essential to assess the objective conditions obtaining in each area in order to determine the critical bottleneck [*Malima, 1974: 26–7*].

The local level branch therefore commanded a fair degree of flexibility in order to be able to respond to local conditions, although this flexibility was constrained by the overall availability of material resources and the specific allocations through central directives. In addition the bank cadres were responsible for 'helping the Peoples' commune to run its affairs efficiently' [*Malima, 1974: 31*] and to this effect organised training in accountancy.

While such decentralisation provides the possibility of state responsiveness to local needs, it does not guarantee it. A responsive local state – this is our third point – requires that the peasantry effectively *demand* material resources and technical assistance from the state sector. This implies not only an effective and developing capacity to plan on the part of the peasantry organised in co-operatives, peasants associations, etc., but also that they can exert political pressure to support their demands. Hence, as we shall argue in more detail below, planning cannot be merely an issue of administering resources in this context, but involves political processes concerning control over resources and making choices about their use.

Finally, under conditions of decentralised planning and of localised (partial) control over accumulation, the *redistributive* role of the central state would have to become more prominent. Decentralised control over accumulation may enhance regional inequalities (as well as intra-regional differences between richer and poorer co-operatives and communes) as a result of a more favourable resource base, or favourable location, as well as better access to state support or interaction with state sector investments. The correction of such inequalities would need positive intervention by the state sector at different levels.

Through its taxation and subsidy policies the central state can attempt to even out such inequalities. For example, 'an important and consistent feature of the Chinese budgetary system has been the much smaller share of revenues retained by rich, industrialised provinces than by poor, backward ones' [*IBRD, 1983, Vol. I: 50*]. In fact, while high-income municipalities such as Shanghai, Beijing and Tianhin retained 11 per cent, 37 per cent and 31 per cent of their revenue, low-income provinces not only retained all their revenues, but also received subsidies from central government [*IBRD, 1983, Vol. 1: 50–51*].

However, there is a limit to which inequalities can be corrected through the mechanism of taxation and subsidies since the latter system presupposes sharp differences in the income earning capacities of different regions. In this respect, spreading the pattern of state investment more evenly among regions may constitute a more powerful redistributive force as it affects the income earning capacity of various regions itself. Saith convincingly argued that the preoccupation with state-centred accumulation may easily lead the central state to pursue an investment pattern which aims to maximise the marketed surplus from agriculture, and thereby favours the better-endowed regions over more backward areas [*Saith, 1985a: 33*].

The need to respond to localised forms of socialist accumulation outside the realm of the state sector may well exert pressure on state investment itself to spread its linkage effects more evenly within the wider economy. However, it must be recognised that such processes remain problematic as is clearly shown in the Chinese experience where regional inequalities were in part accentuated by the investment strategy of the state sector [*Wu, Chung-Tong, 1987*].

At the more micro-level, the specific credit policies pursued by state-owned banks *vis-à-vis* co-operatives and collectives may enhance or even out the tendency to accentuating income differentials. The use of straight financial profitability criteria as advocated, for example, in recent reforms in Vietnam [*Spoor, 1986*] may well entail the danger of building on the best. In contrast, in the discussions concerning the implementation of a new agricultural credit policy in Mozambique, a study group set up by the People's Development Bank put forward a proposal that loans advanced to producer co-operatives should charge a social dividend on the income resulting from the investment rather than a fixed interest rate on capital [*BPD, 1978*]. The latter proposal which involved the principle of 'pay as you earn' in advancing loans was not implemented in practice. At the more superficial level, the main arguments against its implementation were the difficulty of assessing the income of co-operatives and the widespread deficit situation of such co-operatives. *De facto,* these reasons demonstrate the extent to which co-operatives had become an appendix of the state sector.

Health Services as a Vehicle of Transformation

In Nicaragua, not unlike in Mozambique, health centres displayed the slogan 'Revolution is Health' to indicate the centrality of the health of the nation within the revolutionary process [*Bossert, 1984: 213*]. This slogan expresses the fact that, 'it is health rather than survival – both physical and mental health – which is the most basic human need and the one which it is in the interests of individuals to satisfy before any others' [*Doyal and Gough, 1986: 69*]. Within the context of a socialist transition which aims to achieve the convergence between material production and basic human needs, health therefore is bound to be an eminently political issue. The question is thus not merely that investment in people may enhance overall productivity: a position which is typical of human capital theory which sees investment in people as a cost to be balanced against greater returns in terms of profitability. Rather, health is seen to constitute an end in itself.

The social production of formal health care occupies a central – though not exclusive – position with respect to health and illness in society and is profoundly marked by the class character of society [*Doyal, 1979*]. Not surprisingly, within the context of revolutionary change, the question of restructuring health care in accordance with basic needs of the mass of producers becomes an immediate issue. In this section we discuss the critical question of the financing of formal health care and its interlinkage with the specific forms of organisation of the provision of such health care. This also raises the question of the relationship of planning social services to the planning of other spheres of material production.

One prominent view on financing health care in particular (and social services in general) in the context of a transition to socialism argues that wealth must be created before it can be spent on health (and education or other social provisions) and, hence, that the radical transformation of health services cannot be an immediate objective of socialist transition. Any attempt to effect such early transformation under popular pressures may end up jeopardising the revolutionary process itself by stunting the capacity for economic growth and development. This view has been put forward by Seers: 'in the first place, commitments to wage increases, heavy investments in social infrastructure, etc., help a party to gain power, but they greatly complicate its life once it has succeeded. The experience documented here shows that big gains of this type *cannot* be made in the early years of socialist governments' [*1981*]. Hence, the need for a prudent financial policy at the early stages of transition, and this also involves limited expenditures on social services. The basic premises is that any transformation of such services will need to wait till the consolidation and expansion of production provides the necessary finance for it.

Preobrazhensky's view, while different in kind, also combined a recognition of the pressures for *immediate* transformation with an argument for the need for restraint in the early phases of transition:

> From the moment of its victory the working class is transformed from being merely the object of exploitation into being also the subject of it. It cannot have the same attitude to its own labour power, health, work and conditions as the capitalist has. This constitutes a definite barrier to the tempo of socialist accumulation . . . The first, quite obvious difference between the state economy of the proletariat and the typical capitalist economy is the fact . . . in relation to the worker it [= the state economy] begins (but only begins, up to now) to act as a system of production for consumption by the producers [*1926, 1965: 122*].

This conception puts forwards the immediate need to start the process of convergence of production with basic needs in the early stages of the transition, a process which can of course only take place within the constraints of existing production and of the need for accumulation. However, Preobrazhensky saw this process taking place only within the state economy, so that the role of a broader process of change involving the production and financing of transformed social services outside the realm of the state economy was not considered.

The Mozambican approach to health provision outlined above did not restrict health financing to redistribution from central state funds, nor did it restrict its conception of health provision, and pressure for better health, to the provision of curative services. Mozambican health planning did succeed in shifting resources away from curative, hospital-centred medicine, towards preventative and basic curative services, and did make a very considerable effort to integrate public health and nutrition with health services from the start.

In doing this, Mozambique's health services tried to break out of the trap so often described in the Third World, whereby medical services reproduce the pattern of medical provision which is hospital-centred, highly technological and dispensed on a individual curative basis. Such curative policy – although it may have extremely beneficial short term consequences for the individual patient – 'cannot reduce the high incidence of disease, nor raise the general level of health' [*Doyal, 1979: 256*]. Lesley Doyal goes on to point out that in Third World countries the pattern of allocation of resources in health care is extremely maldistributed and denies access to the vast majority of people even to those curative services which would be of value to them. But most important is the problem that, 'in the Third World, curative medicine has become a *substitute* for public health and as a result is inevitably much less effective' [*1979: 256*].

To shift away from this perspective involves two aspects. It involves first a shift in the way central government health budgets are spent. Segal, in his discussion of health care in Tanzania, argues that given the very limited resources, 'a socialist health plan would use this limited amount of money for the maximum benefit of the mass of the population'.

> Like all poor countries, Tanzania suffers from a great deal of disease. Though the economic reality is limiting, it does not mean the country must remain in this state indefinitely: this is because most diseases are preventable. Prevention (with basic curative services) can improve the health of the mass of the people within the tight health budget. It is cheap: it can be effective. It alone can break the vicious circle of disease – treatment – recurrent disease [*1972: 149–50*].

Such a shift in spending pattern alone will not be sufficient, however. There has also to be a sharp change in the organisation of the social production of the new care. In this respect, Walt and Wield point out that an important difference between preventive health care and curative medicine is that the former requires the mobilisation of whole communities to be effective, while the latter normally treats individuals [*1983: 22*]. In other words, preventative care has to be eminently *social* in character (hence, the term 'public health'). This implies that within the context of a society where the peasantry constitutes a significant, if not predominant, share of the population (as well as of its poorest component), health care organisation will need to involve the mobilisation of the peasantry.

Health policy, therefore, to be effective, must draw on and interact with community organisation. Such organisation can help integrate the planning of health care with actions in other 'spheres' such as nutrition, housing, sanitation, etc., which have direct implications for 'economic' planning. Also, it can create the kind of democratic pressures on health service planners which help to create a convergence between production and basic human needs. If it is the case that there is a close connection between the social production of health and illness and the social production of health care, as has been argued for the capitalist West and much of the Third World [*Doyal, 1979*], then both wider production patterns, and health care provision, need to change together if *health* is to become more clearly the aim of all types of production.

This point that the transformation of health care can only be situated within a wider context of change is particularly important:

> For example, the recognition that wider forms of development were important to the promotion of health stemmed in part from experiences of places such as Kerala State in the South-West tip of India. Since its formation in 1956, Kerala has pursued policies of income redistribution through reform of the land tenure system, employment security, free

education at primary level, and some redistribution of health resources away from urban areas. Despite the relative poverty of Kerala compared with some other Indian states (such as Punjab and Maharashtra), by 1981 the people of Kerala had higher literacy rates than any other state, life expectancy at birth was 63.8 years compared to 52 years for all India. And yet during the period the per capita expenditure on formal health services was less than average for all India [*Open University, 1985: 125*].

In constrast, Wolffers argued that the attempt to introduce barefoot doctors in Bangladesh and in Indonesia without any accompanying change in the social and economic context of the rural communities proves to be either ineffective, or else, vehemently opposed by local political structures [*1981: 181–231*]. In fact, a country's health care system will be moulded by the wider social and political structure, rather than the other way around [*Open University, 1985: 125*]. But, in turn, each revolutionary process will need to find concrete ways to integrate health care into the wider process of transformation.

A partially local process of funding health care – of the type attempted in Mozambique – can help promote these aims. The process of mobilising local resources implies the creation of a social surplus and, at the same time, an organised local interest in how that fund is spent. As a result, local funding can have three highly desirable inter-related results. It can add to the total funds available for health care, by mobilising resources which might not otherwise be created, and certainly not created in the form of a fund for social use. Second, the process of mobilising the funds can create a local capacity to control and direct funds, at least partly to benefit the majority. And third, if the creation of the local fund is undertaken through co-operative production, such activity can provide experience in co-operative organisation and create an incentive to socialised production for social use. It is also likely to be socialised production which involves a wider social range of people than may be drawn to scattered co-operatives.

Other Third World countries have also shifted the financing of social production in part to the local level. For example, in China where this specific policy of localised financing of health and education had been carried out to a considerable extent through the development of communes, it has been estimated that 'about 60 per cent of the cost of education is borne by the budget, about 30 per cent collectively, and about 10 per cent privately. The corresponding figures for the cost of health care, apart from medicine, are similar. But the cost of medicine is close to two-thirds of the total, and a substantial portion of this is born privately' [*IBRD, 1983: 66*].

The planning of health care has been in some countries more effectively 'social' than the planning of other forms of production. A consideration of the role of health care in planning transition therefore offers a number of lessons to economic planners. The achievements of health care planners challenge the simple dichotomies between 'social' and 'economic', production and consumption, so beloved for economic planners. The socialising of health planning at the local level challenges these dichotomies by linking the level of production to the level of consumption (if social organisation, and 'labour accumulation' increase local resource creation), and by linking the type of production to the type of consumption (if the organisation of consumption of public health creates at the same time pressure for more appropriate provision).

As a result, socialised activity in 'social' production – which is, in fact, just as 'economic' an activity as agriculture – can help to provide counter-weights to the emergence of an economic strategy which effectively seeks to extract the greatest marketed and investible surpluses from the peasant economy, without due consideration of the impact of such policies on the structure of rural livelihood and on its exchange entitlement. It can create a focus for mobilisation and productive organisation outside the state sector proper, hence providing both pressure on, and valuable lessons for, those concerned with planning other areas of production. It provides a pattern and process of non-state socialised provision, supported but not wholly controlled from above, which can lead the transition to socialisation and adaptation to local needs of more traditional 'economic' activity.

Politics, Planning and Information

The last two sections have both stressed the inseparability of politics and economics in planning transition. They have both been concerned to demonstrate that the rethinking of economic planning strategies involves a change in the political, as well as in the administrative, processes of planning. It is becoming clear – and not only in the Third World[27] – that if production is to provide for need in a pattern different from that which would be expressed through the market, then democratic social involvement in both production and consumption is the only way to achieve this. Local control plays an important role in this, but clearly it is the specific forms of local political organisation which matter, as well as their relation to the overall political process which shapes central direction and planning.

It is not our intention to argue that developing this type of planning is easy and unproblematic, but rather that it is essential if a strategy of socialist development is attempted which aims to effect a broadly-based process of transformation. This is particularly the case if it aims to do so by institutional reforms which locate part of the control over accumulation within newly-emerging socialist institutions outside the realm of the state sector. The implication of such strategy may be a hard one to swallow for the central state as it involves a partial loss of (direct) control over planning, and a shift towards a more interactive pattern, whereby local resource use and consumption decisions are taken and influenced by a wider range of bodies, from co-operatives and peasant associations to various local committees. It also involves leaving a space for markets to function effectively, especially for consumption of goods locally produced on a small scale or by co-operatives.

To effect such change in a planning system involves political struggles in as much as it is influenced by class forces as well as by vested interests of specific groups such as experts in various fields and planners. It is the purpose of this section to briefly pinpoint some of these arenas for struggle which inevitably emerge within a context of reshaping planning.

At the level of the state economy as well as of state planning various forces are at play which militate strongly against the decentralisation of control over accumulation to institutions located outside the state sector proper. These are not merely to do with narrowly-perceived vested interests based on power or prestige, but also relate to fundamental aspects of any process of transition: the character of the organisation of production and consumption in society.

The state sector proper normally emerges out of the nationalisation of the major means of production left behind by the previous regime. As is well known, the mere nationalisation of enterprises (and other institutions) does not necessarily alter the character of the social form of production and exchange. In fact, in the immediate aftermath of revolutionary take-over the issue of preserving productive forces is often seen to be of paramount importance since it is critical to the survival of the revolutionary process itself. Within such a context there is an obvious tension between continuing production within pre-existing moulds and effecting a radical change in the organisation of production.

For example – as argued in Part I – in the experience of Mozambique the state farm sector arose from the nationalisation of settler farms abandoned by their owners after independence. Technical expertise as well as material resources were concentrated on this sector in accordance with the minister's directives to preserve the patrimonium inherited from the colonial economy. However, one specific aspect of this inheritance was the dependence of the profitability of large-scale agriculture on the supply of seasonal labour power by the peasantry. Restructuring state farm production, therefore, would be needed to be done hand in hand with the reorganisation of family agriculture.

However, the state farm sector was planned in an enclosed fashion, and implicitly assumed an unlimited supply of cheap labour power from the peasantry. In principle the formation of communal villages was to be based on the development of collective forms of production – co-operatives and state farms – and hence, communal villages were to be actively involved in the planning of the development of such new forms of production. However, as the case of the transformation of the Limpopo valley clearly showed, the expansion of the state farm sector became centrally planned from the ministry downwards with little or no direct involvement of local structures. In practice, communal villages therefore became reduced in conception to constituting labour reserves for the state farms. Sharp conflicts developed between the state sector and the peasantry in terms of competition for irrigated land [*CEA, 1979b; Hermele, 1986*].

In other words, local politics therefore became divorced from planning the transformation of rural production, and the state farm pursued a policy of recruitment and mechanisation divorced from local needs. The state farms became dominant in terms of landholdings and of production, but this did not significantly alter employment patterns and the conditions of livelihood in the region [*CEA, 1979 b; Hermele, 1986*]. The emphasis on preserving and expanding production forces under state property became the overriding objective which failed to transform patterns of labour use of the colonial economy. A process of change based on more local involvement in the politics of production would still have had difficulty in transforming colonial patterns of exploitation rooted in the organic linkage between labour use of commercial farms and the peasant economy. But such involvement might have given rise to a different process of change, beginning from this crucial interlinkage, and proceeding with a more balanced land use pattern (as between state farms, co-operatives and family farms), lower rates of mechanisation, and the development of more stable patterns of employment in the state sector.

This example raises a related issue. The question of preserving productive forces is often put forward as an issue of maintaining standards in the production and provision of goods and sevices; and this question of standards is often couched in terms of sound technical advice. For example, medical doctors may constitute a strong lobby behind an investment policy centred on curative care in well-equipped hospitals, on the grounds that health care in the new society should at least equal, as well as surpass, the pre-existing levels of care. Similarly, economic planners may argue for accelerating the pace of modernisation of the economy by concentrating investments on big industrial and agro-industrial complexes, on the grounds that these are objectively the most advanced productive forces. This gap between technological precon-ceptions and economic and social aims arises because experts are trained within a given set of social relations which define expertise within a definite social context.

Hence, in Mozambique the shift in emphasis from hospital centred curative care to preventive medicine, combined with a broader infrastructure of basic curative care administered by intermediate health workers, met with considerable opposition from part of the medical profession on grounds that it entailed a significant lowering of the quality of health care. The attempts to introduce courses in public health met with equally strong opposition from many medical doctors and students alike [*Hanlon, 1984: 67–9*]. Similarly, in the training of economists at the university the emphasis was squarely put on preparing managers for state enterprises and surprisingly little attention was paid to analysing the character of the wider economy and the conditions for its transformation. Experts trained in this way will tend to seek solutions strictly within the parameters set by the state sector and its planning framework, and have little feel for the relationships between the state sector and the wider economy.

The question of the democratisation and decentralisation of expertise is therefore of critical importance in any process of transition which attempts to locate part of the control over accumulation in socialised institutions outside the state sector proper. This is particularly important with respect to the expertise involved in the process of planning, which requires the development of the capacity to produce and use information relevant to such planning.

The capacity to operate a simple accounting system is of obvious importance for the development of a local capacity to plan and control production. In Mozambique, colonial domination had left the peasantry largely illiterate and, therefore, after Independence, the peasantry was dependent on state provision of such skills as basic literacy, arithmetic and accounting. There was a successfully broadly-based adult literacy campaign, but the capacity to carry out simple record-keeping for planning purposes within co-operatives was much less successfully developed [*Dolny, 1985*].

There was a debate within the Ministry of Agriculture over this critical issue, with one group insisting on the preservation of good standards in record-keeping. This group favoured the use of double-entry book-keeping carried out by trained technicians located at the district level. The opposing view argued that the state effort should concentrate on imparting minimal skills of elementary book-keeping methods within the scope of members of the co-operatives. The issue, which was repeatedly posed in terms of maintaining high standards of technical expertise, also implied different positions with respect to the location of control over accumulation and planning.

The development of a local capacity to plan an effective decentralised control over planning also implies a change in the flow of information between central state, local state and co-operatives or collectives. Information control and access has to reflect the process of interaction in planning rather than a simple flow of planning data from local level to the centre.

An interesting example of this is given in the case of health planning in China:

> In 1971, for example, when we were told that there were no data on the number of pre-school-age children in China we indicated our scepticism and our belief that such data had to be available in order to plan the production of sufficient doses of immunisation materials. Our hosts responded that such production was based not on reports of the number of children but on the requests for materials from each individual unit. The requests for supplies were aggregated, not the data on population or illness, a concomitant of the decentralised planning and implementation of health services of the period. In other words, we were told that if planning is done locally there is no need for the aggregation of the raw data on which planning is based [*Sidel and Sidel, 1982: 90*].

The essential point is not merely that of administrative convenience through decentralising the planning effort, but the fact that, by developing a local capacity to plan, there develops along with in an understanding of and capacity to fight for local basic needs.

To give a further example, the training of village health workers in Mozambique initially concentrated on imparting skills of preventive care. At the local level, however, many of these workers encountered real difficulties as they could not meet the demand from local people for basic curative care. The result was that, in some instances, people lost confidence in their health workers, with obvious negative implications for the effectiveness of preventative measures. Also, the local community was often unwilling to finance a health worker who could not administer some curative care, and this jeopardised the attempt to decentralise the financing of health care towards the local communities. Subsequently, in order to meet aspirations at the local level the health ministry resolved to provide greater curative skills in the training of health workers [*Barker, 1985: 336*].

We have argued above that the state does not constitute a homogeneous entity and that struggles over the character of planning – as well as over its organisation – reflect as well as act upon differences of interests with respect to economic and social development. In the case of Mozambique, as well as in

Nicaragua, it can be argued that the shift in emphasis towards channelling resources to the peasantry did not mainly originate from within the economic apparatus of the state sector, but was strongly propelled by the military need to enlist the support of the peasantry against externally-backed counter-revolutionary aggression.

In a similar way local institutions do not constitute homogeneous entities but rather reflect struggles over control of material resources within a differentiated peasantry. Hence, a policy which aims to shift resources to the peasantry needs to come to terms with the class character of the peasantry and aim to channel such resources to the broad base of the poorer and middle peasantry. Hence, therefore, political struggle at the local level must embrace not merely the development of socialised production, but also its linkages with the satisfaction of local basic needs and the role of collective self-provisioning therein. The isolated producer co-operative which merely produces a monetary income to be divided among its members is a less potent force for propelling social change than the development of forms of collective self-insurance (health, education, food security, etc.) which require local collective forms of production, as well as taxation for its financing. The latter is more likely to lead to a process where production decisions are linked with the provision of basic needs, while the former may remain at the level of an isolated commercial undertaking which merely benefits its direct members. It is indeed not unusual that co-operatives constitute a vehicle for the richer peasantry to enlarge its access to material resources [*Harris, 1980*]. In this respect, a planning system of which the central objective, in its economic relations with the peasantry, is to increase the marketed surplus may come to constitute an effective blockage to the socialisation of production within the rural economy.

NOTES

1. The authors of this article both worked at the Centre for African Studies, Eduardo Mondlane University, Maputo, Mozambique. During our work there we both learned an enormous amount from our colleagues in the Centre and elsewhere. We are particularly aware how much our ideas are influenced by Ruth First and Aquino de Bragança, Research Director and Director of the Centre, who have both since been killed in the South Africa-backed war which has wreaked such destruction in the country; also by Bridget O'Laughlin and by many of the students who studied at the Centre. None of these people, nor the many other colleagues and friends with whom we worked and who influenced us, have any responsibility for the views we put forward here.
2. This is a marked tendency in the publications of the World Bank [*IBRD, 1981, 1986*]; it is also present in work by much more open-minded academic commentators (see, for example, Evans *et al,* [*1985*] where the market as a relatively undifferentiated phenomenon is counterposed very sharply to the state as the arena of planning. These elisions have tended to drown out those who have argued that there are a variety of possible outcomes, in terms of economic system, from a wider use of markets within a partly or largely socialised system. For another reflection along the latter lines, see White [*1987*].
3. Many Third World socialists, including some in Mozambique, are understandably reluctant to develop detailed economic critiques which can then be turned against them in this manner. This is one of the costs of the current ideological polarisation in the economics profession and in international politics.
4. For example, Zafiris [*1982*].

5. This disclaimer includes those whom we cite in the text which follows, who might not agree with the interpretation we put upon their words.

6. For the sake of this argument we are defining socialist relations of production as production in state or co-operative forms, as opposed to production through private capital and wage labour for private capital owners. We are therefore analysing the process of transition from private *and* peasant relations of production (whose form we discuss only briefly) to state or co-operative production. We are not unaware of the range of definitional and political issues thereby swept under the carpet, in order to keep this article to manageable length; to the crucial issue of democratic involvement we address ourselves in the second section.

7. The best accessible discussions of the impact of the war are offered by Hanlon, [*1984, 1986*].

8. In 1978 the South African government ceased paying part of Mozambican miners' wages as deferred payments in gold at an artificially low fixed price; this colonial arrangement had allowed the Portuguese colonial government in Mozambique to draw the profit from the resale of gold, and until 1977 had provided the biggest single source of foreign exchange to the independent government. It did not appear fully in the balance of payments figures [*First, 1983: 220; Wuyts, 1986: 149*].

9. A second major source of colonial foreign exchange was the payments for transit through Mozambican ports and railways of trade from and to both South Africa and what was then Rhodesia.

10. In 1977, Frelimo estimated illiteracy in Portuguese at 85 per cent in the population above 15 years of age, and this was after two years of literacy campaigns had provided some basic literacy to perhaps half a million people [*Marshall, 1985: 188*].

11. The destruction includes 500 health posts (Speech by the Prime Minister, M. Machungo, reported in Mozambique Information Bulletin February 1987), large numbers of schools, and much of the state farm and communal village infrastructure.

12. Harris, [*1980*] discusses the variation in class origin of those joining co-operatives. See also CEA, [*1979a*] for varying problems of different types of co-operatives.

13. See, for example, the arguments of Richards [*1985*].

14. Saul [*1985: 109*] speaks for example of Mozambican farmers who 'simply retreat' to subsistence agriculture, a retreat which was not in fact possible, given the dependence on outside inputs to keep the agricultural cycle going.

15. An example of this, not further explored here, was the effort to democratise the services and work practices of the Maputo Central Hospital, and problems this brought; see Williams [*1983*].

16. There are good accounts of this debate in English: see Barker [*1985*]; Walt and Wield [*1983*]; Walt and Melamed [*1983*]; Cliff *et al.* [*1986*].

17. Speech of the Governor of the Bank of Mozambique to the Eleventh Session of the Popular Assembly, quoted in *Noticias* (Maputo daily newspaper) 25.3.83.

18. This discussion draws heavily on Mackintosh [*1986, 1987*], and on unpublished consultancy reports by the same author, while working at the Centre for African Studies, for the Mozambican Internal Commerce Ministry, and later for the Swedish International Development Agency. Neither of the institutions commissioning the consultancy work is responsible for our interpretation of the resultant research results in this article.

19. This statement is based particularly on research done in Alto Molocué, an area of fertile land for maize growing, where the farming has since been very seriously damaged by the war.

20. Quoted in *Noticias* (Maputo daily newspaper) 16.2.87.

21. The Mozambican Foreign Minister announced in December 1986 that the foreign debt had reached US$3,000m, mainly consisting of government debt (Mozambican Information Agency (AIM) Bulletin, December 1986).

22. This statement is based on interviews undertaken in 1985.

23. See *Tempo* (Mozambican weekly magazine) 2.8.87 for a brief account of the destruction in Zambezia.

24. Speech by Mozambican President Chissano, on the occasion of an official visit to London, May 1987.

25. USAID, for example, will provide assistance only to the commercial farming sector; the Nordic agencies has expressed doubts about co-operatives, and a very strong preference for financing individual peasant farming (see the Nordic position paper presented to the 1984 SADCC Conference, Lusaka).

26. Some of these arguments are elaborated in more detail in Mackintosh [*1985*].

27. In Europe too, political debate on the failures of state-provided social services to respond to need have led to proposals for more democratic involvement and decentralisation as methods to counter this problem. For two different critiques of the failure, see Le Grand [*1982*], LEWRG [*1979*]; for arguments for democratic involvement, see Mackintosh and Wainwright [*1987*].

REFERENCES

Mozambican Government Sources
Banco Popular de Desenvolvimento (BPD), 1978, 'Relatório sobre a situãçao actual do desenvolvimento agrária e propostas de alteração à politíca de crédito', Maputo.
Comissao Nacional do Plano (CNP), 1985, Direcção Nacional de Estatística, *Informação Estatística 1975–1984*, Maputo.
FRELIMO, 1977, *Directivas Económicas e Sociais*, Maputo.
FRELIMO, 1982, *A Situação Actual em Nosso Pais*, Maputo.
FRELIMO, 1983a, *Relatório do Comité Central ao IV Congresso*, Colecçao 4o Congresso, Maputo.
FRELIMO, 1983b, *Directivas Económicas e Sociais*, Colecção 4o Congresso, Maputo.
Machel, S. 1979a, 'Reforcemos o Poder Popular nos nossas hospitais', Colecçao Palavras de Ordem, FRELIMO, Maputo.
Machel, S. 1979b, 'Façamos de 1980–90 a década da vitória sobre o subdesenvolvimento', Colecção Palavras de Ordem, FRELIMO, Maputo.
Machungo, M. 1987 'The Economic Recovery Programme', Extract from the presentation by the Prime Minister to the People's Assembly, Supplement to *Mozambique News*, No.127, Agência de Informação de Moçambique, Maputo.

Other Sources
Barker, C. 1985, 'Bringing Health Care to the People', in Saul (ed.) [*1985*].
Bell, D., 1983, 'Close-up on rural Health Care', in Walt and Melamed (eds.) [*1983*].
Bossert, T. 1984, 'Health policy making in a revolutionary context: Nicaragua 1979–81', in N. Black D. Boswell, A. Gray, S. Murphy, J. Popay (eds.), *Health and Disease: A Reader*, Milton Keynes: Open University Press.
Centro de Estudos Africanos (CEA), 1979a, 'Sumário preparado à pedido da Direcção Nacional de Habitação para ser utilizado na preparação prévia do Seminário sobre Aldeias Communais de 1979–1980', Maputo.
Centro de Estudos Africanos (CEA), 1979b, 'Problemas de Transformação Rural na Província de Gaza: Um Estudo Sobre a Articulação entre Aldeias Communais Selecionadas, co-operatives agricolas e a Unidade de Produção do Baixo Limpopo', Maputo.
Cliff J. Kanji, N. and M. Muller, 1986, 'Mozambique Health Holding the Line', *Review of African Political Economy*, No. 36, pp.7–23.
Dobb, M. 1966, *Soviet Economic Development since 1917*, London: Routledge & Kegan Paul.
Dolny, H. 1985, 'The Challenge of Agriculture', in Saul (ed.) [*1985*].
Doyal, L. 1979, *The Political Economy of Health*, London: Pluto Press.
Doyal, L. and I. Gough, 1986 'Human Needs and Strategies for Social change', in Ekins (ed.) [*1986: 69–80*].
Ekins, P., 1986, (ed.) *The Living Economy*, London: Routledge & Kegan Paul.
Evans, P. Rueschemeyer, D. and Stephens, E. 1985 *States versus Markets in the World System*, Beverley Hills, CA: Sage.
First, R. 1983, *Black Gold: The Mozambican Miner, Proletarian and Peasant*, Brighton, Sussex: Harvester.
FitzGerald, E.V.K., 1984, 'Problems in Financing a Revolution: the case of Nicaragua', *ISS Working Papers*, Sub-series on Money Finance and Development No.14, Institute of Social Studies, The Hague.
Fitzgerald, E.V.K., 1985, 'Agrarian reform as a model of accumulation: the case of Nicaragua since 1979', *Journal of Development Studies*, Vol.22, No.1, pp.208–26.
Ghose, A.K., 1985, 'Transforming Feudal Agriculture: Agrarian Change in Ethiopia since 1974', *Journal of Development Studies* Vol.22, No.1, pp.127–49.

Griffin, K. and J. James, 1981, *The Transition to Egalitarian Development*, London: Macmillan.
Griffith-Jones, S., 1981, *The Role of Finance in the Transition to Socialism*, London: Frances Pinter.
Habermeier, K. 1981, 'Algodão: dos concentrações à produção colectiva', *Estudos Moçambicanos*, No.2, pp.37–58.
Hanlon, J., 1984, *Mozambique: The Revolution under Fire*, London: Zed Books.
Hanlon, J., 1986, *Beggar Your Neighbours: Apartheid Power in Southern Africa*, CIIR and J. Currey, London: Indiana University Press.
Harris, L., 1980 'Agricultural Co-operatives and Development Policy in Mozambique', *Journal of Peasant Studies*, Vol.7, No.3.
Hermele, K., 1986, *Contemporary Land Struggles on the Limpopo: A Case Study of Chokwe, Mozambique 1950–85*, AKUT (34), Upsala.
IBRD, 1981, *Accelerated Development in Sub-Saharan Africa*, Washington, DC.
IBRD, 1983, *China, Socialist Economic Development*, Vol.I, Washington, DC.
IBRD, 1986, *World Develoment Report*, Washington, DC.
Kaimovitch, D., 1988, 'Nicaragua's Experiences with Agricultural Planning: From State-Centred Accumulation to the Strategic Alliance with the Peasantry', *Journal of Development Studies*, this volume.
Le Grand, J., 1982 *The Strategy of Equality* Allen & Unwin, London:
Lenin, V.I. [*1923*] 1977, 'On co-operation', *Selected Works*, pp.682–7, Moscow: Progress Publishers.
London-Edinburgh Weekend Return Group (LEWRG), 1979, *In and Against the State*, London.
Mackintosh, M., 1985, 'Economic Tactics: Commercial Policy and the Socialisation of African Agriculture', *World Development* Vol.13, No.1, pp.77–96.
Mackintosh, M., 1986, 'Economic Policy Context and Adjustment Options in Mozambique', *Development and Change*, Vol.17, pp.557–81.
Mackintosh, M., 1987, 'Agricultural Marketing and Socialist Accumulation: A Case Study of Maize Marketing in Mozambique', *Journal of Peasant Studies*, Vol.14, No.2, pp.243–267.
Mackintosh, M. and H. Wainwright, 1987, *A Taste of Power: The Politics of Local Economics*, London: Verso.
Malima, K., 1974, 'Some notes on China', Institute of Finance Management, Dar es Salaam, mimeo.
Marshall, J., 1985, 'Making Education Revolutionary' in Saul (ed.), [*1985*].
Meso Lago, C., 1981, *The Economy of Socialist Cuba*, Albuquerque: University of New Mexico Press.
Munslow, B., 1983, *Mozambique: The Revolution and its Origins*, London: Longman.
Nickum, J. 1980, 'Labour Accumulation in Rural China and its Role since the Cultural Revolution', in *Cambridge Journal of Economics*, Vol.2, No.3, pp.273–86.
O'Laughlin, B., 1981, 'A Questao Agrária em Moçambique', *Estudos Moçambicanos* No.3, pp.9–32, Maputo.
Open University, U205 Course Team, 1985, *Caring for Health: History and Diversity*, Milton Keynes: Open University Press.
Preobrazhensky, E. [*1926*] 1965, 'The New Economics', Oxford: Clarendon Press.
Richards, P., 1985, *Indigenous Agricultural Revolution*, London: Hutchinson Education.
Rweyemamu, J.F., Loxley, J. Wicken, J. and G. Nyirabu, *Towards Socialist Planning*, Dar es Salaam: Tanzania Publishing House.
Saith, A., 1985a, 'Primitive Accumulation', Agrarian Reform and Socialist Transitions: An Argument', *Journal of Development Studies*, Vol.22, No.1, pp.1–48.
Saith, A., 1986b, 'The Distributional Dimensions of Revolutionary Transition: Ethiopia', *Journal of Development Studies*, Vol.22, No.1, pp.150–79.
Saul, J. (ed.) 1985, *A Difficult Road: The Transition to Socialism in Mozambique* New York: Monthly Review Press.
Seers, D., 1981, 'Preface' in Griffith-Jones [*1981*].
Segal, M., 1972, 'The Politics of Health in Tanzania', in Rweyemamu *et al.* (eds.) [*149*–65].
Sidel, R. and V. Sidel, 1982, *The Health of China: Current Conflicts in Medical and Human Services for One Billion People*, London: Zed Press.
Spoor, M., 1986, 'State Finance in the Socialist Republic of Vietnam: 1976–1985', *ISS Working Paper*, Sub-series on Money, Finance and Development, No.15, The Hague.
Walt, G., 1983, 'The Evolution of Health Policy', in Walt and Melamed (eds.) [*1983*].

Walt, G. and A. Melamed, 1983, (eds.), *Mozambique: Towards a People's Health Service,* London: Zed Books.

Walt, G., and D. Wield, 1983, *Health Policies in Mozambique,* Third World Studies course material, Open University, Milton Keynes.

White, C. 1983, 'Recent Debates in Vietnamese Development Policy', in White *et al.* (eds.) [*1983*].

White, G., 1987, 'Political Aspects of Rural Economic Reform in China' *IDS Bulletin,* Vol.18, No.3, pp.55–61.

White G., Murray, R. and C. White, 1983, *Revolutionary Socialist Development in the Third World,* Brighton, Sussex: Wheatsheaf.

Williams, R. 1983, 'The Ebb and Flow of Democratisation', in Walt and Melamed (eds.) [*1983*].

Wolffers, I. 1981, 'Masker van de Armoede: Gezondheidzorg in de Derde Wereld', Amboboeken/Baarn.

Wu, Chung-Tong, 1987, 'Chinese Socialism and Uneven Development', in D. Forbes, and N. Thrift, (eds.), *The Socialist Third World: Urban Development and Territorial Planning,* Oxford: Blackwell.

Wuyts, M. 1978, *Camponeses e economia rural em Moçambique,* Instituto Nacional do Livro e Disco, Maputo.

Wuyts, M.E., 1985, 'Money, Planning and Rural Transformation in Mozambique', *Journal of Development Studies,* Vol.22, No.1, pp.180–207.

Wuyts, M.E., 1986, 'Money and Planning for Socialist Transition, the Mozambican Experience', Ph.D. Thesis, Open University, Milton Keynes.

Zafiris, N. 1982, 'Pragmatic Socialism in the People's Republic of Mozambique', P. Wiles (ed.), *The Communist Third World,* London: Croom Helm, 1982.

State and Market in China's Labour Reforms

by Gordon White*

This article sets out to look at how China's labour reforms have been conceived and implemented, and to assess their impact on the urban industrial economy. Labour reform is an area of particular political sensitivity because it engages deep ideological issues relating to the character of socialism, so the political dimensions of labour policy are particularly important in the Chinese case.

Over the past eight years, China's economic reformers have sought to create a more flexible system of labour allocation which will improve labour productivity and increase the flexibility and dynamism of the state sector and the urban-industrial economy as a whole. This reform process has several aspects, of which two are particularly important: (i) at the macro (national) and meso (local) levels, it involves measures to dismantle the previous system of direct state administrative controls over urban labour allocation; and (ii) at the micro level, changes in the status of workers in state enterprises which weaken the previous practice of *de facto* job tenure, encourage employees to move between enterprises and give personnel managers greater power to recruit, discipline and dismiss their workers. Taken in tandem with reforms in the wage system, these reforms are moving in the direction of a more flexible process of labour circulation characteristic of a 'labour market'.

This article sets out to analyse how these reforms have been conceived and implemented and to assess their impact on China's urban industrial economy. I approach the problem not as an economist but with a focus on the political dimensions of labour policy. Labour reform is an area of particular political sensitivity since it engages deep ideological issues rooted in Marxist definitions of 'socialist' and 'capitalist' modes of production. It may pose a challenge to the traditional socialist political commitment to full employment and job security which seeks to rescue workers from the vicissitudes of capitalist labour markets. It raises fundamental questions about the role of labour in a socialist economy. After all, the tepid term 'labour' in reality refers to the urban working class which, in theory at least, is the political rock on which Chinese socialism is founded, in whose interests the Chinese Communist Party claims to exercise state power and who are referred to in the official ideology as 'masters' of Chinese industry. The reforms embody changes in the socio-economic position of Chinese industrial workers and in the relationship between them and their managerial superiors. As such, they involve a redistribution of power and resources which disturbs established interests and generates political opposition and conflict

It is important to clarify the scope of this inquiry at the outset. First, it

*Institute of Development Studies, University of Sussex.

provides a general analysis of the two main arenas of labour policy identified above. I have dealt with specific issues in more detail elsewhere, notably the move to diversify institutional channels of labour allocation through the spread of 'labour service companies' and labour exchanges operating outside the formal network of state labour bureaux, and the attempt to change methods of job-assignment for graduates of higher education [*White, 1987a*]. Second, I focus primarily on industrial labour in the state sector which has been the primary target of labour reform in the post-Mao period. Tables 1 and 2 provide some basic data for 1984 on the relative position of the state sector in general and state industry in particular. As we can see from Table 1, though the state sector only has a small proportion of industrial enterprises (19.2 per cent), it produces the lion's share of GVIO, owns the vast bulk of industrial fixed assets and provides most of the fiscal revenue from the industrial sector.

TABLE 1

CHARACTERISTICS OF INDUSTRIAL ENTERPRISES, 1984

	Total	Of which small	State-owned	Collective	Of which township and town	Other
Number of industrial enterprises						
(thousands)	437.2	430.8	84.1	352.1	217.2	1
		(98.5%)	(19.2%)	(80.6%)	(49.7%)	(0.2%)
Gross industrial output value						
(billion RMB)	703	387.7	517.1	175.8	53.9	10.1
		(55.1%)	(73.6%)	(25%)	(7.7%)	(1.4%)
Fixed assets[1]						
(billion RMB)	588.9	-	517	71.9	28.1	-
			(87.8%)	(12.2%)	(4.8%)	
Profits						
(billion RMB)	84.4	-	70.6	13.8	4.7	-
(as a proportion of total state and collective)						
			(83.6%)	(16.4%)	(5.6%)	
Taxes paid						
(billion RMB)	53	-	44.7	8.3	2.6	
(as a proportion of total state and collective)						
			(84.3%)	(15.7%)	(4.9%)	
Profits and taxes per 100 RMB of original value of fixed assets						
(RMB)	-	-	22.3	30.7	26.1	

Note: [1]Statistics for fixed assets, profits and taxes are only for independent accounting units.

Source: State Statistical Bureau, 1985.

While the state workforce as a whole (including industry and non-industry) is a small proportion of the total workforce (18.1 per cent), it constitutes 70 per cent of the urban workforce (omitting the fourth column in Table 2 from the calculation). The state sector has higher average wage-levels than the collective sector and a lower proportion of female workers.

However, these statistics should be viewed with caution since an unspecified number of 'collective' enterprises (the so-called 'big collectives') have been converted into *de facto* state enterprises and thus belong more properly to the state sector.

TABLE 2

WORKFORCE BY OWNERSHIP SECTOR, 1984

State units	Collective units in cities and towns	Individual workers in cities and towns	Collective and individual workers in rural areas	Joint units	TOTAL
Total workforce (millions)					
86.37	32.16	3.39	353.68	.37	475.97
Total workforce (row percentages)					
18.1%	6.8%	0.7%	74.3%	.08%	100.00
Of which, industrial workforce (millions)					
35.92	16.41	.38	10.34	.33	63.38
Industrial workforce (as a proportion of sectoral workforce)					
41.6%	51%	11.2%	2.9%	89.2%	-
Industrial workforce (as a proportion of total industrial workforce)					
56.7%	25.9%	0.6%	16.3%	0.5%	-
Female workforce(as a proportion of total sectoral industrial workforce)					
33.3%	55.4%	-	-	49.5%	-
Average annual wage (RMB)					
1034	811	-	-	1048	974
Average industrial wage (RMB)					
1071	804	-	-	1007	-

Source: State Statistical Bureau [1985].

Third, the paper does not deal with wage reform, largely because Chinese policy-makers have as yet kept this separate from the issue of introducing a labour market. The main emphasis in wage policy has been on devising methods to link workers' remuneration more directly with the differential productivity of their enterprises; the role of the wage as an allocative device within a functioning labour market has as yet received very little attention (for a critical Chinese view of this separation, see Han [*1986*]. Last, issues of labour reform should be situated within the broader context of China's employment situation and the pressures on the authorities to reduce unemployment: a chronic urban labour surplus, the mounting problems of rural surplus labour, and rural-urban and inter-regional migration (for Chinese analyses of these issues, see Feng [*1982*]. Detailed discussion of these issues is beyond the scope of this article but salient information will be included where relevant.

I. THE PREVIOUS SYSTEM OF STATE LABOUR ALLOCATION AND ITS CONTEXT

On the eve of the reform era in the late 1970s, the Chinese system of labour allocation was highly *dirigiste* even by Soviet and Eastern European standards. The principle of 'unified allocation' which in the early years had originally been intended to apply only to certain strategic skilled groups (notably graduates of colleges and specialised middle schools), was gradually extended to include virtually all new members of the urban labour force [*White, 1982*]. As we can see from Table 3, in 1985 about eight million new workers entered the urban labour force. Although the proportion entering state employment has declined somewhat (from 72 per cent in 1978 to 61 per cent in 1985), state agencies are still responsible for finding jobs for a large majority of new urban workers, both in the state and part of the collective sector). The most significant change since 1978 has been the expansion of the private sector which, by 1985, was providing 13.6 per cent of new urban jobs and largely lies outside the framework of administrative labour allocation.

TABLE 3

PERSONS ENTERING EMPLOYMENT IN CITIES AND TOWNS
(in millions with figures rounded)

Item	1978	1979	1980	1981	1982	1983	1984	1985
TOTAL	5.44	9.03	9.0	8.2	6.65	6.28	7.22	8.14
1. Major Sources								
Labour force in cities and towns	2.75	6.89	6.23	5.34	4.08	4.07	4.5	5.02
Rural labour force	1.48	0.71	1.27	0.92	0.66	0.68	1.23	1.5
Graduates of tertiary education, secondary technical and workers' training schools	0.38	0.33	0.8	1.1	1.17	0.93	0.82	0.89
Others	0.83	1.1	0.7	0.86	0.74	0.6	0.67	0.73
2. Assignment								
State-owned units	3.92	5.68	5.72	5.21	4.1	3.74	4.16	4.99
Collective-owned units in cities and towns	1.52	3.18	2.78	2.67	2.22	1.71	1.97	2.04
Individual workers in cities and towns	-	0.17	0.5	0.32	0.33	0.84	1.09	1.11

Source: State Statistical Bureau [1986: 104].

Along with this system of administrative allocation evolved a *de facto* system of job tenure, not only for workers and staff in state enterprises but also in larger 'collective' enterprises which by the 1970s had become *de facto* state institutions. As of 1983, 96.8 per cent of the state workforce were 'fixed workers' with effective job tenure, the right to remain in their initial enterprise for life.[1] This status also gave them privileged access to certain welfare benefits provided by the enterprise itself, such as medical and labour insurance, housing, child-care facilities, pensions and guaranteed jobs for their children. In fact, state enterprises tended to turn into 'small societies' with mini 'welfare states'. In consequence, state workforces tended to be vary stable, with relatively high levels of overmanning (in Kornai's words [1980: 254] 'unemployment on the job') and relatively low levels of inter-enterprise, inter-sectoral or inter-regional mobility, and with seniority as an important criterion for remuneration and promotion within the firm. This is the system now referred to derogatorily by the economic reformers as the 'iron rice-bowl'.

These phenomena of immobility and overmanning can be traced to a number of basic factors. One factor has been the structural dualism of the urban economy, that is, the socio-economic gap between a relatively privileged state sector (including so-called 'big collectives') and the 'small collective' sector run by urban neighbourhoods, in terms of wages, welfare benefits, job security and social status (for these differences, see Lockett [1986]. This dualism meant that urbanites tried to get 'real jobs' in the state sector and, once there, had little incentive to move out into the 'small collective' sector.

Second, the CCP has been committed to achieving full employment and sensitive to the disruptive potential of urban unemployment. Official spokespeople point proudly to their record of bringing down urban unemployment over recent years. The official statistics are presented in Table 4 (the unemployed are referred to as 'job-waiters').

TABLE 4

URBAN UNEMPLOYMENT

Year	Persons awaiting jobs (millions)	Of which young people[1] (%)	'Job-waiting rate'[2] (%)
1952	3.77		13.2
1957	2.0		5.9
1978	5.3	47.0	5.3
1980	5.42	70.6	4.9
1981	4.4	78.0	3.8
1982	3.8	77.4	3.2
1983	2.71	81.8	2.3
1984	2.36	83.1	1.9
1985	2.39	82.6	1.8

Notes: [1]Between 16 and 25 years old, predominantly graduates of junior and senior middle schools.

[2]This is a ratio of 'job-waiters' to total urban labour force plus job waiters.

Source: State Statistical Bureau [1986: 104].

These statistics under-estimate the extent of the problem, however, since they only include those formally registered as job-seekers and do not include illegal or semi-legal rural immigrants whose numbers have swelled in recent years. This immigration reflects a growing problem of rural surplus labour. In 1982, this was estimated to be about 35 per cent of total rural labour or just over 117 million [*White, 1985: 3*]. In the previous system, this labour surplus was contained through the redistributive mechanisms of the collective system but the spread of household-based 'responsibility systems' in the 1980s has extruded labour from agriculture. Although it is planned to absorb most of the surplus through local diversification and industrialisation in villages and small towns in the countryside, it is also recognised that a certain amount will have to be admitted to the larger towns and cities, as Table 3 indicates. In terms of the total labour force, the World Bank [*1985: 127*] estimates that it will increase by about 180 million between 1981 and 2000, requiring about ten million additional jobs per annum. These pressures pose major headaches for urban labour authorities and will continue well into the next decade.

This 'surplus labour effect' reduces the motivation of workers to leave state jobs and reinforces the administrative controls imposed by a socialist government wishing to prevent unemployment.[2] In a context of heavy population pressure and a rapidly growing labour force, the Party has been pushed to honour its commitment to full employment and respond to the intermittently vocal pressures of urban populations. Thus the apparent success in reducing urban open unemployment indicated by Table 4 conceals the fact that much of this reduction was achieved by converting open unemployment into 'unemployment on the job' in both state and collective sectors.

II. THE REFORM CRITIQUE AND THE DEBATE OVER LABOUR REFORM

China's economic reformers have argued that economic growth in its current 'intensive' phase requires greater factor productivity. The previous labour system was a serious constraint on growth since it was too rigid and centralised, impeding the flexibility needed for a dynamic economy, reproducing unacceptably low levels of labour productivity and retarding technological development. This system should be changed, they argue, to increase labour mobility, give enterprises greater power over the disposition of labour and weaken the job tenure of state workers.[3]

Specifically, they argue that the span of direct state control over urban labour allocation was far too great to be accurate, resulting in misallocations and poor morale. The high degree of administrative centralisation, moreover, meant that economic actors themselves – enterprise managers and individual workers – were rendered inert. Although it was understandable for a socialist government to be sensitive to the need for employment, virtually exclusive concentration on this priority brought considerable direct costs in terms of under-utilisation of labour within enterprises and even greater opportunity costs in that state surplus labour could be employed more productively in the collective and private sectors, particularly in hitherto undeveloped sectors such as services and commerce (consistent with this position, they have sought to encourage the urban non-state and non-industrial sectors). Although a certain amount of frictional unemployment would result, this could be cushioned by state welfare provisions (a dole, retraining and assistance with relocation) and absorbed by a diversifying economic system. To the extent that greater labour flexibility increased productivity in state enterprises, moreover, overall demand for labour would increase. At the micro-level, a change in the job status of state employees from *de facto* tenure to contract would provide, reform economists argue, greater flexibility by allowing 'two choices' or 'two freedoms' (greater opportunity for workers to change jobs and greater discretion for enterprise mangers in handling labour) and would raise labour productivity by concentrating the worker's mind since his/her job performance would determine whether, or on what terms, the labour contract would be renewed.

Accordingly, since the watershed Third Plenum of the Chinese Communist Party's Eleventh Central Committee in late 1978 which ratified the new direction in economic policy, economic reformers have set out to reform the labour system in a number of ways. While the basic principle of state planning was to remain in place, state labour agencies were to play a more circumscribed and indirect role. They would still regulate the overall structure of the non-agricultural labour force, but would use direct administrative controls more sparingly; new labour allocation institutions would be set up outside the state sphere proper; enterprise managers would have more power to recruit and dismiss workers; workers would be encouraged to seek or create their own jobs; the 'iron rice-bowl' would be broken by employing state workers on renewable labour contracts. The end-product was to be greater labour circulation, in effect a regulated labour market.

This paradigm of labour reform has received support and reinforcement from foreign economists and agencies, most importantly the World Bank which sent an economic mission to China in early 1984 and published an exhaustive report on the current situation and future prospects of the Chinese economy in 1985 [*World Bank, 1985*]. The report in the main agreed with both the Chinese reform critique of the previous labour system and the measures proposed to remedy the situation. It also argued that the pace of change (as of 1984) had been too slow and should be accelerated. Specifically, this meant greater freedom for workers to move jobs and greater discretionary power for personnel managers, particularly the power to dismiss workers either for incompetence or in response to changing production needs and market demand. 'Allowing enterprises to release or reject redundant workers would on balance lead to fuller use of China's human potential, despite transitory unemployment' (p.133). In other words, the waste caused by frictional unemployment would be less than the waste caused by 'unemployment on the job'. Temporary unemployment could be eased by state provision and by an economy which was being restructured in ways which generated employment outside industry and the state sector. But the Bank was sensitive to the social and political dangers involved in such measures, noting that labour reforms 'should probably be approached cautiously and gradually' [*World Bank, 1985*]. The report thus echoed the rationale and favoured the practice of the Chinese reformers; it was, moreover, a highly professional and empirically well-based document – as such, it probably strengthened the hand of those Chinese who wanted to accelerate the pace of reform.

To what extent has reformist analysis of the problem and solution in labour policy been unchallenged? There has been a 'debate' on the issue from the late

1970s onwards but this has been limited in several aspects. First, it has not reflected the wide spectrum of opinions on the issue which clearly exists because the views of the disgraced radical Maoists ('followers of the Gang of Four') are excluded; second, while there remains a wide spectrum of views visible in the public arena – from those who only want marginal changes right across to radical reformers who lionise the virtues of a relatively unfettered labour market – the reformist side of the issue (usually in more moderate form) has dominated the debate. It has dominated quantitatively in terms of sheer volume of public material; it has also dominated intellectually by defining the terms of debate, thereby pushing sceptics or opponents on to the defensive, vulnerable to charges of 'conservatism', 'dogmatism' or 'negative thinking'. No well-articulated alternative position has emerged which recognises that problems exist in the labour system but offers a different diagnosis and solution. Partly this reflects the fact that the dominant section of the CCP leadership, led by Deng Xiaoping, has thrown its weight behind the reform analysis, converting it in effect into orthodoxy (dissenting views are thus marginalised, or relegated to the murky utterances of 'some comrades'); partly it reflects the (as yet) apparent absence of such an alternative.

Most participants in the debate recognise that there were problems in the previous labour system: rigidity, misallocation, waste of scarce skills, slack labour discipline, low levels of productivity. However, they vary in their evaluation of the seriousness of these problems, their weight relative to other policy issues and the kind of measures appropriate to solving them. Opponents or sceptics of the reform programme have laid heavy stress on *political and social issues.* They argue that the policy objectives of full employment, job stability and security are fundamental principles which distinguish a socialist from a non-socialist regime and that these commitments must be maintained even though there may be some costs in terms of micro-economic inefficiency. From this viewpoint, the goals of reducing unemployment and raising labour productivity are, in the short term at least, contradictory. This contradiction must be recognised and managed carefully, they argue, both because issues of principle are concerned and because there may be public discontent. The 'iron rice-bowl' thus tends to be seen less as a reflection of unproductive featherbedding or sectoral privilege and more an expression of a socialist concern for job security. The author of one rare public critique, printed in a Guangzhou newspaper, stated a wish 'to cry out for the "iron rice-bowl system" with a heavy heart' since 'many of our revolutionary comrades struggled all their lives so that the people of the whole country could each have an "iron rice-bowl"' [*Yi Duming, 1986*]. The author probably spoke for many, particularly state and party cadres and state industrial workers, when he argued that job security was part of 'the superiority of socialism' while attempts to undermine it, such as the labour contract system, were comparable to a capitalist 'wage labour' system.

Critics also warned that labour reforms would be politically divisive and socially harmful: for example, they could lead to invidious divisions between 'fixed' and 'contract' workers, or between the employed and the unemployed. Open unemployment would also lead to juvenile delinquency and a decline in moral standards.[4]

Critics have also been concerned about the effects of labour reform on the nature of the enterprise. One can detect three mutually reinforcing themes here. First, there is a 'neo-traditional' attitude which views the firm as a family, inspiring quasi-kinship relations of obligation, loyalty and solidarity. Changes which rupture this fabric may bring both social disorientation and economic damage [*Cheng, 1986*]. Second, there is a recognition that lifelong job security appears to have been a factor in the superlative performance of Japanese enterprises; if this was not incompatible with capitalism, why should it not be compatible with socialism? Third, there is a more directly socialist concern that a stable workforce is necessary to enable workers to exercise their rights within the enterprise, particularly in the context of any move towards worker self-management. In the view of one noted economist, for example, a comprehensive adoption of the labour contract system to counter the 'iron rice-bowl' would intensify an already significant shift of power within the enterprises in favour of managers, with the consequence that workers would become 'hired labourers' rather than 'masters' of the enterprise [*Jiang, 1985*].

Views of this kind do not usually signify total opposition to reform initiatives – they tend to lead to counsels of caution and sensitivity in the implementation of policy or to a watering down of the policy (for example, accepting a partial application of the labour contract system). But these critics do suggest that the productivity goals of the reformers can in fact be met by other means: by tightening labour discipline, introducing more effective wage and job responsibility systems, improved training facilities, purchase of more advanced technology, and better relations between managers and workers.[5]

The views of these critics often reflect inflexible attitudes or established interests, as we shall see later, but they do highlight problems in the reformist approach and cannot be dismissed as 'dogmatism' or special pleading. Reformers would do well to heed their warnings about the potential political repercussions of labour reform. Moreover, reform prescriptions do not as yet rest on sophisticated analyses of the internal social relations of enterprises and are therefore unable to answer questions about the extent to which the 'iron rice-bowl' may, along Japanese lines, be economically productive in certain contexts – the discipline of industrial sociology has yet to emerge in China. However, the economic arguments of the critics are less cogent, partly because they do not hang together, and partly because they do not appear to work very well, judging from attempts over the past eight years to strengthen managerial controls or design productivity-enhancing incentive schemes. The reform argument does have considerable force, that is, that such measures cannot be effective as long as workers have guaranteed employment *in a given firm,* nor can firms operate effectively in a market environment without greater managerial freedom to redeploy and if necessary prune their workforces. That this will create (hopefully temporary) unemployment is undeniable, but, from a political point of view, the key question is whether such movement towards a labour market can be squared with continuing socialist commitments and institutions. I shall address this question in the Conclusion of this article.

III. CLEARING THE IDEOLOGICAL GROUND

In the era of post-Mao reform, policy has led ideology by the nose, a process given official sanction in the Dengist slogan of 'practice as the sole criterion of truth'. To cite a recent example, the notion of 'the initial stage of socialism' which was given official blessing at the Thirteenth Party Congress in October-November 1987 was clearly arrived at inductively as a summary response to, and justification for, the policy changes of the reform era [*Zhao Ziyang, 1987*].

Likewise, since the reformist innovations in labour policy lead in a market direction, policy-makers sooner or later must confront the question of the ideological status of the notion of a 'market in labour power'. In the Marxian canon, acceptance of a market in labour power requires the recognition that labour power is a commodity; since this is a defining characteristic of a distinctively capitalist mode of production, it would appear to be incompatible with any notion of the role of labour in a socialist economy. The non-commodity nature of labour power has been a central tenet of Chinese Marxism-Leninism until the 1980s, a theoretical axiom which was compatible with, and provided a rationale for, the administrative system of state labour allocation. To the extent that existing ideology is a congealed rationale for previous practice, it poses problems for the reformers. In an 'ideocratic' polity of the Chinese state socialist kind, practical policies must be clothed in a suitable ideological raiment; radical changes in policy require changes in ideology which can provoke charges of 'revisionism' from opponents. In essence these debates reflect different conceptions of socialism – the traditional Marxist-Leninist view and a reform view of a society based on a 'socialist commodity economy'. The rarefied debate over 'labour power markets' reflects this basic divide.

The debate on this issue has proven contentious, both among the reformers and between them and their opponents, and mirrors the debates over policy. The reformers have been faced with the decision about how far to go in the process of theoretical revision: at the least some kind of cosmetic tinkering, through various kinds of fudging to an outright attempt to revise fundamental principles. As the reform process deepened and the reform leadership gained more political confidence in the mid-1980s, the ideological frontiers have been gradually pushed back and previously heretical ideas have received a public airing.

The range of views reflected in the public debate, conducted in both academic journals and mass circulation organs, has been surprisingly wide. Answers to the basic question 'Is labour power a commodity under socialist conditions?' have ranged from an unambiguous 'no' to an emphatic 'yes', with various shades of opinion in between. The debate has also included the issues of whether or not there can or should be unemployment under socialist conditions, and the political significance of the principles of job security and guaranteed employment as social rights.

The traditional ideological position, that labour power is not and cannot become a commodity under socialist conditions, appears to retain a lot of support among both analysts and policy personnel. We can take Hu Chen [*1986*] as one representative of this school. He argues that labour power is not a commodity under socialism for two basic reasons: first, 'public ownership is practised and the labourers jointly possess the means of production and are the masters of the means of production. We cannot say that labourers are selling labour power to themselves'; second, the worker's wage does not represent the value of his/her labour power but 'the value of income distributed according to his work':

> The content of the value of labour power is only the value of the means of subsistence needed by labour power for expanding production, but the content of the value of income distributed according to work is much wider. In addition to the value of the labourer's means of subsistence, it also includes the value of enjoying and developing such means as well as collective welfare, awards, bonuses and so on.

Hu Chen's position is distinctive in that he separates the questions of whether labour power is a commodity and whether a 'labour power market' can exist, affirming the latter and denying the former. Other analysts have preferred to avoid the term 'market in labour power', preferring less sensitive terms such as 'labour services market', 'job market', 'labour market' or 'labour resources market'.[6] This school, which denies that labour power is a commodity under socialist conditions, is conservative ideologically, in the sense that it does not wish to revise a fundamental principle. But ideological conservatism, the denial that labour power is a commodity or refusal to use the term 'labour market', does not necessarily betoken policy conservatism. Some analyses (for example, Wu Kaitai [1986], combine this position with support for thoroughgoing labour reforms (for example, a comprehensive labour contract system for state workers). Clearly the relationship between theory and practice is somewhat elastic, as we have seen in the case of Soviet Union where something very similar to a labour market operates while the concepts of labour market or labour as a commodity have not been admitted into official vocabulary [Nove, 1980]. One can be theoretically conservative and practically innovative.

On the other hand, some reformers wish to go further by changing the theory to fit a new reality, arguing that it is important to recognise that labour is also a commodity within the wider framework of the 'socialist commodity economy' which is the overall aim of the economic reform. They criticise as naive the traditional view, that since workers own the means of production, they can hardly sell labour power to themselves [Zhuang Hongxiang, 1986]:

> In socialist society although the means of production are under public ownership, they are not combined directly with labour power in a simple manner. This combination is achieved through recruiting and hiring, with one side paying the wages and the other hiring out its labour power... Although labourers are the elements that constitute [an enterprise], an individual labourer cannot be equated with this body. The seller and buyer of the labour power are two different legal persons.

For Zhuang, the fact that labour power remains a commodity is determined by 'objective economic law': The reason is that since social products are commodities, the materialised and animate labour which constitute the cost of commodities must be a commodity. While Zhuang traces the issue to underlying economic realities, other reformers, notably Zhao Guoliang [*1986*] and Dong Fureng [*1986*], emphasise that the answer to the question whether or not labour power is a commodity depends on the nature of the labour system in reality. In the previous system of administrative labour allocation, the freedom of individual labourers and hiring enterprises was severely curtailed and there was very little in the way of genuine exchange – there was thus no labour market and labour power was not a commodity. However, if this were to be reformed, particularly through the introduction of a labour contract system, then labour power would in fact become a commodity. The key issue, they argue, is to use reforms to *transform* labour power into a commodity, an act which requires prior recognition that this is indeed possible, nay unavoidable, in a socialist context. Here these radical reformers are, implicitly or explicitly, arguing against the view of their more moderate colleagues who, while willing to concede that goods and services are commodities, are unwilling to extend the same status to labour.

In essence, these differences between more radical and moderate reformers reflect different responses to a basic political challenge: the establishment of a new, harmonious relationship between three political levels: Marxist economic theory, operational ideology and specific policies. The first level is that of the Marxian economic canon which is in theory immutable but in practice malleable, thanks to its lacunae and inconsistencies. The second level is the reigning operational ideology of the day, a congealed derivation of our first level which may vary according to country, phase, or nature of the dominant leader, and is the terrain of debate and conflict at the higher reaches of the Party. The reformers are in effect trying to create a new operational ideology which rejects previous Maoist or Stalinist casts of thought, and both reflects and legitimates the need for new economic policies.

This attempt to reconstitute the relationship between theory, ideology and policy is complicated by two important political factors. First, there is another level of ideology which one might call small-i as opposed to big-I ideology, that is, the values of mass publics shaped (or not shaped) by decades of socialist rule. This phenomenon, which Western political science views in terms of 'political culture', is important to the extent that mass attitudes have been moulded by the previous operational ideology (in the Chinese case, the most important influence has probably been Maoism) and to this extent they conflict with the new ideas of the reformers. As we shall see in our later discussion of the attempt to introduce the labour contract system into state enterprises, many, perhaps most, state industrial workers hold 'traditional' socialist views about job security under socialism and are sceptical about the reforms.

Second, disagreements at both levels of ideology, at both elite and mass levels, are linked in more or less systematic ways to specific sets of social interests. At the elite level, the 'traditional' view, which denies that labour power is a commodity, reflects and reinforces the power and status of those party and state managers responsible for organising the previous system of administrative labour allocation. At the popular level, the 'traditional' view reflects the interests of workers in the relatively privileged state sector (in relation to their counterparts in collective industry) and an established practice of job tenure. Both these factors posed powerful political obstacles to the economic reform process.

Ideological debate and ambiguity thus reflects political disagreement among the Party leadership and the clash of attitudes and interests in society at large. As of 1987, reformers had yet to agree on a new definition of the role of labour in the new 'socialist commodity economy'. But this intellectual task is dwarfed by the political task which it overlays: that of arriving at a new definition of the actual status of labour in a new form of 'socialism'. Are they in fact offering state industrial workers a better deal in the new type of commodity-based socialism than in the traditional kind? If they are unable to carry this political conviction, they are vulnerable to the attack of opponents of reform, notably residual Maoists, who would denounce the labour reforms as evidence of 'capitalist restoration'.

Influential reformers such as Dong Fureng are aware of this problem and are at pains to point out that, although labour may be a commodity in the post-reform economy, this has fundamentally different meanings under capitalism and the new form of socialism. There are similarities – notably the separation of interests between seller and buyer, their separate legal identities and their freedom to enter into a contractual exchange – but these are outweighed by the differences:

> In different economic relations, wage labour or the system of wage labour also reflects different economic relations ... In capitalist production relations, the system of wage labour reflects the relationship between the exploiting class of capitalists and the exploited class of workers. However, in a socialist economy the system of wage labour reflects the relationship of equality and mutual benefit. *The fundamental difference lies in to whom the surplus products belong and whose interests they serve* [*Dong, 1986*] [emphasis added].

Questions of intellectual cogency aside, the key political problem here lies in the realities of labour's position in the post-reform economy. Whether one is talking about labour's status within the enterprise or in the economy at large, will it be better off than before and what will be the key 'socialist' institutions and policies which serve to differentiate the new labour system from that characteristic of capitalism? I shall address this issue in the conclusion. Before then, it is useful to investigate the extent to which China's labour reforms had actually been realised by early 1987 – this is the theme of the next section.

IV. CHANGE AND CONTINUITY IN THE CHINESE LABOUR SYSTEM

(a) Macro-level Reforms: Towards a Labour Market?

The central thrust of macro-reform has been towards '*destatification*'. In terms of specific reform policies, this involved, on the one side, a redefinition and reduction of the direct regulatory role of state agencies; on the other side, the devolution of decisions over labour allocation from state labour bureaux (both central and local) to non-state agencies of various types. Although the state would continue to engage in labour planning, this was conceived in terms comparable to the kind of 'manpower planning' characteristic of mixed economies. Although direct controls over certain strategic categories of specialised labour might still be necessary (notably college graduates), their numbers would be reduced and greater power over their disposition was to be given to training and hiring institutions and to individuals themselves. Regulation of other categories of labour was to become more indirect. For example, local labour bureaux, rather than assigning workers to enterprises by administrative fiat, were to play more of a recommendatory or intermediary role, that is, workers would apply to a bureau which would forward their names to appropriate enterprises which would have the power of vetting, acceptance or rejection. The decision to 'recommend' would ideally reflect both planning priorities and the labour demands put forward by individual enterprises. Labour bureaux were also to hand over part of their functions to non-state agencies, notably various kinds of 'labour service companies' (LSCs). Individuals and groups have also been encouraged to create their own jobs by setting up private and collective businesses without state administrative assistance or financial support. Urban labour bureaux have also been called on to *extend* their role to facilitate mobility of labour between enterprises and to 'cushion' the frictional unemployment which is an inevitable outcome of a successful reform programme. Labour bureaux would take responsibility for labour shed by enterprises, arranging interim welfare benefits and retraining and eventual reassignment to other units.

Deregulation was to be accompanied by a corresponding *increase in the labour allocation power of enterprises,* as part of the wider move to expand the 'autonomy' of basic units of production. Many reformers argued that the supervisory role of labour bureaux should be minimal and enterprises should take most major decisions on personnel matters. If they needed more workers, they should be allowed to advertise, deal with applicants directly and establish their own recruitment methods and criteria. They should also have the right to 'lure away' labour from other units, using their increased power to offer wage incentives. Even more crucial, argued the reformers, was the right of enterprise managers to dismiss workers – without this, any attempt to increase market regulation of the economy would founder.

The third major element of the redivision of power over labour allocation was the attempt to *increase the choice available to individual workers and professional staff.* Greater freedom, it was argued, would increase the general efficiency of labour utilisation, and, in particular, protect specialised personnel against the arbitrary dictates of personnel cadres in enterprises or state organs.

As of 1987, although there had been some movement in these directions, reform economists regarded progress as disappointing. There has been no decisive change in the labour allocation system. The degree of administrative direction remains high, most notably for labour in the state sector but also in the urban economy as a whole. State labour bureaux at various levels still dominate labour allocation, though some of their previous responsibility for details has been devolved to other institutions, notably Labour Service Companies (LSCs) and enterprises. I have discussed these changes in detail elsewhere [*White, 1987a*]; what follows is a synopsis of that account.

The key level of decision is still the Centre in Beijing and the key institution is the Ministry of Labour and Personnel (MLP). The MLP still regulates, directly or indirectly, three labour sectors: (i) the strategic groups described earlier; (ii) labour for state-owned enterprises under central management. Both (i) and (ii) are subject to 'directive plans', expressed in terms of labour quotas determined by the MLP and transmitted down to local labour bureaux; (iii) urban labour generally (including the collective sector) which is subject to a more flexible 'guidance plan' designed to regulate the activity of local governments, which have a planning role *vis-à-vis* state enterprises under local administration and collective enterprises in their localities.

Although the reforms envisaged a loosening of controls over category (iii) through local deregulation, the directive element in local labour allocation also remains dominant, though there have been some moves towards limited devolution. Let us take Beijing municipality as an example. The process of drawing up the city's *labour plan* has not changed since 1979. It is based on an estimate of the needs of enterprises and offices within the city, each of which submits an estimate of its labour requirements to the labour and wages office of its superior bureau which then communicates with the municipal Labour Bureau. The ensuing *recruitment plan* draws on three sources of labour: the strategic groups under centralised 'unified allocation' who must be given priority; junior and senior middle-school graduates from the city (and left-over graduates from the previous year who are 'awaiting employment'); and people with jobs who want to move. The actual process of assignment to a state enterprise is handled by three agencies in concert: the enterprise, the relevant functional bureau's labour office and the city labour bureau (and/or its affiliate labour service company).

At this recruitment stage of the labour allocation process, there have been some changes since 1979, in Beijing and elsewhere. Previously, local labour bureaux not only assigned a numerical quota to an enterprise but also chose and dispatched the individual workers. Since 1979, the enterprise has been given greater say in evaluating and choosing individual workers (within the quota) and recruitment methods have been improved and standardised (through various forms of examination). Job aspirants can apply through a local labour bureau, or through one of the new labour service companies (on which more below) or directly to the enterprise. Local labour bureaux do retain some controls: for example, to enforce a rule of gender equity if an enterprise refuses to accept female labour for no defensible reason.[7] Enterprises also complain that they are often forced to accept unnecessary (and often unwilling or unsuitable) workers because the local labour bureau is desperate to find places for registered local job-seekers, or is trying to fulfil a quote for one of the strategic groups stipulated by the MLP.

The other significant change has been the rise of the 'labour service company' (LSC) (for a more detailed discussion, see White [*1987a*]). Although LSCs were originally set up to find jobs and provide training for entrants into the labour force, many have developed into a sort of holding company with their own enterprises, operating in the interstices of the urban economy, creating rather than finding jobs. By the end of 1984, they employed about 5.5 million people (about 4.5 per cent of the total urban labour force).

Although all LSCs are dependent on their sponsoring agencies, be they government bureaux or enterprises, they do enjoy a degree of operational independence. This gives them greater scope to weave their way through the highways and byways of the planning system and the urban economy than their sponsoring organs; they act like a kind insitutional 'fixer'. Indeed, one of their major strengths is their ability to go out to bat for their own collective enterprises by extracting resources, by hook or by crook, from an economic system which is still basically inimical to the non-state sector (most notably the procurement of materials in scarce supply and still mainly distributed by the state materials allocation system).

If we situate LSCs in the overall system of labour allocation, however, one comes to ambivalent conclusions about their value as an instrument of economic reform. As agencies of labour management, they in fact act to extend the power of the state labour bureaucracy and the principle of non-market allocation into the urban collective sector. As such, they are an integral element of the state labour system. From a market reform perspective, therefore, their role is highly problematic. On the positive side, however, they have brought an element of decentralisation and competition into urban labour allocation. They also help to reduce the pressure on state jobs which most urban job aspirants still regard as the only 'real' employment LSCs have expanded and eased entry into the collective sector, helping to legitimate employment there and defend the interests of this sector against the state economy.

In fact, LSCs are a hybrid entity: they straddle both state and collective sectors and serve to cocoon collectives within a quasi-state integument. They provide greater flexibility in urban labour allocation but extend the practice of non-market allocation into the non-state economy. Rather than facilitating the operation of labour markets, they contribute to a kind of 'state pluralism' in a system of non-market allocation.

Looking at the planning system as a whole, though further changes in methods of labour planning are envisaged over the next few years, they are hardly radical and their economic implications may well be problematic.[8] But, to be effective, such reforms depend on success in other areas of reform policy. Improvements in labour productivity rest upon the overall calculus of enterprise behaviour which, in turn, depends on the environment faced by enterprise managers and the nature of the social dynamics within enterprises.

As the Chinese economic planning system continues to operate, it exerts inadequate pressures for greater microeconomic efficiency in the use of all resources, not merely labour. On the labour side specifically, the 'surplus labour' effect and the continuing political commitment to full employment exacerbates the problem. Not only do enterprises have little difficulty in obtaining the labour they ask for, but they are frequently forced to accept extra labour above their requirements. The chronic overmanning of Chinese state enterprises reflects both sets of pressures, one arising from the economic logic of a directive planning system and the other from the political (and ideological) imperative of achieving full employment, in a situation of chronic surplus labour.

In such circumstances labour productivity cannot be improved merely by changing methods of labour allocation, but by introducing other reforms which create pressures on the enterprise to economise in its use of all resources, not merely labour. In the area of labour reforms, their prospects for success depend on the extent to which labour authorities have shifted their real (as opposed to the declared) priority from creating employment towards raising labour productivity. This shift depends heavily on the relative influence of political forces in favour or against the reforms. One of these forces is the enterprise itself, to which we turn in the next section.

(b) Micro-Level Reforms: Managerial Power and the 'Iron Rice-Bowl'

How successful have the reformers been in changing the position of labour in the enterprise? We can discuss this question under two headings: first, the division of power over labour between state agencies and state enterprise managers and, second, the question of the job status of state workers and the attempt to break the 'iron rice-bowl'. On the former issue, enterprise managers have increased their power over labour decisions in recent years, but far less than reformers would have liked. They are still bound by mandatory numerical quotas but have greater power to choose individual workers rather than accept a batch allocated by the local labour bureau. In some sectors, moreover, such as construction and transportation, state enterprises have greater power – and the collective sector still greater – in selecting, managing and rewarding labour. Moreover, administrative controls over state enterprises mainly apply only to certain categories of worker, namely, 'fixed' and 'contract workers'. Enterprises have far greater power to recruit short-term labour without state approval or subject to limited state supervision: these include 'temporary workers', recruited according to seasonal needs, or 'rotation workers' for short-term work in particularly unpleasant or demanding jobs. It should be remembered, moreover, that these freedoms and restrictions are in the formal realm only; enterprises can, and do, increase their powers over labour by informal means outside the scrutiny of state labour bureaux. In spite of this, however, the pressures and constraints posed by state labour agencies are still considerable, a situation which many managers resent.

Our second micro-issue concerns the job status of workers within the state enterprise. As we have seen, reformers view the existence of a virtual tenure system to be a major constraint on increasing labour productivity and encouraging labour flexibility. However, their attempts to weaken the principle of the 'iron rice-bowl' by putting state workers on labour contracts have run into a great deal of resistance from those workers, and from some managers who view the reform as disruptive or adminstratively burdensome (for a detailed analysis of the reaction of different groups to the labour contract system, see White [*1987b*]). Although the policy was launched in 1982, progress has been very slow: by the end of 1986, only 5.24 million state workers were on contracts, about 5.6 per cent of the total. Although a new policy offensive to introduce labour contracts was launched in mid-1986, one cannot expect rapid progress. This means that enterprise managers still have very limited ability to lay off workers, either in response to the enterprise's changing labour requirements or to workers' bad performance. According to statistics for 1986 drawn from 14 provinces and cities, only 0.007 per cent of the state workforce were fired for 'violation of discipline'.[9]

But have other changes in the urban economy over recent years increased the incentives for state workers to move jobs? Limited progress in introducing wage reforms in the state sector means, among other things, that wages still do not serve as signals to channel labour (notably from low to high performance state enterprises). On the other hand, there are some indications that the previously rigid dualism between state and collective enterprise is breaking down to some extent. The greater freedoms enjoyed by urban collectives and private businesses have opened up opportunities and increased incentives for state workers to move jobs independently. Some collectives are now able to offer terms and conditions of work superior to state enterprises, tempting state workers to leave the security of their 'iron rice-bowls'. Research in China in mid-1987 suggests that, in some sectors, such as textiles, state enterprises are having trouble both attracting and keeping labour: in some textile mills, for example, workers are often prevented from leaving when they wish [*White and Bowles, 1987*].

There has also been some halting progress in increasing the circulation of specialised/professional labour. The new 'talent exchange agencies' have spread from city to city but as yet are operating on a very small scale. Movement for skilled professionals is still not easy, not the least because their original units refuse to let them go even if another unit wishes to recruit them. The MLP itself has an office which tries to adjudicate this kind of dispute. In some sectors, however, mobility seems to have increased significantly. Members of the Beijing Chinese Academy of Social Sciences (CASS), for example, complained that a lot of younger academics had been leaving recently, partly because wages are low and partly because they think that 'if you stay at the academy, you are a worm; if you go out, you are a dragon'. Others were enticed from Beijing by the prospect of becoming bigger fish in the provinces.

To sum up for both macro and micro levels, labour reform has encountered a good deal of scepticism and resistance and overall progress has been disappointingly slow from the viewpoint of the reformers. Although the economic environment (that is, the existence of a large and chronic labour surplus and the lack of complementary changes in other areas of economic policy) is clearly impeding reform at this stage, there are certain key political factors which have played an important role in conditioning the reform process. We turn to these in the first part of our concluding section.

CONCLUSIONS

(i) Some Remarks on the Politics of Labour Reform

Why have labour reforms run into such heavy weather and made so little progress? It would be tempting to adopt the familiar view that they have been impeded by the conservative vested interests of the state bureaucracy, in this case the state labour bureaux.

Chinese experience suggests that this argument does have some explanatory force. There is evidence that state labour agencies are in fact reluctant to devolve anything but relatively marginal powers to lower-level units. The enunciated principle, indeed, proclaimed by both the MLP and local labour bureaux, is to 'control the big things and decentralise the small'. Moreover, the new ancillary agencies, the Labour Service Companies, have a marked tendency to behave like state agencies. Clearly the principle and practice of comprehensive state labour regulation is still firmly in place, though more 'pluralistic'. Once such a complex institutional network has been established and consolidated over more than two decades, it is difficult to shift.

But to rely on a 'bureaucratic vested interest' explanation alone would be misleading in two respects. First, it would imply that state labour authorities were purely conservative bodies and, second, that their behaviour was determined merely by their own institutional interests. Both such conclusions are unwarranted.

State labour authorities are subject to strong external pressures both pro and anti reform. Pressure for reform comes from CCP leaders pursuing the elusive goals of macroeconomic dynamism and microeconomic efficiency; from enterprise managers who would like greater power over their own workforce and resent bureaucratic interference; from part of the workforce themselves, notably young, skilled (and potentially mobile) workers, or highly trained professionals, who dislike being told where to work after graduation and resent the lack of freedom to move on to better jobs. On the other side, there are powerful pressures to blunt the impact of reform or retain the status quo. The key factor here is the continuing problem of surplus labour which threatens politically unacceptable levels of unemployment. These circumstances, and the fears they inspire, produce widespread scepticism when reform economists praise the putative benefits of labour markets, or the virtues of unemployment as a stimulus to productive effort. It would be very difficult for the CCP to revoke its commitment to maintaining full employment to the greatest extent feasible.

This commitment has created over the past two and a half decades a kind of institutionalised patron–client relationship between the Chinese state and its urban constituents: the state takes on the role of provider (sometimes described as the 'donative state') and the clientele comes to depend on the state and expect its bounty. There is thus a mass constituency to retain state labour controls which coincides with and reinforces the institutional interests of state labour agencies.

The anti-reform influence of this political relationship is buttressed by certain interests within state enterprises, who see dangers in any expansion of a labour market: enterprise managers who fear losing their best workers to more successful enterprises – state, collective or private; workers who fear that the reforms will threaten their jobs or conditions of work. Within state enterprises, in fact, an implicit social contract has developed over the past three decades whereby workers exchange their quiescence and cooperation for managerial/state guarantees of job security and material welfare. Thus the basic character of Chinese enterprises is a powerful brake on current labour reforms.

If these implicit 'social contracts' – between state and society at large and between managers and workers within enterprises – are threatened, the legitimacy of the state is called into question and there is the danger of mass discontent and resistance. Policy-makers are keenly aware of this latter prospect and talk of the need to proceed cautiously with labour reforms for fear of disturbing 'social peace'.

In sum, state labour agencies are locked into political relationships which are as yet inimical to thoroughgoing reform and resistant to change. Moreover, they are charged with achieving two objectives – relieving unemployment and raising labour productivity – which, though not incompatible in theory, have strong 'trade-off' elements whereby improvement in one may lead to deterioration in the other, at least in the short term. Since labour policy and labour organisations embody these basic political contradictions, it is hardly surprising that progress towards significant labour reform has been slow.

(ii) The Future of the Reformist Vision

One strong message from the preceding analysis is that, if the reformers are to succeed, they must carry with them those whose interests are affected and whose values are challenged. Do the reforms really offer a 'new deal' for Chinese labour (and managers) compared to the traditional labour system? It is all very well for reform economists to enthuse about 'labour flexibility' or speculate on the economic advantages of unemployment (for example, Cheng Feng [1987]) but they will not be the ones to bear the brunt of adjustment.

At the broadest level, this is a question of whether they can offer a practical vision of a 'socialist commodity economy' wherein the advantages of markets can be combined effectively with the advantages of socialist planning and institutions, that is, an economically more dynamic and productive, less bureaucratic form of socialism which offers faster income growth and greater socio-economic opportunity while retaining the basic distinictive socialist concern for full employment and job security. Alternative future scenarios are not unlikely: either a 'half-way house' which encounters the characteristic problems of a market economy while retaining many of the negative features of the old administrative planning system, or a 'post radical market reform' scenario in which workers are prey to powerful managers and the vicissitudes of a labour market.

In the short and medium term, it is the basic economic and political realities analysed earlier which will continue to determine the pace and direction of the reform and maintain a balance between certain features of the old and new labour systems. Political leaders will continue to lend one ear to reformist paeans of the market and the other to their own political values and the demands of their various political constituencies.

The most favourable environment for rapid reform is a situation in which incomes and opportunities are expanding rapidly, thereby minimising the zero-sum element of adjustments in the labour system. But, though the performance of the Chinese economy over the past eight years has been impressive, labour officials are sober about the problems ahead. The normal increase in the urban labour force will be swelled by labour 'shaken out' by industrial rationalisation (particularly if the bankruptcy law is allowed to bite) and the increasing flow of labour from the countryside. Political pressures to expand employment through state action will remain high – the Minister of Labour, Zhao Dongwan, has already promised that urban unemployment will be held down to two per cent, its 1986 level, for the rest of the decade.[10] Other social objectives, such as correcting regional inequalities, will also prompt labour planners to retain some direct controls (particularly over the employment of college graduates).

At the same time, the reform policies designed to encourage greater labour flexibility will also be pursued, at both macro and micro levels. Frictional unemployment will probably increase as industry restructures and the labour contract system will be extended within state enterprises. Recent experience suggests, however, that these measures will be introduced cautiously and with the accompaniment of complementary policies to cushion their impact, notably a state welfare system to retrain and reallocate the unemployed and a system of legal and institutional safeguards to protect the rights of workers involved in labour contracts.[11] One theoretical expression of this attempt to combine elements of traditional socialist concern with greater labour flexibility is the redefinition of the notion of the right to employment: it involves the basic right to a job, but not any particular job in any particular firm (one writer refers to this distinction in terms of the difference between 'major and minor concepts of the iron rice-bowl').[12]

There are signs, moreover, that as the labour system takes on certain market attributes such as differential wages and contractual exchanges, hitherto dormant worker organisations will step in to defend the rights of their members – the trade unions[13] and 'workers' representative congresses' within enterprises. While they do not figure largely in the programme of the reform economists, such organisations would seem to be natural products of a commodity economy, capitalist or socialist. This is but one aspect of a wider process of institutional growth or regeneration stimulated by the reforms, finding its counterpart on the managerial side in the rise of trade associations, entrepreneurs' associations and chambers of commerce. We appear to be witnessing the birth of a new form of 'civil society' in response to the advance of market socialism. But this is a subject for another article.

NOTES

Abbreviations

CREA   Joint Publications Research Service, *China Report: Economic Affairs*, Washington
FBIS   *Foreign Broadcasts Information Service*
GMRB   *Guangming Ribao* (Glorious Daily), Beijing
RMRB   *Renmin Ribao* (People's Daily), Beijing
SWB: FE   BBC, *Summary of World Broadcasts: Far East*, Reading

1. This figure was supplied by Professor Wu Dingcheng of the CASS Institute of Economics: see White [*1985:7*].
2. For a review of development economics literature on structural unemployment and surplus

labour in Third World context, see Martin Godfrey, *Global Unemployment: The New Challenge to Economic Theory* (Brighton, Sussex: Harvester Press, 1986). For a Chinese discussion of the impact of surplus labour, see Zhao Lukuan, 'On China's Employment Problem under Conditions of Relative Labour Surplus', *RMRB*, 2 March 1982, p.5, in *FBIS* 048.

3. For an example of reformers' arguments, see Ye Ming, 'In making the best possible use of manpower, put the stress on "flexibility"', *GMRB*, 7 Aug. 1980, in *CREA*, No.84 (1980).

4. For example, see the interview with a veteran army officer in Hongkong's *Zhengming Daily*, 24 July 1981, who linked growing unemployment with growing prostitution and criminal violence (translated in *FBIS*, 27 July 1981).

5. For example, Yi Duming [*1986*] makes these points as does a local labour bureau official from Hebei province in *Hebei Ribao* (Hebei Daily), 13 April 1982, in *FBIS*, 26 April.

6. For advocacy of a 'job market', see Wei Jie [*1985*]; for use of the term 'labour resources market', see Wang Jue and Xiao Xiu [*1986*].

7. For evidence on job discrimination against women, see Chi Yuhua and Chen Jin, 'Zhang Guoying, Vice-President of the All China Women's Federation, Calls for Eliminating Discrimination Against Women', *RMRB*, 31 July 1987, in *SWB: FE* 3640.

8. For example, the MLP wishes to shift from 'directive' to 'flexible' planning methods, namely, instead of setting an overall quota for the number of workers in an enterprise, the allowable number is to be linked to increments in the gross value of the enterprise's output (GVO) that is, if GVO increases by one per cent, the workforce can increase by 0.3 per cent. To the extent that marginal increases in GVO thus surpass labour increments, labour productivity can be improved, argues the MLP. A more radical reform would abolish labour quotas altogether by substituting the wage plan only for the current labour and wage plans. Wage targets will be based on prescribed incremental ratios and these would be enforced 'by regulations and statistical methods', with the banks and the newly established auditing offices playing an important monitoring role [*White, 1985*].

9. *Zhongguo Xinwenshe* (China News Agency), Beijing, 5 Aug. 1987, in *SWB:FE* 8643.

10. Reported by Moscow Radio, 3 August 1987, in *SWB: FE* 8637.

11. For a recent discussion of these measures, see Cao Guiying, 'Several Questions Concerning Population and Employment', *RMRB*, 16 March 1987, in *FBIS* 057.

12. Commentator, 'Is the "Iron Rice-Bowl" Something We Cannot Bear to Part With? – On Reform of the Labour System', *RMRB*, 18 Nov. 1986, in *SWB: FE* 8428.

13. Consider, for example, the complaints about extension of working hours by the Vice-Chairman of the All-China Federation of Trade Unions, voiced in *Gongren Ribao* (Workers Daily), 4 March 1987, in *SWB: FE* 8520.

REFERENCES

Cheng Feng, 1987, 'A Fresh Understanding of the "Waiting for Employment" Problem', *Jingji Ribao* (Economic Daily), 18 April, in *SWB: FE* 8569.

Cheng Tizhong, 1986, 'An Inquiry into Certain Problems Concerning a Comprehensive Implementation of the Contract System', *Zhongguo Laodong Kexue* (Chinese Labour Science), No.5 (May) pp.10–12.

Dong Fureng, 1986, 'A Brief Discourse on the Labour System and Labour Power as a Commodity', *GMRB*, 4 Oct. 1986, in *SWB: FE* 8397.

Feng Lanrui, 1982, 'Six Questions Concerning the Problem of Employment', *Selected Writings on Studies of Marxism*, No.1, Beijing: Institute of Marxism-Leninism-Mao Zedong Thought, Chinese Academy of Social Sciences.

Godfrey, Martin, *Global Unemployment: The New Challenge to Economic Theory*, Brighton, Sussex: Harvester Press, 1986.

Han Zhiguo, 1986, 'The Labour Force Remains a Commodity under Socialist Conditions . . .', *GMRB*, Beijing, 2 Aug., translated in *SWB: FE* 8351.

Hu Chen, 1986, 'Opening Up a Labour Power Market Is Not Based on Regarding Labour Power as a Commodity', *GMRB*, 25 Oct. 1986, in *SWB: FE* 8412.

Jiang Yiwei, 1985, 'If All Workers Are on the Contract System, It Will Not Be Conducive to the Socialist Character of the Enterprise', *Jingji Tizhi Gaige* (Economic Structural Reform), No.1 pp.11–13.

Kornai, János, 1980, *Economics of Shortage,* Vol.A, Amsterdam: North-Holland.

Lockett, Martin, 1986, 'Small Business and Socialism in Urban China', *Development and Change,* Vol.17, No.1 (Jan.) pp.35–67.

Nove, Alec, 1980, 'The Labour Market in the Soviet Union', *New Society,* 10 April, pp.58–9.

State Statistical Bureau, 1985 and 1986, *Statistical Yearbook of China 1985, 1986,* Hong Kong Economic Information and Agency.

Wang Jue and Xiao Xiu, 1986, 'Tentative Analysis of the Labour Resources Market', *GMRB,* 12 July 1986.

Wei Jie, 1985, 'A Socialist Job Market Should Be Established', *GMRB,* 10 Aug. 1985.

White, Gordon, 1982, 'Urban Unemployment and Labor Allocation Policies in Post-Mao China', *World Development,* Vol.10, No.8, pp.613–32.

White, Gordon, 1985, *Labour Allocation and Employment Policy in Contemporary China,* Brighton: Institute of Development Studies, University of Sussex.

White, Gordon, 1987a, 'The Changing Role of the Chinese State in Labour Allocation: Towards the Market?' *Journal of Communist Studies,* Vol.3, No.2 (June).

White, Gordon, 1987b, 'The Politics of Economic Reform in Chinese Industry: the Introduction of the Labour Contract System', *China Quarterly,* No.111 (Sept.).

White, Gordon and Bowles, Paul, 1987, *Towards a Capital Market? Reforms in the Chinese Banking System,* China Research Report No.6, Brighton: Institute of Development Studies, University of Sussex.

World Bank, 1985, *China: Long-Term Development Issues and Options,* Baltimore, MD; London: Johns Hopkins University Press.

Wu Kaitai, 1986, 'Reforming the Labour System Does Not Mean Opening Up the Labour Force Market', *Jingji Ribao* (Economic Daily), 6 Dec., in *FBIS* 243.

Xue Muqiao, 1981, *China's Socialist Economy,* Beijing: Foreign Languages Press.

Yi Duming, 1986, 'In Defence of the "Iron Rice-bowl" System', *Yangcheng Wanbao* (Canton Evening News), 23 Feb., translated in *CREA,* No.347.

Zhao Guoliang, 1986, 'A Brief Discussion on Socialist Labour as a Commodity', *GMRB,* 23 Aug., in *SWB: FE* 8357.

Zhao Ziyang, 1987, 'Advance Along the Road of Socialism with Chinese Characteristics', Peking Radio (domestic), 25 Oct., translated in *SWB: FE* 8709.

Zhou Xiuqiang, 1980, article in *RMRB,* 23 July, in *FBIS,* 25 July.

Zhuang Hongxiang, 1986, 'Recognising Labour Power as a Commodity Will Not Cause the Negation of the Socialist System', *GMRB,* 7 Sept. 1986, in *SWB: FE* 8368.

The State, Planning and Labour: Towards Transforming the Colonial Labour Process in Zimbabwe

*by Nelson P. Moyo**

The transition to socialism involves a number of interrelated and often contradictory processes: on the one hand, the need to transform colonial structures; while, on the other hand, because of the necessity to avoid economic collapse, productive forces must be preserved. Planning in such a context should address the issue of the transformation of colonial-capitalist labour processes in the early stages of the transition as colonial labour regimes enter crisis. The Zimbabwean experience shows that the emphasis on preserving productive forces – while an important aspect of transition – can provide a convenient platform for those forces in society which have little interest in fundamental change.

INTRODUCTION

Zimbabwe inherited an economy characterised by uneven development, possessing, on the one hand, a modern industrial and commercial sector which was primarily designed to serve the interests of the minority white settler community, yet one which was notably dependent on foreign monopoly capital and technology, and, on the other hand, a low productivity and generally underdeveloped peasant sector. These colonial features of the economy were summarised most vividly in the first government economic policy statement, *Growth with Equity* (1981) in the following terms:

> economic exploitation of the majority by the few, the grossly uneven infrastructural and productive development of the rural and urban economy, the lopsided control of the major means of production and distribution, the unbalanced levels of development within and among sectors and the consequent grossly inequitable pattern of income distribution and of benefits to the overwhelming majority of the people of this country, stand as a serious indictment of our society. So does the imbalance between predominant foreign ownership and control of assets on the one hand and, on the other, limited local participation as also and more especially the past colonial dispossession of land and other economic assets and the consequential impoverishment of the masses of the people . . . (p.1).

Emphasising the point of linkage between the two sectors, the Three-Year Transitional National Development Plan (TNDP) 1982/83 – 1984/85 said,

*University of Zimbabwe.

'the two sectors, however, are not functionally separate and of particular importance in this regard is that the one, the modern sector, has historically fed on the other'. The above two statements together capture, on the one hand, the essence of the problems and contradictions of capitalist development under colonialism and, on the other, the urgency of tackling those problems. The policy document went on to state the government's determination to undertake 'a vigorous programme for the development of the country' with the ultimate objective of establishing 'a democratic, egalitarian and socialist society'.

But the achievement of the goal of growth with equity, let alone that of a truly socialist society, is not an unproblematic process as the experience of other Third World countries which have embarked on this path has shown. For this will involve a number of interrelated and sometimes contradictory processes involving, on the one hand, the need to transform the colonial economic structures while, on the other hand, and because of the necessity to avoid economic collapse or chaos, preserving productive forces. The preservation of the productive forces has crucial significance in Zimbabwe not only because their development had reached an advanced stage under colonial rule but also because of the instructive experiences of Zimbabwe's closest neighbour and ally, Mozambique.

The need to preserve productive forces was stressed in the introductory chapter of the TNDP which said

> While the inherited economy, with its institutions and infrastructure, has in the past served a minority, *it would be simplistic and, indeed, naive to suggest that it should, therefore, be destroyed in order to make a fresh start.* The challenge lies in building upon and developing on what was inherited . . . (p.1).

These concerns are real and every socialist experience must confront them in one way or another.[1]

But a word of warning is perhaps appropriate here. What we are saying is that even if a party and the state are committed to constructing socialism, the issue of preserving and developing productive forces, and of simultaneously transforming existing production relations is one riddled with tensions. Moreover, as Lenin knew well, and as the Chinese also stressed through their experience, these tensions also reflect class struggle.[2] This is very much the case in Zimbabwe as we shall show later. Thus, while transformation is a protracted process, there are definite forces within society who have no interest to do so, and these will often hide as well behind the emphasis on preserving productive forces.

We must elaborate a little further on this point. Productive forces do not exist in a vacuum, but bear the stamp of the social relations of production. What is inherited from the past is not just technologies and people with varying skill levels, but capitalist labour processes set within capitalist relations of production which themselves are situated in varying concrete contexts: colonial settler-based capitalism in Zimbabwe with, however, strong dominance of foreign capital.

The task is to transform the colonial capitalist labour process. It is important, in this respect, to understand the labour power/labour dichotomy, the crucial concept in Marxist economic theory that delineates the essential non-exchange relations of the capitalist economy. Labour power, the commodity which is exchanged in the labour market, is the human capacity to work. Labour, on the other hand, 'is the active, concrete, living process carried on by the workers; its expression is determined not only by labour power but also by the ability of the capitalist to exploit it' [*Gintis, 1976: 37*]. The aim of the capitalist is to extract as much surplus value as possible from the labourer. Three factors determine the extraction of surplus value: first, the length of the working day, that is, the number of hours that the labourer has to work each day; second, the intensity of labour related to how hard the labourer works or is driven or motivated by the capitalist employer; third, the productiveness of labour which results in more goods being produced in the same amount of time and with the same intensity of labour. The bringing together of large numbers of workers under one roof requires control and co-ordination. Under capitalist relations of production such control tends to be authoritarian and coercive.[3]

Although some recognition is given to it, transforming the labour process is generally seen as being outside the domain of planning. In summary, planning must address the issue of the transformation of the labour processes if at all it is concerned with advancing socialism. The issue is not merely one of seizing the commanding heights of the economy through nationalisations, but also of reorganising production and labour processes. Admittedly, this cannot be done overnight, but a clear strategy is needed so as to be able to identify tactical interventions. In this respect, the concrete conditions need to inform strategy. In the case of Zimbabwe we need a clear understanding of colonial history in general and of the UDI period in particular, for during the UDI regime the state was not just a *laissez-faire* state but a strongly interventionist one. The state itself invested significantly in public enterprise within key sectors of the economy and aided private as well as public capital to subordinate black labour under their command. Hence, the inherited economic structure was comprised of a mixture of public and private enterprises (the latter mainly under control of foreign capital) and both relying heavily on the state to structure their profitability through keeping black labour cheap and compliant. This is reflected in the organisation of the labour process and of the employment relationship. Hence, issues which will be of major concern in the transition period include:

- the question of *confidence*: not merely the fear of nationalisation, but also the question of labour and its control;
- the incorporation of Zimbabweans into management and ownership within a basically unchanged structure of control;
- the state and the working class: will the state propel workers' power within public enterprises and the private sector or will it ally itself with capital against labour?

These are fundamental issues of planning which have become fudged. My article attempts to highlight their importance and to put them back on the agenda.

THE COLONIAL INHERITANCE

An important feature of the colonial economy is that far from being *laissez-faire,* it was actually subject to close state regulation or 'planning', especially with respect to the creation and continued reproduction of labour power. For example, pre-Second World War colonial development which centred around the white agrarian bourgeoisie who were aided to capture large portions of the most fertile and well-watered land from the African peasantry was not just a question of creating more land for settler agriculture, but a way to restrict the scope of peasant agriculture and of drawing labour from the peasantry. Herein lies the origins of the 'success' story of white commercial agriculture. Arrighi [*1967*] wrote about the two main consequences of land apportionment: first, it ensured an expanding supply of labour to white farms, mines and industry as the productivity of peasant agriculture progressively became undermined and peasants were thrown on to the job market[4] and, second, it divided the economy into non-competing racial groups by restricting competition on produce and labour markets as well as other individual spheres.[5]

Many studies that describe the impressive growth and technological development of the manufacturing sector up to the collapse of UDI tend to ignore the repressive labour regime that accompanied it. The colonial form of production organisation was based on very tight control over black unskilled and semi-skilled labour by white managements. White workers, on the other hand, formed a labour 'aristocracy', which possessed the skills and jealously guarded their 'skilled' jobs. The state not only propelled the industrialisation process but also shaped the conditions for cheap black labour while acting as a bulwark for the white skilled workers.[6] But the expansion of capitalist industry involved the need for the flexible use of labour and came into conflict with the racial character of the division of labour.

At first capitalist employers relied on unskilled labour recruited on a migrant basis. With the rapid growth of industry and the shortage of skilled labour, many employers began to make efforts to stabilise the African labour force for use in industry. Many 'welfare' schemes designed to stabilise labour, such as hostel or compound accommodation, rations, etc., were installed. But, broadening the base for black labour while keeping it cheap propelled changes in the organisation of the labour process, in the employment relation and the structure of the labour market.

Major battles were fought between white skilled workers and capitalist employers who pushed ahead with job fragmentation to bring in semi-skilled African workers.[7] The main objective of the capitalist employers was not just to 'de-skill' the white workers but to use the less expensive semi-skilled labour more flexibly and thus increase profits.

The potential of semi-skilled African workers since the beginning of the Second World War was recognised by the Todd Select Committee when it said

> Since the beginning of the Second World War . . . there has been the beginning of what can fairly be described as an industrial revolution. In the older industries Africans have learned to do jobs of a higher grade

than labourers' work and, in a number of cases, to do fully skilled work. At the same time, new industries have been established on mass production lines where, except for a small number of European supervisors and European engineers to maintain and repair the machinery, practically the whole labour force consists of Africans; and it has come to be realised that the aptitude of Africans for this type of operative work, and the availability of large numbers of them, is one of the most important factors favourable to the development of modern secondary industry in this country (p.5).

While under the 1959 Industrial Conciliation Act (Chapter 267) the definition of 'employee' included all races, the Act was not designed to facilitate the growth of African trade unions. Its basic feature was control of unregistered trade unions, all of which were African. While unregistered trade unions were given no status under the law they were nevertheless closely watched – they were required to notify the Registrar of their existence, supply copies of their constitution, keep books of account, etc. In presenting the Bill to Parliament the Minister responsible[8] admitted and confirmed that 'to provide for these associations is nothing more than a control measure' (Col.1547). Moreover, the road to registration was meant to be as hard as possible. According to the Minister, the Bill was not meant to 'open the door wide to full trade union rights for all overnight' (Col.1547).

The change in the labour law was not a benevolent act. It was a result of, on the one hand, the struggles and growing militancy of the black labour movement and, on the other hand, a response to changes at the level of production which brought blacks into semi-skilled work. The 1959 legislation did not, however, apply to agricultural and domestic workers whose conditions of service continued to be governed by the Masters and Servants Act. Another important feature of the Act was the protection afforded to 'minority interests' or skilled members of a trade union. While no person could be excluded from a trade union on the grounds of race, colour or religion, the constitution of a trade union could provide 'for its membership to be divided into branches on the basis of class of work or enterprise or the place of work or business or the sex or the race or colour of the members, or otherwise' (Section 50(3)(b) p.64).

During UDI, the Rhodesia Front government took more steps to protect and enhance the interests of the white artisan class. They tightened surveillance over National Industrial Council Agreements and the organisation of apprenticeship training. A classic example of the government's protection of white journeymen was revealed in a confrontation between the Ministry of Labour and the Transport Operators' Association in 1976, following the recommendations of the sub-committee of the National Industrial Board of the Transport Operating Industry set up to, *inter alia,* 'investigate the work performed by unskilled and semi-skilled employees in the workshops of establishments in the industry'. The sub-committee's report, which recommended a major fragmentation of skilled jobs, was rejected by the Ministry on the grounds that there were many operations which either infringed on journeymen's work or could not be satisfactorily identified with the 'Agreements' jobs (a reference to the Motor Industry Agreement which the Ministry claimed was the 'parent body'). The Transport Operators' Association objected strongly to the Ministry's position and to the fact that certain sections of their recommendations had been referred to the Industrial Council of the Motor Trade. Why should recommendations of a sub-committee of the Industrial Board for one industry be referred to another, they charged? They rejected the suggestion that the Motor Trade was the 'parent body'.[9]

The Rhodesian Front government also passed many amendments to the Industrial Conciliation Act designed either to protect white journeymen or to keep a tight lid over black trade unions.[10] It is clear from the foregoing that colonial capitalism was not based on *laissez-faire,* but was characterised by a strong interventionist state. Private capital had come to rely on the state to support it, particularly with respect to labour. It will want to perpetuate the pre-independence form of production organisation.

PLANNING AND LABOUR IN POST-INDEPENDENCE ZIMBABWE

In this section we focus on the implications of planning for transforming labour. In this respect, the land question and the emancipation of the peasantry have been in the forefront of post-independence policy debates. As we have seen, peasant agriculture progressively became marginalised under colonial rule through the expropriation of fertile and rain-fed land and discriminatory pricing and marketing policies. The communal lands were thus reduced to 'labour reserves', with able-bodied men leaving to seek wage employment. These effects were felt more strongly in the areas with lower agro-ecological potential.[11] Remittances of migrant labour became and continued to be a major source of peasant incomes and, in some cases, a condition of agricultural development.[12]

The coming of independence opened up possibilities for restructuring the relationship between the state and the peasantry. Real transformation would require amongst other measures a significant redistribution of good land to the peasantry.[13] This will create more employment and incomes for the rural population. It must be recalled that driving African peasants on to dry and infertile land was the major cause of labour migrancy. Provision of more land must be accompanied by changes in the forms of production organisation and in the social relations of production in farming. The resettlement programme has progressed slowly with some 36,000 households resettled by 1986.[14] Among the obstacles to a more thoroughgoing land redistribution programme is the Lancaster House Constitution whose 'Bill of Rights' provisions restrict the government's ability to acquire land except on a 'willing seller willing buyer' basis of land that is 'underutilised'. The result is that only abandoned farms in the drier and poorer areas have been available to the government.[15]

Moreover, most of the resettlement schemes have been of the Model A type of individual plots rather than the Model B involving co-operatives. The latter held the promise of a real transformation of social relations of production in farming – but has so far faced immense problems due to lack of capital, technical support and management.[16]

The attempts by government to enforce changes in the status of farm workers, have met with resistance from the large-scale commercial farms who have responded by rapidly displacing labour for capital.[17] Thus, attempts at radical land reform have encountered severe limitations not only from the Lancaster House Consitution but also from the perceived need to preserve the existing productive forces while simultaneously opening up further opportunities for individual accumulation which entrench interests against fundamental change.

Faced by all these problems actual government policy has shifted towards channelling more resources to the communal areas, with lesser emphasis on resettlement.[18] Recent research shows that this will fuel further differentiation in the countryside.[19] It has been shown, moreover, that the post-independence increase in marketed output by the peasantry has not meant lesser vulnerability of its poorer strata who continue to suffer from hunger and malnutrition.[20] This will accelerate the movement of the rural poor and unemployed in search of wage employment at a time when formal employment is contracting.

PLANNING AND THE COMMODITY LABOUR POWER

The preceding discussion has indicated that in the colonial period labour power was a commodity but not set within the framework of a free market. The context was, rather, of heavy state intervention and political subjugation of the black working class and the peasantry.

Post-colonial development cannot therefore merely consist of liberalising or freeing the labour market from its racially segregated fragmentation, but must involve conscious steps to allocate labour with the aim of reducing unemployment and providing stable livelihoods to the producing classes. This is a critical issue of planning. But what really has happened? At independence, capitalists had two main concerns: first, they were fearful about the prospect of expropriation or nationalisation of their assets and, second, they were worried about the loss of control over labour as this was bound to undercut their chances for further accumulation. These conditions were guaranteed under the colonial state which was not sensitive to the needs of the black workers and the peasantry. The fear was that the black government would give too much power to the black workers and that this could disrupt the balance of power in industry with serious consequences for capitalist accumulation. 1980 and 1981 indeed saw wild-cat strikes and challenges of managerial power by industrial workers. Among the main demands of the strikers were: higher wages, dismissal of hated white managers/supervisors, reinstatement of dismissed workers, etc. However, the governement used its weight and moral authority to stem the labour unrest and inserted itself between the capitalist employer and the workers as the guardian of labour discipline. More emphasis came to be placed on increased productivity and the development of 'good communications' between workers and employers. The call for discipline and stability was to underscore the need to preserve productive forces. But it was clear also that the struggle was over the content of independence.

Sachikonye [*1986*] has provided a useful account of the strike wave of 1980–81.[21] He, however, seems to subscribe to the view that the strikes were 'disorganised' and that they were a result of 'a poor state of communication between management and workers in most firms'. 'The strikes', he said, 'had thrown into broad relief the yawning gap in communication flows while management was particularly worried by the militancy displayed by workers in conflicts on the shopfloor' (p.257).[22] Sachikonye also, in my view, puts undue emphasis on the 'weakness' or 'ineffectiveness' of trade unions which he says 'could not be counted upon to articulate workers' demands or restrain their members from spontaneous industrial action' (p.255). It is widely known that crippling and weakening the trade union movement was a priority agenda of the colonial state. That did not, however, kill the rank and file movement.

The significance of the 1980–81 strikes is that the workers themselves rose spontaneously countrywide to demonstrate their hatred of the exploitative and repressive system of colonial capitalism which was characterised by low wages and surplus control of labour. The strikers demanded not only higher wages but also changes in the authoritarian system of management. What needs to be highlighted, in my view, is the way the state responded by moving quickly to contain the strike movement and thus aligning itself firmly with capital but all in the name of the 'national interest'. The retreat of the state was further demonstrated in the case of the agro-industry strikes in 1985 involving plantation and factory workers in private (mainly TNCs but also large-scale commercial farmers) and parastatal enterprises based mainly in Manicaland (for coffee and tea) and Chiredzi (for sugar). In July 1985, the government had announced a new minimum wage of $143,75 for agro-industrial workers. But the entire industry – apparently with the support of the Ministry of Lands, Agriculture and Rural Resettlement – applied for exemption from the new minimum wage, arguing that they were unable to pay due to very low world prices and input costs. At first the Ministry of Labour refused to consider blanket exemptions, pointing out that the law allowed employers facing economic hardships to apply for exemption on an individual basis. As the employers dug in and threatened retrenchment of thousands of workers, the state was forced to give in. The strategy of the employers was to force a distinction between plantation workers and those who worked in the factories. In the final settlement plantation workers were awarded a new minimum wage of $85 per month while factory workers received $110 per month.[23]

Two significant pro-labour measures taken by government through emergency powers were the introduction of the legal minimum wage from July 1980[24] and regulations barring employers from dismissing workers except with the approval of the Minister of Labour. This represented a significant departure from colonial labour policy. The regulations are a continuing bone of contention between the employers and the government. Government sees the measure as a means of maintaining employment, whereas the employers see it as an infringement on their right to hire and fire. The difficult years of drought and recession and the problems of foreign exchange shortages opened the way for employers to rationalise labour processes. First, many employers resorted to short-time working on the basis of three or four days in a working week, but second, many found ways to retrench workers although government's regulations served as a mitigating factor.[25]

Recently, there has been renewed pressure on the government to revise the 'no firing and no hiring' regulations which, employers claim, oblige them to keep 'lazy' and 'unproductive' workers. Employers are particularly unhappy about what they call the 'red tape bureaucracy and time-wasting delays that clog up the justification process'.[26] The Chief Justice of Zimbabwe recently put himself firmly on the side of the employers when he said of the Labour Relations act

> The Act forces employers to keep unproductive workers and to shut their doors to would-be future employees who may prove to be better workers. There must be competition on the labour market. The general impression is that the Labour Relations Act says: 'thou shalt not dismiss a lazy worker. If you do, the heavy hammer of the Ministry of Labour will descend on your skull'.

The Chief Justice added

> This policy cannot be right in a country in which unemployment is high. I have good reason to believe that the attitude of lazy workers would change tomorrow were employers to have a free hand in the control and management of labour. They would dismiss unproductive workers and employ hard-working ones.[27]

It is clear from the above what the real preoccupation of the employers is about: it is to discipline the workforce – by using the stick of unemployment. The response of the government to pressure by the employers will be important in defining or redefining future state-labour and state-capital relations, that is, for the future of industrial relations in Zimbabwe. One of the early measures taken by the majority government in 1980 was the establishment of Workers' Committees in all industrial establishments. Workers Committees were reconfirmed under the Labour Relations Act 1985 which repealed the Industrial Conciliation Act of 1959. Does the Labour Relations Act actually given more power to the workers and their organisations? Will it facilitate the transformation of the capitalist labour process? Nzombe has commented that while it recognises the right of workers to organise Workers' Committees and trade unions, it contains very severe restrictions designed essentially to control the workers' organisations and to prevent them from using the strike weapon to achieve higher wages and better conditions.[28] The right to strike is so severely limited under the law that it becomes virtually impossible to conceive of a legal strike. An extensive role is given to state officials to ensure industrial peace.

While the economic stabilisation programme initiated in 1982 did help to achieve external balance, it had the effect of placing a heavier burden on wage-earners through reduced formal sector employment and substantial increases in the prices of basic foodstuffs.[29] Government freezes on wages from 1982 also had the effect of reducing real wages. More recently, government has committed itself to take further adjustment measures aimed, *inter alia*, at reducing the budget deficit. Government has also agreed, in principle, to institute a process of trade liberalisation. It remains to be seen what the effect of these will be on employment and labour.

RESTRUCTURING THE LABOUR PROCESS

Government policies and plans must be seen against the backdrop of a deteriorating domestic and international economic climate. While between 1980 and 1981, following independence and liberalised foreign exchange allocations, the economy grew very rapidly achieving GDP growth rates of 11 per cent and 13 per cent respectively in real terms, the economic climate changed markedly in the period 1982–84 due to a combination of the worst drought and international recession which plunged the country into severe balance of payments problems. The end of 1984 saw the beginnings of recovery with a good agricultural season while 1985 was a very good year with a GDP growth rate of about ten per cent. But this was short-lived as the economy dived into recession again in 1986 with little prospect of real growth in 1987.

Since 1982, government economic policy came to focus more on achieving external balance – with negative consequences on growth, employment and income distribution.[30] Planning in the context of a declining economic climate will clearly have to be much more than merely directing investment and stating priorities in the use of resources (important though these dimensions of planning are) but also has to address the organisation of production and the transformation of labour itself.

My research on this theme is in progress. My main focus is on labour processes in the manufacturing sector. So far, I have done research in two engineering companies as well as a comprehensive study on the Clothing Industry National Employment Council. Work on the Motor Industry National Employment Council is continuing. All this material still has to be processed and analysed fully. What follows are therefore my preliminary thoughts which are necessarily tentative and incomplete. The restructuring of labour processes necessarily involves political struggles, and needs organising on the basis of worker education and increased participation in decision-making by the workers in ways which limit certain avenues of capitalist accumulation. This is an issue of politics as well as economics, and it involves struggles since verbal commitment to socialism is not always backed by real commitment.

In their book on African industrialisation, Barker *et al.* [*1986*], show how an increasing division between mental and manual work had developed in Tanzanian enterprises as a consequence of the growth in the size and influence of management and engineer personnel in relation to production workers. This typical colonial division of labour tends to exclude most of the workers from planning, designing and control tasks which become exclusively the jobs of managers and engineers. The skilled tasks performed by production workers included quality control and repair and maintenance work.[31]

The point was made earlier that the colonial form of production organisation was based on a very tight control of black labour by white managements. Under this division of labour, management and supervisory staff do not do manual work. They merely exercise control over production processes and over workers. The top managers and engineres are still overwhelmingly white seven years after independence. The capitalist owners seem to want to keep things that way. The Deputy Prime Minister, Simon Muzenda, made a scathing attack on the mining industry in 1987. He said the government was concerned that in the middle to senior management in both technical and administrative areas there seemed to be 'a preserve' for whites while black Zimbabweans remained confined to senior positions in personnel or industrial relations. He said:

> A number of black Zimbabwean engineers with relevant qualifications have had to leave some private companies out of frustration. It is inconceivable that seven years after independence, the corporate policies of our mining companies still reflect the old attitudes of basing advancement in a job on racial lines – While it is not the government's intention to promote incompetent people to higher positions, it is still not right that advancement be based on race, and so it is hoped that this phenomenon will be redressed in the very near future.[32]

An important question that arises is: what has been the result of government intervention to promote a black managerial class and the acquisition of shares by the state in private enterprises? One result has simply been incorporation into existing, essentially capitalist, structures and institutions. Such an outcome amounts to co-optation not transformation. The main issue shifts towards control over surplus value, that is, a division of surplus value between national and foreign control. It becomes very much planning without transformation and, hence, the demand for capitalist efficiency grows stronger. The substitution of black for white managers and the process of co-optation are reflective of the tension between preserving productive forces within a process of transition and building up forces which counter such transition itself. Training of both managers and workers is clearly very important. The training of a management cadre has tended to reproduce technocrats with little or no political commitment. And besides rudimentary on-the-job training by firms to meet their immediate needs, the training of shop-floor workers has been neglected. The result is that a hierarchical division of labour still persists and can only lead to the alienation of shop-floor workers. The older workers with a lot of experience, but still on the minimum wage, have no hope because they realise that they have little formal education. While some are keen to improve themselves through further education, the environment at work is not conducive to study. By the end of the day they are so tired they cannot do anything.

Interviews with workers in the engineering firms so far covered in our study show no increase in confidence that things have changed in the direction of giving more power to the workers to influence decision-making at the enterprise. While Workers' Committees have been established and continue to confront management with workers' demands, their powers are very limited. And it is almost impossible to use the strike as a weapon of struggle. All decisions about investment, production levels, employment, and so on, are preserves of the board of directors and top management.

Works Councils – a joint Committee of workers representatives and management – have also been established. In theory, Works Councils are meant to promote workers' participation in decision-making in the enterprise, but in reality they are used as a means of communicating management decisions downward. They also discuss issues of discipline, the need to increase productivity, and welfare matters.

CONCLUDING REMARKS

The preceeding discussion suggests that however you look at planning, you cannot do that successfully without looking at the dynamics of production and work processes. The argument of 'preserving the productive forces', a strong issue in post-independence Zimbabwe, is an argument for preserving those labour processes that fuelled colonial industrialisation. The government of independent Zimbabwe is now faced with the problem that both public and private enterprise had come to rely on this system to maintain their momentum of growth – not growth with equity but growth at the expense of labour. The 'loss of confidence' after independence is a reflection of workers' opposition to this system of exploitation and private capital's unease at the government's socialist philosophy. To restore productivity, one either has to re-instate the conditions of colonial exploitation, or seek new and better ways of organising production. This is an issue of planning, but not merely a technocratic one. Less authoritarian, higher-productivity and participatory methods of organising work in industry should be possible. However, the issue of preserving productive forces, although a real issue, is often a convenient excuse for inaction. There seems to be a reluctance at present to proceed too rapidly with widespread nationalisation of industry, but a number of nationalised industries are in existence already. Perhaps a start could be made in the numerous parastatals or even in those enterprises where the government has a sizeable equity, for example, the many companies wholly or partially owned by the Industrial Development Corporation. In other words, there is a lot that can be done now to try to unlock the potential productivity of workers by making it possible for them to govern their own work activities.

At present, the employment relation in public enterprises is structured along similar lines to that of the private sector. The appointment and training of managers for public enterprise have not been within a perspective of 'red and expert'. A lot more emphasis could be given to worker education and workers and their organisations could be given more space to influence managerial decisions.

NOTES

1. In his criticism of the ultra-left, Lenin [1982] stressed the need to keep a balance between the simple task of 'expropriating the expropriators' and the more difficult one of introducing and consolidating 'country-wide accounting and control' of production and distribution in the expropriated or nationalised enterprises.

2. For a discussion of the Chinese experience in industrial organisation see Bettelheim [*1974*] and Lockett [*1980*].
3. Gartman [*1978*] distinguishes two types of capitalist control: basic control, a type of authority which is necessary in any large-scale production of use values regardless of the relations of production under which production takes place; and surplus control, which is necessitated by the antagonistic nature of production relations under capitalism.
4. By putting a definite limit to the land available for African permanent occupation, the Land Apportionment Act ensured that the African system of shifting cultivation had to be transformed to one of continuous cultivation, which, given the type of soils allocated to the Africans, led to severe soil erosion and consequent decrease in the productivity of the land. See also Palmer [*1977*], Munslow [*1985*], Ranger [*1985*].
5. In 1969, during UDI, the segregation of land on a racial basis was reaffirmed and intensified under the 1969 Land Tenure Act. The fundamental principle of the Act was to ensure that the interests of each race were paramount in their respective areas. The Act made the ownership, leasing and occupation of land by one race in another's area more difficult. The restrictions were more stringent for urban (especially residential) land than for rural land.The measures ensured that Africans could not acquire business stands in city or town areas outside designated African township areas (Parliamentary Debates, Vol.75, 15 Oct., 1969). At the same time, about half a million acres of land was taken away from the Purchase Areas scheme and 'unreserved land' which had been available for purchase and occupation on a non-racial basis was ended and most of the area (about 5.5 million acres out of a total of six million acres) was reclassified as European. The removal of Africans 'illegally' occupying European land was intensified. (See H. Dunlop, 'Land and Economic Opportunity in Rhodesia', *The Rhodesian Journal of Economics,* Vol.6, No.1, March 1972).
6. The pattern of 'white' and 'black' jobs in industry came to be established under the 1934 Industrial Conciliation Act which left out the Africans from the definition of 'employee' and denied them the right to organise in trade unions.
7. Among the major battles were those waged in the Motor Industry in the early 1960s. The employers were pushing for the fragmentation of journeymen's jobs so that black semi-skilled and unskilled could do those jobs. The white trade union representatives, on the other hand, were opposed to any dilution of journeymen's work.
8. See Legislative Assembly Debates, 12 Feb., 1959 (Cols. 1536–1558).
9. See 'Papers re objection to amended amendment' (No.10), June 1976 and also 13th, 14th and 15th Reports of the Industrial Board of the Transport Operating Industry.
10. See P.S. Harris [*1973*]), 'The 1973 Amendment to the Industrial Conciliation Act', *The Rhodesian Journal of Economics,* Vol.7, No.3. Reports of the Secretary for Labour show that less strikes were recorded in the period after UDI than a few years before UDI.
11. Weiner [*1988*] discusses recent trends in land use and agricultural production in LSCF and CAs and evaluates land use forms under the resettlement programme. See also Weiner *et al.* [*1985*].
12. A number of studies have shown that the more well-to-do communal households are those with access to non-farm sources of income such as wage income which they use to buy tools and inputs. See, among others, Weiner [*1988*]; Jackson (on-going research).
13. See Coudere and Marijsse [*1987*]; D. Weiner [*1988*].
14. The TNDP had envisaged that some 162,000 households would be resettled by mid-1985. There are two main models of resettlement schemes: Model A for individual households and Model B for producer co-operatives. Many observers feel that the resettlement scheme is perhaps too land-extensive (as compared, for example, to Kenya's) and that more people could be resettled if the scheme was made more intensive. See the Cliffe Report [*1986*]; Weiner [*1988*]; and Kinsey [*1983*].
15. Land has to be paid for immediately and in full – in some instances, in foreign currency. Almost 50 per cent of the cost of resettlement (estimated at $50m at end 1985) had gone to land purchase alone (see Cliffe Report).
16. See the Cliffe Report [*1986*].
17. Some writers, notably Muir *et al.* [*1982*], argue that the rapid drop in employment in the LSCF sector was due to the rise in the minimum wage. See also the ODI paper.
18. Communal farmers have benefited from the substantial increases in the prices of controlled commodities as well as from increased credit and extension services. Ironically, they also

benefited from the drastic cuts in resources going to the resettlement programme starting in 1983 (ODI Paper, p.136), Coudere and Marijsse [*1987: 4*], Cliffe Report [*1986: 8*].
19. In their study of six villages in Mutoko, Coudere and Marijsse [*1987*] found that income inequality was to be found not between the villages or between agro-ecological zones but *within* villages (p.15). Second, that '*those societies (villages) with the lesser interference of market and state, thus less inserted in a money economy and more dependent on subsistence, experience a lower mean income but also less inequality*' (p.16).
20. See Moyo *et al.* [*1985*].
21. Sachikonye [*1986*], 'State, Capital and Trade Unions'.
22. The lack of 'communication' between workers and managements was a major concern of the Ministry of Labour under Minister Kumbirai Kangai who took a personal interest in diffusing strikes by going round the country urging the strikers to return to work.
23. *The Herald,* 27 Nov. 1985.
24. A number of studies have shown that the minimum wage legislation increased real wages until about 1982 but that thereafter, with the introduction of the government's stabilisation programme, wages have fallen in real terms. See the ODI Paper.
25. Mkandawire [*1985*], 'The Impact of the Recent World Recession on the Zimbabwean Economy', Lusaka, ILO, Dec.
26. See speech by Mr. H.E. Behr, Chairman of the Institute of Directors of Zimbabwe, *The Financial Gazette,* 20 Nov. 1987.
27. The Financial Gazette, 6 Nov. 1987. The Chief Justice was speaking at a luncheon held by the Zimbabwe Chamber of Commerce.
28. S. Nzombe's research on some aspects of the Labour Relations Act of 1985 is in progress.
29. ODI Paper.
30. ODI Paper, op. cit.
31. Barker *et al.*[*1986*].
32. *The Herald,* 16 May, 1987.

REFERENCES

Arrighi, G., 1970, 'Labour Supplies in Historical Perspective: A Study of the Proletarianisation of the African Peasantry in Rhodesia', *Journal of Development Studies,* Vol.6, No.3, April.
Arrighi, G., 1967, *The Political Economy of Rhodesia,* The Hague: Mouton.
Bettelheim, C., 1974, *Cultural Revolution and Industrial Organisation in China,* New York: Monthly Review Press.
Barker, C.E., Bhagavan, M.R., Mitschke-Collande, P.V. and D.V. Wield, 1986, *African Industrialisation: Technology and Change in Tanzania,* Aldershot, Hants: Gower.
Braverman, H., 1974, *Labour and Monopoly Capital,* New York: Monthly Review Press.
Cliffe, L., 1986, 'Policy Options for Agrarian Reform in Zimbabwe: A Technical Appraisal', paper submitted by FAO for the consideration of the Government of Zimbabwe.
Coudere, H. and S. Marijsse, 1987, '"Rich" and "Poor" in Mutoko Communal Area', Centre for Development Studies, University of Antwerp, Belgium.
Doeringer, P.B. and M.J. Piore, 1971, *Internal Labour Markets and Manpower Analysis,* Lexington, MA: Heath Lexington Books.
Edwards, R., 1978, 'Social Relations of Production at the Point of Production', *Insurgent Sociologist,* Vol.8, Nos.2–3.
Edwards, R., 1979, *Contested Terrain: The Transformation of the Workplace in the Twentieth Century,* London: Heinemann.
Elger, A., 1979, 'Valorization and Deskilling: A Critique of Braverman', *Capital and Class,* Vol.7.
Friedman, A.L., 1977, *Industry and Labour: Class Struggle at Work and Monopoly Capitalism,* London: Macmillan.
Gann, L.H., 1965, *A History of Southern Rhodesia, Early Days to 1934,* London : Chatto & Windus.
Gartman, D., 1978, 'Marx and the Labour Process: An Interpretation', *Insurgent Sociologist,* Vol.8, Nos.2–3.
Gintis, H., 1976, 'The Nature of Labour Exchange and the Theory of Capitalist Production', *Review of Radical Political Economics,* Vol.8 No.2 (Summer).
Gordon, D.M., 1972, *Theories of Poverty and Underemployment,* Lexington, MA: Lexington Books.

Harris, P., 1974, *Black Industrial Workers in Rhodesia,* Gweru, Zimbabwe: Mambo Press.

Jackson, J., 1986, 'The Determinants of Rural Incomes and Food Security: A Preliminary Assessment of the Topography of Poverty and Hunger in Zimbabwe's communal areas', Department of Rural and Urban Planning, University of Zimbabwe, Nov.

Kinsey, B.H., 1983, 'Emerging Policy Issues in Zimbabwe's Land Resettlement Programmes', *Development Policy Review,* Vol.1, No.2, Nov.

Lenin, V.I., 1982, *On Workers' Control and the Nationalisation of Industry,* Moscow: Progress Publishers.

Lessing, D. *The Children of Violence of Rhodesia,* Books 1–5.

Littler, C.R., 1982, *The Development of the Labour Process in Capitalist Societies,* Aldershot, Hants: Gower.

Lockett, M., 1980, 'Bridging the Division of Labour? The Case of China', *Economic and Industrial Democracy,* Vol.1.

Marglin, S.A., 1976, 'What do Bosses do?' in A. Gorz (ed.), *The Division of Labour,* Atlantic Highlands, N.J: Humanities Press.

Marx, K., 1965, *Capital,* Vol.1, Moscow: Progress Publishers.

Mkandawire, T., 1985, 'The Impact of the Recent World Recession on the Zimbabwean Economy', Lusaka, ILO, Dec.

Moyo, N.P., Moyo, S. and R. Loewenson, 1985, 'The Root Causes of Hunger in Zimbabwe: An Overview of the Nature, Causes and Effects of Hunger and Strategies to Combat Hunger', *ZIDS Working Paper,* Sept. 1985.

Munslow, B., 1985, 'Prospects for the Socialist Transition of Agriculture in Zimbabwe', *World Development,* Vol.13, No.1, Jan.

Muir, K., Blackie, M., Kinsey, B. and M. de Swardt, 1982, 'The Employment Effects of 1980 Price and Wage Policy in the Zimbabwe Maize and Tobacco Industries', *African Affairs,* Vol.81, No.323.

Murray D.J., 1970, *The Governmental System in Southern Rhodesia,* Oxford: Clarendon Press.

Palmer, R., 1977, *Land and Racial Domination in Rhodesia,* London: Heinemann.

Ranger, T.O., 1985, *Peasant Consciousness and Guerrilla War in Zimbabwe,* Harare: Zimbabwe Publishing House.

Sachikonye, L.M., 1986, 'State, Capital and Trade Unions', in I. Mandaza (ed.), *Zimbabwe: The Political Economy of Transition 1980–1986,* Senegal: Codesria.

Steele, M.C., 1970, 'White Working Class Disunity: The Southern Rhodesia Labour Party', *Rhodesian History,* Vol.1.

Weiner, D., 1988, 'Land and Agricultural Development', in C. Stoneman (ed.), *Zimbabwe's Prospects,* London: Macmillan (forthcoming).

Weiner, D., Moyo, S., Munslow, B. and P. O'Keefe, 1985, 'Land Use and Agricultural Productivity in Zimbabwe', *The Journal of Modern African Studies,* Vol.23, No.2.

Wield, D., 1981, 'Manufacturing Industry', in C. Stoneman (ed.), *Zimbabwe's Inheritance,* London: Macmillan.

Government of Zimbabwe Publications

Growth With Equity: An Economic Policy Statement, Harare, Feb. 1981.

Three-Year Transitional National Development Plan, Vol.1, Nov. 1982.

First Five-Year National Development Plan 1986–1990, Vol.1, April 1986.

Socio-Economic Review of Zimbabwe 1980–1985, 1986.

Budget Statement, 1987.

Report of the Select Committee on subject of Native Industrial Workers' Union Bill, March 1956 (Chairman: G.S. Todd).